Authority and Alliance
in the Letters
of Henry Adams

Wisconsin Studies in American Autobiography

WILLIAM L. ANDREWS
General Editor

Authority and Alliance in the Letters of Henry Adams

Joanne Jacobson

THE UNIVERSITY OF WISCONSIN PRESS

The University of Wisconsin Press
114 North Murray Street
Madison, Wisconsin 53715

3 Henrietta Street
London, WC2E 8LU, England

Printed in the United States of America

Library of Congress Cataloging-in-Publication Data
Jacobson, Joanne.
    Authority and alliance in the letters of Henry Adams /
Joanne Jacobson
    176 pp.   cm. — (Wisconsin studies in American autobiography)
    Includes bibliographical references and index.
    ISBN 0-299-13440-7 (cloth) ISBN 0-299-13444-X (paper)
    1. Adams, Henry, 1838–1918—Correspondence—History and criticism.
    2. Historians—United States—Correspondence—History and ciriticism.
    3. American letters—History and criticism. I. Title. II. Series.
    E175.5.A2A4   1992a
973'.07202—dc20   92-7894

In memory of Beatrice Levin Goldberg
who wrote letters to me at the very beginning,
to whom I wrote letters at the very end

Let us consider letters—how they come at breakfast,
and at night, with their yellow stamps and their green stamps,
immortalized by the postmark. . . . Venerable are letters,
infinitely brave, forlorn, and lost.

Life would be split asunder without them.

Virginia Woolf, *Jacob's Room*

Contents

Acknowledgments

I feel very fortunate to be able to say that I have never felt entirely alone with this project, and I am happy, finally, to have the opportunity to thank the many people who have served as allies in my completion of it.

This book has changed a great deal over the past decade; but I have always sought in writing it to maintain the critical and intellectual spirit of Wendy Deutelbaum and of Robert Sayre, and I have always thought of them as readers. Many other friends and colleagues have read and helpfully criticized portions of the manuscript: Margaret Nelson, Virginia Jackson, Margaret Dickie, Christopher Wilson, Jennifer Nelson, and Katherine Sonderegger. I am also indebted to Cecilia Tichi and to John Carlos Rowe for their attentive, useful evaluations. Tamar Mayer's aggressive theoretical priorities and patient, thorough readings of revisions show throughout the entire book. At the University of Wisconsin Press, William Andrews and Barbara Hanrahan have been steady sources of reliable, thoughtful advice, and of calm, and Raphael Kadushin has been consistently helpful. Over the past year Saundra Segan Wheeler, George Wheeler, Joan Haahr, Carole Silver, and Judith Neaman have supplied all manner of aid and sustenance—and helped me not only to complete this book but, equally important, to feel part of a community in New York. Richard McCann has been unflagging in his confidence in my work and in his support of it. And Tahl Mayer has provided essential distraction and an essential reminder of priorities outside the text. The American Council of Learned Societies provided funding which enabled me to devote a full year to writing. Finally, I want to thank my entire family, especially my parents: I know that I have not always paused to explain my self-absorption to those who have borne the brunt of it, but I hope that they can see in these pages the effects of their love and their encouragement.

I am grateful to the following for the permission to reprint portions of letters: Alexander R. James; the Houghton Library, Harvard University; the John Hay Library, Brown University; the Harvard Law School Library; the Library of Congress; the William R. Perkins Library, Duke University; the New-York Historical Society; the Henry W. and Albert A. Berg Collection, the New York Public Library, Astor, Lenox and Tilden Foundations; the Van Pelt Library, the University of Pennsylvania; the University of California Press. Letters from *The Correspondence of Walt Whitman*, edited by Edwin Haviland Miller, are reprinted by permission of New York University Press, copyright © 1961–1977 by New York University. Quotations from the Adams Papers are from the microfilm edition, by permission of the Massachusetts Historical Society; reprinted by permission of the Harvard University Press from *The Letters of Henry Adams*, Volumes 1–6, edited by J. C. Levenson, Ernest Samuels, Charles Vandersee, and Viola Hopkins Winner, by permission of the Harvard University Press.

A portion of "Conclusion: The Resisting Letter," was first published in *Biography: An Interdisciplinary Quarterly*, Fall 1991, copyright © 1991 by the Biographical Research Center.

Authority and Alliance in the Letters of Henry Adams

Introduction: The Letter
at the Margins

The Conditions of Letter Writing: Cultural Conflict
in the Late Nineteenth-Century United States

As a literary form, the letter has been marginalized by its own necessity. Until quite recently, most readers have taken for granted letters' literal presence in daily lives, assuming that, with actual business in the world, their task is plainly mimetic: "There is the artist writing literary works and there is the man writing letters," Stephen Crane's editors, for example, pronounced firmly in their introduction to Crane's collected letters; and a reviewer concluded, similarly, from Raymond Chandler's correspondence, "A good letter . . . uses the voice its writer thinks with, the voice he talks aloud to himself with. It is . . . pure, uncluttered."[1] A virtual obligation of literacy, the modern letter has, at least since its eighteenth-century incarnation, occupied a critical limbo, marking the margins of "literary" discourse.[2] Lacking the authority of publication, lacking such formal and imaginative prerogatives as autonomy, unity, and closure, the letter's prose has seemed unauthored; women's reliance on the form is both telling and unsurprising, a clear sign of the form's marginal literary status.[3] Only within the last decade have readers begun to challenge the assumption that the letter is rhetorically innocent, and to recognize the strategies of performance and construction which the form makes available to writers.[4]

This book uses Henry Adams's letters to argue that radical cultural change in the late-nineteenth-century United States intensified a set of complex rhetorical imperatives which the letter was ideally positioned to serve. For Adams, as well as other contemporaries of his, the letter straddled a set of rhetorical boundaries which were crucial to the conditions of transition taking place during this period: between public and private; between literary and nonliterary; between elite and democratic discourse. If its location at these

3

boundaries clouded the letter's formal status, that marginality also gave the letter substantial advantages in the management of transition, especially as a source of strategies of resistance and control. Territorial, subversive, Adams's letters prove that the form's permeable rhetorical boundaries preserved the negotiable status of authority, and sustained parity between correspondents as a central imperative of writing.

This politicized critical language—"marginality"; "territory"; "resistance"; "subversion"; "control"—reflects the heightening of cultural conflict in the turn-of-the-century United States. Two events conveniently encapsulate this struggle for cultural hegemony: the 1893 World's Columbian Exposition in Chicago, and the Progressive Reform movement. In both of these cases, an established elite tried to preserve its authority over a newly emergent working and immigrant class; in both cases, the emerging mass culture proved a powerful source of resistance to the consolidation of elite control. The contrast between Daniel Burnham's pristine, classically ordered White City and, at the margins of the fair, the commercial amusements on the Midway and the increasingly fractious city itself, is often used to figure conflict over the authority to define and dominate "America" and "civilization" taking place in American society.[5] At the same time, the growth of urban commercialized leisure-time institutions like amusement parks and dance halls demonstrates the force with which the new mass culture displayed behavior that challenged genteel standards of sexuality and public comportment; while reformers' efforts to impose middle-class values demonstrate the unarticulated (and largely unacknowledged, even forbidden) presence of class tension at the root of reform itself.[6] Even such putatively radical Progressive reformers as Lincoln Steffens were unable to recognize the extent to which their claims about the democratic responsibility of "the people" were based on middle-class assumptions about access to the political process.[7] If, for instance, the development of art museums and municipal orchestras helped to democratize high culture, control of the institutions which brought art to "the masses" remained for the most part in the hands of an existing set of cultural stewards, whose authority was legitimated rather than diffused by their leadership.[8] Each of these cases constituted a kind of border dispute: in each, as cultural boundaries were redrawn, lines of loyalty among those of common values and status were fixed and reinforced.

As these examples suggest, transition in the industrializing United States assumed highly territorial proportions, and space emerged as an arena of conflict over dominance and control. The increasing emphasis on planning in U.S. cities during this period was reflected not only in the Columbian Exposition but in projects as diverse as George Pullman's company town outside Chicago and settlement house maps of inner city wards; Jane Addams's famous pronouncement that Pullman was "A Modern Lear" not only expressed

Addams's doubts about Pullman's benevolence as an employer but, equally, represented Addams's own vision, as a competing reformer, of the future of the American city.[9] Subsequent labor and race riots dramatized the violent potential of such turf battles.[10] Industrialization also disrupted existing territorial patterns by altering the relationship between public and private space. Some of the resulting changes were highly gendered: the rise of commercialized leisure-time amusements, for example, not only shifted the allocation of public space but also released restraints on working-class women's public behavior in mixed company, and increased their social autonomy; the rise of the department store during this period, on the other hand, contributed to the isolation of middle-class women from the industrial capitalist workplace and their transformation from producers into consumers.[11] More generally, the development of the X-ray forever altered the boundaries between interior and exterior and, at the same time, professionalized authority over previously personal space.[12] And innovations in transportation, communications, and medical technology had, throughout the industrializing West, the effect of democratizing physical space and making newly accessible the opportunity to travel and to gather and exchange information which had previously been the preserve of an elite; in Vienna, Emperor Franz Joseph felt so threatened by these changes that he banned telephones and electric lights from the royal palace.[13]

Like the turn-of-the-century American city, the turn-of-the-century American text became the site of increasingly intense conflicts over territory and parity. The rise of literary realism in the United States signaled many late-nineteenth-century American writers' recognition of the fact that cultural transition was transforming the conditions of authorship.[14] Realism spoke for these authors' conviction that writing was obligated politically, that considerable power was located in the authority to assign "literary" status and to grant access to "literature"; to control meaning and to define "truth."[15] These political questions have remained embedded in frequently gendered inequities between "realism" and "local color"; more directly, many late-nineteenth-century American writers made the problematic status of authorship and of narrative convention central issues in their texts.[16] Realism's commitment, on the one hand, to democratizing subject matter and audience and, on the other hand, to reinforcing the centrality of the literary text as a site of political struggle in which, inevitably, writers would retain unequal advantages suggests the difficulty for these writers of resolving their own conflicts about literary authority.[17]

The letter's ambiguous literary status might seem to consign the form to the margins of such conflicts; yet that marginality actually proved rhetorically advantageous under conditions in which "legitimacy" was an explicit subject of contention. The letter's ability to sustain alliances among correspondents was well suited to the imperative of negotiating and reinforcing loyalties, which was amplified under these conditions of transition. Moreover, in his letters Adams was able, simultaneously, to resist obligation to public discourse and to constitute a private alternative to it in rhetorical terms very much like the spatial ones in which so much contemporary cultural conflict was expressed. Henry Adams's commitment to correspondence speaks for the letter's ability to broker such conflicts from the literary margins: there he could retain control over rhetorical territory by controlling access to exchange, by retaining authority as a writer, and by constructing and sustaining a community of allied readers.

The Conditions of Letter Writing: Henry Adams's Commitment to the Form

If the letter was ideally positioned to negotiate cultural conflict, Henry Adams was ideally positioned to take advantage of the letter. For Adams, letter writing was in a quite real sense inevitable. He grew up in a family with a distinguished epistolary tradition, under the tutelage of a father who insisted that "there is no species of exercise, in early life, more productive of results useful to the mind, than that of writing letters."[18] Contributing to the family tradition and maintaining its high standards were part of what being an Adams had come, by Henry Adams's lifetime, to mean. Since the founding eighteenth-century generation of John and Abigail Adams, letter writing had become deeply embedded in family members' sense of duty and prominence: the Adamses have been called "the premier American letter-writing family," and many of them regarded letter writing as "almost an Adams privilege, like the mission to England or the keeping of the republican conscience."[19] Henry Adams's father shouldered the responsibility of editing collections of family correspondence, and two of Henry Adams's brothers, Brooks and Charles Francis, Jr., used the family letter collections extensively for family biographies. Henry Adams himself came to regard the family's epistolary achievement with considerable pride: he insisted to his friend Charles Milnes Gaskell, from Quincy in October of 1869, "In the way of letters there is nothing [in American literature] but my old great-grandmother Abigail Adams's that are worth reading . . ." (II, 168).[20] And Adams passed on that sense of respect and those daunting expectations to his wife, who moaned to her father from Florence in November of 1872, "Life is such a jumble of impressions just now that I cannot unravel the skein in practical, quiet fashion. Oh, for the pen of Abigail Adams!"[21]

Just as family inculcated a letter writing tradition into Henry Adams, family also made the form's location at the boundary between private and public attractive and advantageous to Adams. By the end of the nineteenth century, the Adamses' century and a half of public service had given them visibility, heightened by family members' own publication of family documents, which was unique in the country. All four brothers of Henry Adams's generation, John Quincy Adams II, Charles Francis Adams, Jr., Brooks Adams, and Henry Adams himself—who actually recalled from correspondents and destroyed a substantial portion of his letters—were anxious about their privacy, and made strong efforts to maintain control over public access to their letters and personal papers, and to family documents.[22] As both a source of privileged information and a treasured accomplishment, Henry Adams's correspondence was written under considerable pressure to meet family standards and, quite possibly, to claim a public audience; yet, at the same time, Adams could use letter writing to contain his obligations to public discourse and to protect the private status of exchange.

Perhaps more important, the letter's ambiguous rhetorical location, between withdrawal and engagement, offered Henry Adams an ideal means of negotiating his own highly ambivalent cultural loyalties. The alienation for which Adams made himself famous proves difficult to locate precisely. Adams retained a considerable investment in the distribution of power, and, as Carolyn Porter has shrewdly demonstrated, despite his disclaimers in *The Education* and in many of his letters, he actively sought power as a political journalist and reformer until his wife's death in 1885.[23] As a member of the class whose hegemony was challenged by the rise of industrialization and by immigration, Adams often experienced change as threatening; his anti-Semitism stands out as one especially ugly instance of his class loyalty.[24] Yet Adams was also restless with the insular conformity of the New England elite, whom he described impatiently in a letter to Henry James in November of 1903, long after he had left Boston for a Washington which he found less stultifying, as the "type bourgeois-bostonien" (V, 524). While Adams looked back longingly to medieval Europe and its spiritual synthesis, he also remained quite friendly toward the cause of modern technology and its engineering prowess.[25] Henry Adams has become the exemplar of a cultural tradition hopelessly at odds with the conditions of industrial capitalism: from Washington in January of 1911, he described himself pointedly to Elizabeth Sherman Cameron as "feeling strangely outlawed" (VI, 409). Yet Adams also left a body of work whose willingness to experiment with new language and new theoretical formulations for historical change marks him as one of the most modern writers of his age.

Henry Adams's commitment to letter writing needs to be seen in the light of these ambivalences, for the form proved highly amenable to negotiating them. The "marginality" which Adams so consistently claimed for himself, as "a child of the seventeenth and eighteenth centuries . . . required to play the game of the twentieth," is more accurate as a gauge of his rhetorical stance than as a description of Adams's political or cultural location.[26] To the extent that class is a matter of expectations, then the fact that Adams "took for granted that this sort of world, more or less the same that had always existed in Boston and Massachusetts Bay, was the world which he was to fit" may certainly have proved to be a burden; but Adams's lifelong proximity to power seriously calls that claim into question.[27] Far from neutral carriers of information between correspondents, Adams's letters were aggressive, sophisticated actors in a series of negotiations for parity and control: in this sense, Adams's political environment served in his correspondence as a source of rhetorical imperatives rather than as subject matter. Adams's claims to marginality enabled him to retain the advantages of ambivalence (lack of public obligation, responsibility, and risk) without engaging ambivalence's disadvantages (potential isolation, loss of entitlement and status).

Adams's *Letter to American Teachers of History*, which he had privately printed in Washington in 1910, and which he distributed to a list of history teachers and university presidents, helps to illuminate the rhetorical agenda set by Adams's conflicted cultural loyalties, as well as Adams's reliance on the letter as a means of negotiating those conflicts.[28] In this last of his extended prose works, Adams provided his fellow historians with a radical critique of the profession. Like *The Education*, the *Letter* remained poised between Adams's recognition of the intellectual rigidity of historiographical tradition, wedded to chronologically shaped order, and his own quite traditional unwillingness to abandon history's ongoing obligation to serve a human need for coherence. Adams was impatient with the "literary class" of historians who remained bound by their suspicion of the law of entropy toward which modern science seemed to be heading, and even insisted that to ignore the initiatives of science was for historians to risk ahistoricity: "A society in stable equilibrium is—by definition,—one that has no history and wants no historians" (*Letter* 4, 186). Yet Adams remained loyal, at the same time, to a language of models and theories which was already being challenged by historical relativists in the early twentieth century: "The idea that the entire sidereal universe could have gone on for eternity dissipating energy, and never restoring it, seemed, at the least, unreasonable . . ." (*Letter* 11).[29] Most important, Adams turned to the letter as a rhetorical model for negotiating that conflict. While he took the aggressive step of directly addressing the members of his profession, Adams also refused to publish the essay or to have it reviewed—and he not only called the volume a "letter" but attached to the original volumes and personally signed a prefatory letter, addressed "Dear Sir," and dated 16 February 1910.[30] This preface drew firm boundaries between the writer's responsibility to a potentially intrusive public and his right to the prerogatives of privacy: "[the *Letter*] is a domestic matter, to be settled at home before inviting the world to interfere" (*Letter* iv). Even more directly, Adams insisted that the *Letter*'s

"epistolary" informality and lack of closure enabled him to sustain the unresolved quality of inquiry which he was seeking in the text:

> If I call this volume a letter, it is only because that literary form affects
> to be more colloquial or more familiar than the usual scientific treatise; but
> such letters never require a response, even when they invite one; and in the
> present case, the subject of the letter involves a problem which will certainly
> exceed the limits of a life, already far advanced, so that its solution, if a
> solution is possible, will have to be reached by a new generation. (*Letter* vi)

Here Adams himself acknowledged that the letter was not inevitably for him
primarily a medium of exchange; it was, instead, primarily an alternative condition of discourse, which preserved an arena within which the writer remained
protected from obligation either to formal convention or to a public audience.

Thus Henry Adams had unusually good reasons to write letters. Adams
also produced an unusually large body of correspondence, which has claimed
for him an unusually respectful reputation as a letter writer. Especially in the
last half of his life, after his wife's death had left him lonely and restless, Adams
traveled almost incessantly, and letters became a necessity for him. And even
when old age began to slow him down physically, letter writing retained a routine place in his daily life.[31] By virtually any standards, Henry Adams was a
good letter writer: he was skilled with language, and language mattered to him;
his closeness to many of the most important people and events of his day gave
him access to compelling material; and, as the sheer bulk of the new six-volume
edition of his letters plainly demonstrates, he made a serious commitment to
writing letters. In turn, critics have long taken Adams's letters seriously, and
acknowledged them as central to his achievement as a writer: "among the fruits
of Adams's mind, his letters come very close, at the very least, to holding first
place," Newton Arvin, for example, closed the introduction to his 1951 collection of Adams's letters; and one of the editors of the new edition of Adams's
letters writes, thirty-five years later, "These letters are in a class of their own
in nineteenth-century American literature, comprising a major literary work
equal to, if not surpassing, *The Education of Henry Adams* and *Mont-Saint-
Michel and Chartres*."[32] Other readers have claimed that Adams's letters
"establish their author as probably the foremost epistolarian in American literature"; that Adams was "decidedly first among American letter writers," and
that his letters are "the best thing of their kind in American literature."[33]

Yet despite their appreciation for Adams's skill as a letter writer, until quite
recently virtually none of Adams's editors or readers has questioned the letters' rhetorical innocence: "The letters speak for themselves and require no
comment," Adams's first official editor, Worthington Chauncey Ford, emphati-

cally concluded his brief preface to the first volume of Adams's published letters, which appeared in 1930.[34] In particular, many readers have sought in
Adams's letters access to intimate, firsthand information which might fill in
what the guarded, cryptic *Education* had left out: "If these letters result in
making Henry Adams better and more humanly known than he can be from
the detached examination of himself in the 'Education,'" Ford continued later
in his preface, "my purpose will be accomplished"; "The letters are more meaningful, finally, when read in connection with *The Education*—not because they
essentially contradict or alter the self-portrait Adams there draws of himself,
but because they confirm it," one of the first book-length studies of Adams's
work asserted, similarly, in 1951.[35] Other readers have looked to—and
trusted—Adams's letters as documentary source material on the United States
during his lifetime: "This is a good book," a 1931 review of Ford's first volume
began,

> beautifully made, conveniently arranged, and endlessly interesting to read.
> As a supplement to the curiously successful *Education*, it is, of course, in-
> valuable; but as the partial record of a distinguished American's contact
> with the political, educational, and cultural life of his country, it is even
> more important.[36]

In the same spirit, a recent reviewer of the Harvard edition of the Adams letters regrets that Adams's service in the U.S. Legation in England during the
Civil War deprived later readers of Adams's gifts as a historical witness: "His
letters during the secession crisis form one of the most penetrating analyses
we have of the nation moving from politics to combat, and when Adams went
to England and was unable to see the Civil War at close hand, America lost
a great account of that war."[37] Many readers, in short, have counted on
Adams in his letters as a reliable narrator: "The intellectual story they tell is,
quite naturally, much less artfully shaped and organized than that in the Education, but it is a more complex, shifting, indecisive, and credible story,"
Newton Arvin wrote in the introduction to his 1951 collection of Adams's
letters.[38]

However, the same social, literary, and political advantages which made
his letters so "endlessly interesting" and so "credible" also put Henry Adams's
letters in a rhetorically sensitive position, for they intensified the tension
which the letters had to negotiate between private and public, and between
elite and democratic discourse. In turn, the letter's location at the margins
of "literary" discourse gave Adams rhetorical advantages which were especially
well suited to negotiating those specific conflicts. Under these conditions of
transition and territoriality, "writerly" concerns with authorship and audience paralleled "political" concerns with authority and alliance: in each case,

control and parity emerged as central imperatives; and in each case, control and parity emerged as mutually dependent. Henry Adams's letters demonstrate the rhetorical agility with which the form was able to meet those needs for Adams, and the lifelong commitment which he made in service to them as a letter writer.

This book approaches Henry Adams's letters in roughly chronological order, focusing on the letters to a selection of key correspondents in which Adams developed, in maturing succession, his mastery of the medium. The choice to examine Adams's letters as an autonomous text represents an effort to look at the letter writer as an *author*; to examine the degree to which the form provided Adams with strategies for constructing an alternative discourse that did not necessarily depend for validation on his correspondents' responses. This critical stance is meant neither to preclude nor to invalidate analysis of correspondences as systems of exchange but, instead, to enable discussion to focus on the tension between private and public discourse which gave much of Adams's letter writing its imperative and its sustaining strategies, and on the role which the form's permeable rhetorical boundaries played in Adams's negotiation of that tension.

Chapter 1 examines Henry Adams's early letters, to his older brother Charles Francis Adams, Jr., and to his friend Charles Milnes Gaskell, as an arena within which Adams could claim authority as a writer and use that authority to negotiate parity with his correspondents. While Adams initially used his letters to his older brother to emulate his brother's example and to prove his worthiness of family expectations, writing these letters steadily shifted for Adams into an effort to consolidate his own, autonomous authority as a writer. In turn, Adams validated and protected his bond with Gaskell, outside the sphere of family, by displaying his mastery of an elite rhetorical tradition. Chapter 2 demonstrates how equalizing authority between correspondents became less important in Adams's succeeding letters than allying both correspondents in private, shared opposition to public discourse. Within the insular rhetorical environment which he created in his letters to his friends Gaskell, Henry James, and John Hay, Adams made intimacy subversive: both Adams's anti-Semitism and his stance of public silence served as weapons of exclusion which drew aggressive boundaries around a territory of privileged speech; and, at the same time, Adams's letters also served as the symbolic currency of a community within which meaning was privately coded and circulated among allies. Chapter 3 shows how Adams emerged more aggressively as author in the letters of the last half of his life, following his wife's 1885 suicide, when both parity and disparity receded as rhetorical priorities. These letters—to his younger brother Brooks Adams, to his friend Elizabeth Sherman Cameron, and to her daughter Martha Cameron—ceased to rely so heavily on a world outside their own boundaries, either as a source of validation or as an object of resistance. Instead, each of these sets of letters openly employed fictionalizing strategies to construct and sustain its own distinct version of "reality," in terms which were advantageous to Adams himself.

Chapter 4 examines both of Adams's novels, *Democracy* (1880) and *Esther* (1884), and his *Mont-Saint-Michel and Chartres* (1904) and *The Education of Henry Adams* (1907) in terms of the consistently problematic status of audience and authorship for Adams. In the context of his work as a unified, interpenetrating whole, Adams's concerns in the letters with authority and alliance emerge as fundamentally writerly concerns, and establish the fundamentally *textual* status of the letters. Adams's efforts to control readers' access to meaning in these texts, and to resist obligation to the mass literary marketplace by privatizing his relationship with readers, dramatize the enduring centrality for Adams of tension between private and public. At the same time, Adams's effort to ally himself, as author, with a responsive readership testifies to his commitment to the possibility of overcoming his own doubts about the viability of authorship and about the viability of an audience with cultural loyalties like his own.

The Conclusion fixes more sharply the stance of resistance—to public discourse; to narrative; to unity; and to closure—as a defining quality of the letter as a form, at least under the conditions of cultural transition in the late-nineteenth-century United States. Seen in the context of the letters of two other contemporary writers, Alice James and Walt Whitman, Adams's letters confirm the form's ability to exploit its own permeable rhetorical boundaries, as a source of strategies for negotiating difference and parity. Together, these three correspondences demonstrate the extent to which the letter's location at the margin between private and public has enabled letter writers to occupy rhetorical ground within which they can retain control over discourse and, at the same time, count on a responsive audience.

1   Negotiating Parity

Henry Adams never turned either casually or innocently to letters. From the very start, letter writing was heavily charged for Adams, bound up with the problem of negotiating parity—with claiming and defending authority, and with constructing and sustaining alliances. Adams used his early letters, to his older brother Charles Francis Adams, Jr., and to his friend Charles Milnes Gaskell, to reposition himself in increasingly authoritative stances with respect to his correspondents. His mastery of language in these letters was highly politicized, for it enabled Adams to challenge the condition of inequality between himself and his correspondent under which each exchange opened and to move, steadily, toward a collaborative posture: Adams's letters to his older brother legitimated writing as a source of validation within the context of family; his letters to Gaskell confirmed writing, in turn, as a source of validation between peers. Thus these letters immediately challenge assumptions about the form's passive status, for they served Adams not only as records but as agents of transition.[1]

During the period from 1858 through approximately 1877, arguably the most fluid and the most publicly engaged of his life, Adams's emerging commitment as a writer played a central role in his growth to maturity, and letter writing played a central role in Adams's struggle to carve out an autonomous place for himself within the demanding Adams family. After graduating from Harvard in 1858, Adams studied and traveled in Europe until 1860, when he returned to the United States to serve as private secretary to his father; first in Washington from 1860 to 1861, when Charles Francis Adams, Sr., served in Congress, and then in London from 1861 to 1868, when Charles Francis, Sr., was appointed American ambassador to the Court of St. James. During his early years in Europe, Adams began submitting travel "letters" for publication; later, from Washington and from London, Adams began working as a "correspondent" for a number of Boston and New York newspapers. When the

Adams family returned to the United States in 1868, Henry Adams returned to Washington, this time on his own, to devote himself full time to reform journalism. During the succeeding years, Henry Adams made three of the most formal professional and personal commitments of his life: he served as assistant professor of history at Harvard from 1870 through 1877 and as editor of the prestigious *North American Review* until 1876; and Adams married Marian (Clover) Hooper in 1872, when he was thirty-four years old.

The letters which Henry Adams wrote to Charles Francis Adams, Jr., and to Charles Milnes Gaskell during these years of transition into adulthood, from his graduation from college in 1858 until the completion of his term as a college professor in 1877, actively participated in Adams's negotiation of difference. In them Adams learned to use language to broker a set of essential changes in his relations to his correspondents: from emulation of his older brother to differentiation from him; from earning intimacy with Gaskell to protecting the stability of that intimacy. If, over the course of these transitions, the context of parity steadily shifted for Adams, his reliance on letter writing as a source of validating authority and alliance grew increasingly consistent and more confident.

The Economy of Family: Henry Adams's Early Letters to Charles Francis Adams, Jr.

The importance of letter writing as an Adams family tradition and duty made it wholly appropriate for Henry Adams to turn to correspondence as a proving ground; and developing proficiency as a letter writer initially meant to Adams demonstrating his worthiness of family expectations. But in his first correspondence, with his older brother Charles Francis Adams, Jr., Henry Adams entered an exchange within which the act of writing created a shifting power economy, for in these letters Adams learned to use language to claim and to consolidate autonomous authority.[2] Just three years older, Charles Francis Adams, Jr., was the family member to whom Henry Adams felt closest when he set off for Europe after graduating from Harvard and began writing letters home. Charles turned out, also, to be the Adams brother most susceptible to the pressures of being an Adams: he remained deeply held by the intertwined needs of proving himself, in public, a distinguished citizen in the family tradition, as a soldier in the Civil War, a land speculator, and president of the Union Pacific Railroad; and of carving out, in private, a clearly marked place for himself in the family within which he would always remain, after John Quincy Adams II, the second son.[3] Henry Adams's transition in these early letters from imitating to resisting his older brother's example was, therefore, very much tied to changes in his relationship to family. Directly confronting Charles Francis, Jr., with increasingly aggressive language, these early letters to his older brother provided Henry Adams with a set of rhetorical strategies for constructing, rather than resolving, difference from his family.

Initially Henry Adams's letters to his older brother provided him a safe, private place where he could begin writing, where he had a familiar audience whose response he could anticipate and trust, and a model which he could emulate. Adams counted on his older brother as an ally in family battles. "The Governor wants us to marry," he exclaimed in frustration from Switzerland in August 1859, in response to their father's pressure; "Well and good. Like other fathers who can afford it, he is willing to allow us so much. I say, take it and if there's any trouble about it, don't back down as if it was your fault" (I, 53–54). And Adams counted on his older brother's presence in the family, just ahead of him, for confirmation of his own instincts. "We are considerably in the same box, brother mine," Henry wrote to Charles in one of his earliest letters, from Berlin in February 1859,

> and what applies to me, applies also, with slight alterations, to yourself. As you say, there are differences between us, and my character isn't your's; in fact, I know many respects in which I wish it were; but still we have grown up in the same school. . . . (I, 23)

In turn, Adams looked up to Charles Francis, Jr., in the family hierarchy, and sought approbation from him in his earliest letters. His very first letter to Charles, for example, from Berlin in November 1858, presented Adams's plans for the future to his brother with earnest, naive clarity:

> you ask me, what my plans are, here and in life. . . .
> As for my plan of life, it is simple, and if health and the usual goods of life are continued to me, I see no reason why it should not be carried out in the regular course of events. Two years in Europe; two years studying law in Boston; and then I propose to emigrate and practice at Saint Louis. (I, 4)

In this context of unequal expertise, Adams's earliest letters cast his older brother as a kind of writing master to whom he bound himself as apprentice, fresh out of college on his first trip to Europe. Adams presented the challenge of sparring with his older brother in their correspondence as an opportunity to gain valuable experience as a writer rather than as competition. "No doubt it's good practice, this fencing with each other . . . ," he insisted to Charles from Dresden in November of 1859 (I, 67). Writing to Charles from Berlin in February 1859, Adams positioned himself in respectful deference to his brother's judgment: "I will pay your last letter the compliment to say that it had effect enough over me to make me feel unpleasantly for two days. . . . though your criticisms are rather hard on me, I acknowledge that you are wholly

in the right" (I, 18). And three months later, from Dresden in May, Adams
sighed with envy at his brother's skill and with the drudgery of his own efforts:

> I wish I could write as long as you, and I admire your last exceedingly.
> You've made a first-rate letter out of common-place materials. But the truth
> is, though I have probably a thousand things to your one to say, I get so
> tired of writing them that it comes hard. However I'll do my worst and let
> her go. (I, 40)

Writing steadily emerged in Henry Adams's earliest letters to his older
brother as a kind of performance—converting the raw "common-place" into
the belletristic "first-rate"—calculated to display skill and to win approval. From
very early on, asserting his own presence as author began for Adams to take
priority over asserting himself as either narrator or protagonist; and Adams
quickly learned in these letters to exploit the tension between narration and
authorship. Continuing the same May 1859 letter, for example, Adams relayed
to Charles Francis, Jr., the news of his unnerving entrance, at the age of twenty-
one, at a Dresden wedding:

> I was shown up stairs and had taken off my coat and was calmly drawing on
> a pair of gloves, when the servant opened the folding-door and I was horri-
> fied at seeing before me an army of white dresses and sternly fixed counte-
> nances arranged in order, and all staring, gravely as if it were a funeral, at
> me as if I were the coffin. With that grace and suavity of manner for which
> I am famous, I marched up and stormed the phalanx by a series of bows. I
> did attempt one speech at a person whom I supposed to be the father of the
> bride, but he looked so alarmed and seemed so thoroughly overwhelmed
> with his white cravat, that I backed off and took to flight without an answer.
> Probably I should have remained smirking in the middle of the floor all the
> evening if I hadn't caught sight of one of my Fraüleins [sic] grinning at me.
> I bolted at her and began chattering nonsense fluently. Admired the bride's
> dress as in duty bound. She wore all white, as is necessary, and a myrtle
> wreath on her head, fastening her veil and a bouquet of white flowers in
> her hand. The bridegroom who had just that day received his promotion as
> Ober-Lieutenant or 1st Lieutenant, was very polite to me, probably because
> I had presented to my four Fraüleins, his sisters, bouquets all round just
> before they set off to the church; a piece of extravagance which I had in-
> tended should cost me six dollars but which through a stupid blunder of the
> gardener who didn't understand my German and sent smaller bouquets than
> I ordered, only did cost one Am. dollar and a half. So here I ensconced
> myself, behind the muslin, and talked idiocy till all the officers and guests
> had arrived. (I, 42)

This letter provided a stage on which Adams could experiment with language and assert to his older brother his seriousness about writing. Approaching the drawing room door and preparing himself to face the social test on the other side, as protagonist Adams displayed in this scene an uncomfortable mixture of self-consciousness and ineptitude, which dramatized the naiveté of his social ambitions. But as the scene's author Adams managed to sustain the credibility of a different set of ambitions. Already Adams was paying evident attention to craft, manipulating unexpected prepositions—"one speech *at*"—and strategically selecting puns and figures: "all staring, gravely as if it were a funeral, at me as if I were the coffin." Already he could render tension between the pressures of convention and the underlying strain of comprehension and feeling; already he could adopt an ironic tone toward himself. His skill with words emphatically belied Adams's characterization of himself as incoherent, "chattering nonsense fluently." In investing such care in writing this event, Adams was making a commitment to writing as his chosen mode of participation in it—identifying himself as someone who wrote about parties rather than someone who attended them—as surely as the German words, "Ober-Lieutenant" and "Fraüleins," which he dropped casually here and there confirmed the mastery of local culture which the letter's narrative denied. Most important, in facing Charles Francis, Jr., so decisively as a writer, Adams established the literary status of these early letters, and determined that the grounds on which he would earn his older brother's approval and, eventually, equalize exchange between them would be literary.

While these early letters to Charles sustained a protected environment within which Adams could try out the skills requisite of "a first-rate letter," they also sowed the seeds of changes which would inevitably alter the condition of disparity under which Henry Adams had begun writing to his older brother. Charles Francis, Jr.'s, own example steered his younger brother toward publication, ushering Henry Adams into a literary arena where neither Charles's authority, nor correspondence with his family, felt sufficient. It was Charles Francis, Jr., who encouraged his younger brother to put his time in Europe to constructive use by writing about his experiences there, and who even offered to use his editorial connections to place Henry's work in the United States. But as Charles led their correspondence out of privacy, parity became contested between Adams and his brother, and Adams's letters to Charles became an important ground on which that contest would be fought. Adams thanked Charles for his sponsorship, for example, from Berlin in January 1859, "I acknowledge gratefully your offer to negotiate for me about any article I may care to write" (I, 15)—but he quickly began to resent Charles's elevated expectations of him: "Were you intoxicated when you wrote I am to 'combine in myself the qualities of Seward, Greely [*sic*], and Everett'?" he exclaimed, a month later, again from Berlin; "Mein lieber Gott, what do you take me for? . . . I know what I can do, and I know what a devilish short way my tether goes . . ." (I, 20). Adams seemed to count on his older brother as a partner and a disciplinarian: "we may consider ourselves a case of modern Romulus and Remus, only omitting their murderous propensities," he continued, in the same letter; "What is still more, we are beautifully adapted to work together; that is, *you* are. I stand in continual need of some one to kick me, and you use cow-hides for that purpose. So much the better. Continue to do so" (I, 23). Yet while Adams submitted himself to Charles's guidance, he also anticipated the moment when he would veer from the path which his older brother had set. "I'm glad that you approve my Gymnasium course," he wrote from Berlin in March 1859; and then insisted, in the same letter, "I shall stick to my present course, which up to a certain point is identical with your plan. When that point comes, I'll be ready to decide" (I, 28).

When Adams did, eventually, complete the two "letters" on his Prussian gymnasium which his older brother had solicited, they remained a source and a sign of unresolved conflict about Adams's ability to meet the standards which his brother had set for him. Adams himself described the essays, to Charles from Dresden in May 1859, as "very poorly written and excessively stupid," and admitted that they were "in a wholly unpublishable state" (I, 40–41). And Adams's lack of maturity as a writer showed in the work itself, where he lamely undermined his credibility with his audience: "I believe I've now told you as much as you will care to read. At all events if you can get no definite ideas from all this, you would get no more thought were I to spin out this letter to a book. . . ."[4] Yet if Adams quietly acceded to his older brother's decision not to submit his early writing for publication, he was unwilling to submit passively to Charles's criticism of his use of his time in Europe. Six months later, in November 1859, Adams was standing up to his brother in a tone whose steady calm bespoke self-confidence which the experience of a year in Europe on his own—experience which Charles could not claim—had clearly given him:

> I acknowledge . . . that so far as my plan went, I have failed and done little or nothing. At the same time I feel for myself convinced that this year has been no failure, but on the contrary is worth to me a great deal. . . . if I am a humbug . . . I shouldn't have done any better if I'd remained in Boston. . . .
> (I, 65)

Continuing the letter, Adams acknowledged the political charge of this exchange by producing a counterattack which turned Charles's criticism back to its source in openly competitive—and openly writerly—terms:

> This contest of purpose; this argument about aims, you began against, or if you will, for me. You blame me very fairly no doubt, and try to protect your-

self from retaliation by pleading guilty; a sort of Yankee Sullivan tactics, hitting a lick and going down. Face the music yourself. I acknowledge I've failed but I believe I've discovered a treasure if I can but use it. But you. . . . Why do you recommend writing, to me who have been hurrying around Europe like a steam engine and am so busy with learning that I can't spare a second . . . when you yourself are smouldering worse than I, when you have never published a word so far as I know. (I, 66)

In using the language of "contest," "argument," "blame," and "retaliation," in fixing Charles's approach as "tactics," Adams acknowledged the extent to which writing had become an arena of conflict between his brother and himself, and the extent to which exchanging letters had become for Adams a means of challenging the imbalance of rhetorical power between the two of them.

If correspondence with Charles Francis, Jr., provided Henry Adams with his first literary sponsor and audience, the conflicts over audience and authorship in which writing these letters engaged Adams pressured him to acquire literary authority equal to his older brother's. In February 1860, Charles began publishing pseudonymously in the *Boston Daily Advertiser* a series of essays on Washington politics. Closely following his brother's lead, Henry wrote to Charles from Dresden, in March, with the idea of experimenting under Charles's wing with the same sort of thing as he traveled through Europe:

> Your Washington letters, my boy, have stirred me up. As you know, I propose to leave Dresden on the 1st of April for Italy. It has occurred to me that this trip may perhaps furnish material for a pleasant series of letters, not written to be published but publishable in case they were worth it. This is my programme. You may therefore expect to receive from week to week, letters from me, beginning at Vienna and continuing so long as I don't get tired of it. What the letters will be about depends of course on circumstances. . . . you can do just what you choose with them so long as you stick by your own judgment. . . . But it needs a critic to decide what's copper and what silver and I suppose you have courage enough not to be afraid to tell me in case my coinage should turn out copper or copper-gilt. So gird on your sword and don't be idiotic enough to bother yourself with family affection or brotherly sympathies. (I, 106)

Simultaneously ambitious and modest, this letter eagerly placed Adams in his brother's improving hands; for his part, Charles arranged to have Henry's work published in the *Boston Daily Courier*, beginning in April of 1860. This nascently professional "programme" eased "correspondence" and "letters" out of the private context of exchange between two brothers, even as submitting to his older brother's final judgment on his work's "publishable" status protected Adams from taking a public risk alone. Almost immediately, Adams began to see letter writing as a means of consolidating his own authority as a writer,

within a family which expected some kind of ambitious commitment from its
sons. That meant for Adams, in part, using letters to establish his independence of the terms for success—public service, the law—which had become
conventional among Adams males (terms which continued to pose obstacles
for Charles himself). A month after his first travel letter had appeared in the
Courier, Adams wrote to his older brother from Rome, in May 1860:

> I read Gibbon. Striking, very. Do you know, after long argument and
> reflexion I feel much as if perhaps some day I too might come to anchor
> like that. Our house needs a historian in this generation and I feel strongly
> tempted by the quiet and sunny prospect, while my ambition for political
> life dwindles as I get older. (I, 149)

If he was not to be "political" in the Adams family tradition, Adams needed,
he felt, to claim some other turf of his own, and letter writing offered him the
chance to take tentative steps toward becoming the "historian" of his generation. Adams's published travel letters attest to the efficacy of that arrangement
for him, for while he maintained in them the conceit of a familiar relationship with his reader, he was also able to give his prose more formal polish, using
irony and repetition to establish a more consistently assertive and ambitiously
literary voice for himself: "Here I was at last, then, face to face with one of
the great events of our day," he wrote dramatically from Palermo in June 1860,
painting the scene of Garibaldi's revolt as a set piece:

> It was all perfect; there was Palermo, the insurgent Sicilian city, with its
> barricades, and its ruined streets with all the marks of war. There was that
> armed and howling mob in the square below, and the music of the national
> hymn, and the five revolutionary cannon. There were the guerilla [sic] cap-
> tains who had risked their lives and fortunes for something that the worst
> envy could not call selfish. And there was the great Dictator, who, when
> your and my little hopes and ambitions shall have lain in our graves a few
> centuries with us, will still be honored as a hero, and perhaps half wor-
> shipped—who knows!—for a God.[5]

In December 1860, Adams wrote to Charles Francis, Jr., from Washington:

> I propose to write you this winter a series of private letters to show how
> things look. I fairly confess that I want to have a record of this winter on
> file, and though I have no ambition nor hope to become a Horace Walpole,
> I still would like to think that a century or two hence when everything else
> about us is forgotten, my letters might still be read and quoted as a memo-
> rial of manners and habits at the time of the great secession of 1860. (I, 204)

Despite his disclaimers, locating himself in the tradition of Walpole as a writer of familiar letters confirmed the seriousness of Adams's ambitions as a writer and committed him to pushing the private limits of his letters to his older brother. In addition to the travel letters which he published from Europe in the *Courier* from April through July of 1860, and the *Advertiser*, from Washington over the period from December 1860 through February 1861, Adams reported for the *New York Times* for the six months between June 1861 and January 1862.[6] The power of reaching a larger audience—even under the sponsorship of his older brother—proved so seductive to Adams that writing to Charles lost some of its imperative for him. At one point in June 1861, from London, Henry actually referred Charles to his published letters rather than writing directly to him: "My letters in the Times will give you pretty much all I have to say about politics" (I, 243).

The two brothers' divergent Civil War experiences helped Henry Adams separate from Charles Francis, Jr., and helped, finally, to draw the differences between them to a head in Adams's letters.[7] Initially Adams's Civil War correspondence with his older brother established a collaborative stance, attempting to contain difference within the tactical exigencies of a family political strategy. Charles Francis Adams, Sr.'s, ambassadorship to England placed the entire family in an extremely awkward position during the war, when British sympathies for the Confederacy ran strong, especially after Southern cotton supply lines to the English textile industry were cut. Secretly the two brothers worked in tandem as publicists for their father's policies during the early years of the war, as "correspondents" to the *New York Times* and the *Boston Advertiser*. Over the next six months, Henry Adams published in the *New York Times*, under the anonymous signature of "Our Own Correspondent," a set of essays meant to lay out publicly and defend his father's efforts, as American ambassador, to prevent a break between the United States and England. Adams warned in his first "letter," for example, which appeared in June of 1861 on the heels of England's official refusal to take the side of the Union, "*If our Government forces the evil to a head by resenting the course the Ministry have taken, it will infallibly create trouble here . . .*"; and he praised his father's cool, reasoned response: "It seems plain, however, that Mr. ADAMS at least means to take no step without due care. . . ."[8] In the face of English support for the Confederate military, Adams cautioned calm, consistently trying to maintain his father's policy of restraint. "Very grave rumors found currency that the Ministry were thinking of recognizing the Southerners. . . . Now, however, matters have much brightened up," he reassured his American readers in the confusing wake of the first battle at Bull Run.[9] Concurrently, Adams's letters to Charles Francis, Jr., helped, privately, to coordinate his newspaper campaign with his brother's. "Feeling as I did in the matter [of the Queen's Proclamation of Neutrality], of course I did my best in my letters to the Times to quiet rather than inflame. If you choose you can suggest to the Advertiser a leader developing the view which I take. . . ," Adams advised Charles Francis, Jr., from London in June 1861 (I, 238); and, a month later, "As a counter-part to my letters in the Times, I am looking round here for some good paper to take you as its American correspondent" (I, 244).

Broadening the arena of "correspondence" was central in creating a symmetry of authority between Henry Adams and his older brother, and in holding competition between them in check—temporarily—within a set of common tactical imperatives. Adams's letters were, in fact, first collected under the rubric of the family's Civil War correspondence, and their editor presented, and justified, collecting the letters as a record of the family's shared historical mission: "the description of social conditions, the discussion of public questions, and the wide relations held by the writers, make them a contribution to the social, military and diplomatic history of the War of Secession, unequalled in scope and concentrated interest."[10] Under the delicate and heightened political conditions within which Adams wrote letters to his older brother and "letters" to newspapers, supporting Charles Francis Adams, Sr.'s, diplomatic positions took precedence over Henry Adams's adoption of an autonomous political stance. Adams's political reasoning as both a personal and a newspaper correspondent largely followed his father's, as in the November 1861 *Trent* incident, in which an American ship captain boarded the British mail steamer *Trent* on the high seas and seized two Confederate envoys en route to England and France. The questionable legality of this event made representing the United States extremely difficult for Charles Francis Adams, Sr. and brought the United States and England to the brink of war, and Henry Adams used his *New York Times* column on behalf of his father's effort to protect British neutrality: "[U.S. Secretary of State Seward] . . . *has only to reassert the old principles of American history, and, while refusing to obey the mandate of this Government, to offer to yield at once to a request based on the American theory of neutral rights.*"[11] Charles Francis Adams, Sr., himself used the family correspondence to clearly state his position, in a letter to Charles Francis Adams, Jr., from London on 27 December 1861: "It is unlucky for me that I was bred up in declared hostility to the arbitrary dogmas against neutral rights. . . ."[12] And Henry Adams echoed his father in a letter to his older brother the next day, from London:

> Again, about the Trent affair. Our lawyers have shown a strange want of close logic. The seizure of the commissioners can only be justified in one of two ways. If Seward sticks to his rebel theory, he must claim a right to do that which is most repugnant to our whole history and sense of right. He must defend a violation of the right of asylum. (I, 267)

Yet even as the diplomatic necessity for confidentiality drew a crucial line between private and public "letters" and rallied both brothers to a common cause, the interpenetration between these two kinds of "correspondence" also helped to consolidate Adams's own authority in private exchange with his older brother. Adams's role as a newspaper correspondent exploited the proximity to power which he had gained as a member of the American legation and gave him new confidence as a writer. While his newspaper work was, of course, public, its authorship had to remain a secret, even from Charles Francis, Sr., in order to avoid compromising either their father's diplomacy or Henry Adams's political observations. Sharing that secret helped to equalize exchange between Adams and his older brother, and Adams could confide in Charles Francis, Jr., "I am myself more uneasy than I like to acknowledge in my public letters" (London, September 1861, I, 250). Yet the experience that he gained as a member of the legation and as a journalist also made Adams considerably less amenable to submitting to his older brother's authority. Adams had taken in determined stride Charles's criticism of the travel letters which he wrote for the *Boston Daily Courier* and the observations on the Washington political scene which he published in the *Boston Daily Advertiser*, informing his older brother from Washington in December 1860,

> I received a letter from you last night, almost wholly occupied with criticisms on my Advertiser letters. What you say is perfectly true and I am and have been as sensible to it as you. Naturally it is hard at first for a beginner as I am, to strike the key note; still I think I can manage it in time; and meanwhile criticise away as much as you please. (I, 212)

But while such letters consigned Adams to his brother's "judgment" about "what's copper and what silver," less than a year later Adams faced his brother's letters with criticism of his own. "In your last letters I am not a little sorry to see that you are falling into the way that to us at this distance seems to be only the mark of weak men, of complaining and fault-finding over the course of events," he wrote sternly to Charles, from London in October of 1861; "In mere newspaper correspondents who are not expected to have common sense or judgment, this may be all natural, but you ought to know better . . ." (I, 256).

Two December 1861 events decisively weakened the tenuous containment of disparity in Adams's letters to his older brother: the *Boston Daily Courier*'s exposure of Adams's authorship of an article, "A Visit to Manchester: Extracts from a Private Diary"; and Charles's enlistment in the Union army. In necessitating his resignation from the *New York Times* correspondence, the first represented the loss of Adams's public, if anonymous, podium for his writing; the second represented the loss of Adams's advantage over his brother as a participant in war affairs, as his brother became an officer in the cavalry.

Although the main thrust of his article (which Charles Francis, Jr., had placed with the *Courier*) had been to provide Henry Adams's American readers with an evaluation of the British cotton industry's response to the Northern cotton blockade, under the assumption of anonymity Adams had also taken the liberty of satirizing the London society which had shunned him: "In London the guests shift for themselves, and a stranger had better depart at once as soon as he has looked at the family pictures. . . . In London one is regaled with thimbles full of ice-cream and hard seed cakes."[13] Unfortunately Adams's article was excerpted in a number of English newspapers, including the *London Times*, which responded with cutting remarks of its own on Adams's resorting to gossip in "a document which evidently purports to be in the nature of a State paper."[14] Clearly his public exposure was personally embarrassing to the already self-conscious Adams. More important, Adams felt that the *Courier*'s revelation put his anonymity as the *New York Times*'s London correspondent newly at risk, threatening his integrity as a member of the American legation, his credibility with the *Times*, and his father's trust. As a result, Adams felt forced, immediately, to quit his *Times* column, as well as all his other newspaper correspondence, and he wrote to Charles Francis, Jr., from London in January 1862, and asked for his brother's help in withdrawing discreetly from these obligations:

> The Courier in putting my name to my "Diary" has completely used me up. . . . for the present I shall cease my other writings as I am in agonies for fear they should be exposed. . . . Couldn't you write to [the *Times* editor] and explain without mentioning names why his London correspondent has stopped for a time. My connection with him must on no account be known. The Chief [Charles Francis Adams, Sr.] as yet bears this vexation very good-naturedly but another would be my ruin for a long time. I don't want him ever to know about it. (I, 269)

Although Adams hoped to pick up the slack by "stretching my private correspondence as far as possible" (London, January 1862, I, 278), he felt the narrowing of his range keenly. "Do you understand how, without a double personality, *I* can feel that *I* am a failure?" he moaned to Charles from London in February 1862 (I, 282).

Almost immediately following the *Courier* incident and Charles's enlistment, Henry Adams's letters expressed a renewed sense of inequality between himself and his older brother. The letters which he wrote to Charles during the war often took Adams's measure against his older brother's achievements as a soldier, and measured his brother against his own achievement as a political writer and aide.[15] The letters at first threatened to sink under Adams's sense of uselessness, as he watched passively from the sidelines Charles's engagement in one of the central male dramas of their generation. "Meanwhile," he wrote from London in March of 1862,

> it worries me all the time to be leading this thoroughly useless life abroad while you are acting such grand parts at home. . . . My pen is given up. The risk in using it became too great and the consequences of a discovery would have been utterly destructive. Here I am, more dry-nurse than ever, dabbling a little, a very little in society; reading a little; copying a great deal; writing nothing, and not advancing an inch. I envy you who at least have an enemy before you. My enemy is only myself. (I, 284–85)

Adams's letters to Charles made frequent comparisons between the two brothers which located Adams at a distinct disadvantage. "Hard as your life is and threatens to become, I would like well to share it with you in order to escape in the consciousness of action a little of the struggle against fancied evils that we feel here" (I, 305), he complained restlessly from London in July 1862; and from London in March 1863 he groaned to Charles, only half tongue in cheek, "While you are resolving into the primitive wild Injun among the regions where Captain John Smith once roved to considerable effect, I am becoming every day more and more the man of rules and conventionalities" (I, 335).

But if Adams's anxious differentiation of himself from Charles in his letters at first only exposed his sense of his own inadequacy, eventually difference from his older brother emerged there as a sign of Adams's strength. "I find myself, I think, of use, and am well content to be here. . . ," he wrote, firmly, to Charles from London in December 1862; "On the whole I would infinitely prefer to be here to going into the army . . ." (I, 319). While Adams's first response to the Union defeat at Bull Run had been to request that his older brother obtain a military commission for him—"I wish to have a commission and if you succeed in arranging it, let me know at once," he wrote immediately from London in August 1861 (I, 247)—after he had settled into his own diplomatic position Adams began to question the military model on which his older brother depended for validation. "I congratulate you on your Captaincy if it be a cause of congratulation," he wrote doubtfully to Charles from London in January of 1863; "You know I look on the service merely as a necessary duty" (I, 324); and a month later: "military men in Europe . . . are the greatest curse and nuisance in existence" (I, 331).

Charles must have played a part in inciting his younger brother to turf battles; appealing to Henry's insecurities about experiencing the war as a reader, Charles wrote to him from Virginia in January 1863,

You may say that my mind is lying fallow all this time. Perhaps, but after all
the body has other functions than to carry round the head, and a few years'
quiet will hardly injure a mind warped, as I sometimes suspect mine was, in
time past by the too constant and close inspection of print.[16]

And Adams himself was not above dismissing what lay beyond his reach; "You
don't catch me entering the army now. Donner-r-r-wetter! it would be like
entering college Freshman when all one's friends were Seniors," he wrote to
Charles from London in May of the same year, exposing his sense of having
already lost irrecoverable ground (I, 348). In fact, Adams never quite shook
off the shame that he felt in sitting out the war as a chaperone for the family
women. "It hardly seems consistent with self-respect in a man to turn his back
upon all his friends and all his ambitions, during such a crisis as this, only for
the sake of conducting his mother and sister to the opera, and to ride in Rot-
ten Row," he confided to his older brother from London in July 1863 (I, 369);
and he groaned from Windermere, in September of the same year, "all your
regiment of cavalry isn't half the bother to you that my squadron of female irreg-
ulars is to me" (I, 379). Yet even such anxious comparisons helped Adams to
assert satisfied claims to achievements of his own. "My hand could at best use
a rapier," he insisted to Charles from London in May of 1863,

It is not made for a sabre. I should be like a bewildered rabbit in action, being only trained to counsel. My place is where I am, and I never was so necessary to it as now. All thoughts of escape even for a day, have vanished. We
are covered with work, and our battles are fierce and obstinate. (I, 348)

Appropriating the rhetoric of combat for his own "battles" against humiliation, Adams undermined his characterization of himself as useless and cow-
ardly; "My place is where I am," he accepted with finality. "I write and read;
read and write," Adams wrote plainly to Charles from London in October of
the same year (I, 401); and a month later he defended his insularity:

although I believe I did once know an attaché, such is not the case now. . . .
You, my dear Brother Imperator, will probably sneer a bitter sneer at me for
this neglect of opportunities. To skulk away like this, when I might make
myself so necessary—so useful and so well known! . . . But . . . in maintaining a mysterious reserve on public affairs, I believe I can best maintain our
own dignity and alone retain any good position. (I, 406–7)

When Charles was discharged from the army, seriously ill, in June 1865, Henry
Adams used the differences in their wartime experiences strategically, to insist on his own gifts as an observer and thinker. "I shall get along," he wrote
confidently to his older brother from London in December 1866, "and if I am

in the end what you in your sublimity call a failure, I shall still have enjoyed what I, in a spirit of more philosophical and milder tendency, consider a rounded and completed existence" (I, 515).

By the end of the Civil War, Adams's letters to his older brother had adopted a stance of disengagement, cementing his commitment to writing as a weapon of autonomy in a family committed to public service and resisting exchange with his older brother as unlikely to be advantageous. In a November 1867 letter from London, for example, Adams wrote to Charles:

> John [Quincy Adams II, their oldest brother] is a political genius; let him follow the family bent. You are a lawyer, and with a few years patience will be the richest and the most respectable of us all. I claim my right to part company with you both. I never will make a speech, never run for an office, never belong to a party. I am going to plunge under the stream. For years you will hear nothing of any publication of mine—perhaps never, who knows. I do not mean to tie myself to anything, but I do mean to make it impossible for myself to follow the family go-cart. (I, 557)

This passage's shrill language of uncompromising extremes—"never," "nothing," "impossible"—reveals the strain of transition for a still-maturing Adams. Such letters not only justified but actively created distance, carving for Adams a path out of the orbit of "the family go-cart"; plotting the boundaries between "John"—"you"—and "I"; protecting the writer from obligation to others' expectations.[17] "As to the future, I know that the prospect is misty, but I have made my plans and am ready to begin the march;" Adams announced again to his older brother a month later, from London, decisively demanding space of his own, "for march it will have to be, since Boston is not big enough for four Adamses, and I claim my right to remain, what I have been for ten years, an independent cuss" (I, 561). And after returning to Washington after the war, Adams resisted becoming reengaged in a correspondence within which he had managed to renegotiate the disempowering effects of difference:

> I see you are getting back to your old dispute with me on the purpose of life, by means of an attack on my self-esteem. . . . My path is a different one; and was never chosen in order to suit other people's tastes, but my own . . . . Your ideas and mine don't agree, but they have never agreed. You like the strife of the world. I detest it and despise it. You work for power. I work for my own satisfaction. You like roughness and strength; I like taste and dexterity. For God's sake let us go our own ways and not try to be like each other. (II, 33)

The insistent boundaries drawn by such letters attest to the extent to which Henry Adams's letters to his older brother had become a site of competition, especially as his correspondence with Charles Francis, Jr., helped to confirm Adams's increasing professionalism as a writer. While their public writing "programme" had previously had a collaborative effect on Adams's letters to Charles, during the period following the war it evolved into a source of friction. In addition to providing the encouragement which had launched his younger brother there, Charles himself also wrote for the *Boston Courier*, and after the war both Adams brothers began writing for the *North American Review*. Despite Charles's seniority, Henry Adams treated his brother's claims to that territory as trespassing. "Damn you, you are treading on my toes" (I, 511), he blasted Charles from Berlin in November of 1866, in an argument over material for articles in the *North American Review*. Adams's letters to Charles adopted an aggressive, often hostile stance, which emphatically reversed the assumptions of disparity with which the correspondence had begun and reduced the imperative of alliance between them. From London in July 1867, for example, citing Charles's own request for stern criticism—"you ask for it, and, by the Prophets, you shall have it" (I, 544)—Adams delivered a lengthy, detailed response to a *North American Review* manuscript of his brother's, first taking apart Charles's argument point by point and then demolishing Charles's style:

> You wrote better than this at College. Your affectations are intolerable. You flounder like an ill-trained actor in your efforts to amuse and to be vivacious. Nervousness thrusts itself out in your sentences as in your ideas. One seeks in vain for that repose and steadiness of manner, on which alone an easy and elegant style can rest. (I, 545)

Turning the tables on his older brother with the accusation of youthful awkwardness, Adams used their writing outside the correspondence to drive a wedge between him and Charles rather than, as before, to mutualize their efforts. Adams's arrogant air firmly positioned him on autonomous turf, inviting from Charles only defensiveness or withdrawal. Despite the fact that the two brothers collaborated on a series of railroad reform articles which they published in 1871 as *Chapters of Erie and Other Essays*, Henry Adams's critiques of his brother's writing remained stubbornly resistant to the kind of rhetorical compromise which would have encouraged exchange between them. "As for style, I am rather surprised at your criticism . . . ," he wrote in response to Charles's article "Railroad Inflation" in the *North American Review*, from Washington in January 1869, rising up to lash back with unrelenting sharpness at his older brother's judgment; "Polish be damned. I never tried to polish in the sense of smoothing. . . . That is all I have ever said of your style—get rid of your tricks" (II, 12). Charles himself seems to have shared, and contributed to, his younger brother's defensiveness, for he published anonymously a long critical review of Adams's 1879 *Life of Albert Gallatin* in the *Nation*.[18] Moreover, Charles's acerbic self-justification to the editor of the *Nation* suggests how deeply issues of territory and even loyalty and betrayal entered into exchange between the two brothers: "If Henry and his wife can't stand that, but insist on pure and solid taffy, he'd better stop writing. My good sister-in-law don't favor me much now, and if she finds it is I who dared criticize her adored Henry, my goose will be finally cooked. . . ."[19]

"As you know, I loved Charles," Henry Adams was later to confide to Henry Cabot Lodge at his older brother's death in 1915, "and in early life our paths lay together, but he was a man of action, with strong love of power, while I, for that reason, was almost compelled to become a man of contemplation, a critic and a writer" (VI, 705). Like his 1867 resolution to "make it impossible" for himself to follow "the family go-cart," Adams's insistence that he was "almost compelled" by Charles's "action" and "power"—and, perhaps, by his own impulse to emulate his older brother's example—to make a different claim for himself reveals the enormous pressure to achieve parity under which Adams's earliest letters, to Charles Francis, Jr., labored. In all these letters, Adams's sense of territoriality feels central: the strategies which he developed in them for consolidating his own authority honored boundaries and hoarded difference. This wariness toward Charles eased only near the very end of Adams's life, when chronic illness had exhausted Adams and parity ceased to feel either so fragile or so important to him. He could then write to his older brother, from Washington in November of 1912, and remember their relationship with more generosity: "Thanks for your letter which is a turning back to our youth quite in the spirit of love and bounty" (VI, 565).

The Economy of Comradeship: Henry Adams's Early Letters to Charles Milnes Gaskell

Near the end of his stay in England and after his return, in the late 1860s, to the United States, Henry Adams turned away from writing letters to his older brother. When the English aristocrat Charles Milnes Gaskell replaced Charles Francis Adams, Jr., as Henry Adams's major correspondent, the locus of validation in the letters shifted from family to class and peer group. Like his correspondence with Charles Francis, Jr., Adams's correspondence with Gaskell began, after they met in April 1863 in Cambridge, under conditions of disparity: the son of a British M.P. who would eventually occupy his own seat in Parliament, Gaskell was impeccably connected among the English landed gentry; and although Gaskell was several years younger he could offer Adams the entrée into a literary and intellectual circle of male peers in London for which Adams had been hungry throughout his entire, isolated stay during the Civil War years in England. As he wrote to his older brother from London in October of 1864 after his first visit to Gaskell's family home, Adams felt grateful to Gaskell for providing him "a species of quiet success, so curiously different from the usual stiffness of English society . . ." (I, 451). Like his early letters to Charles Francis Adams, Jr., Henry Adams's early letters to Charles Milnes Gaskell were rhetorical performances calculated to earn Adams parity with his correspondent. But while Adams's letters to his older brother had used strategies of differentiation to broker transition, his letters to Gaskell used strategies of bonding to control difference. Adams came to count on Gaskell's steady presence, and he sought Gaskell out in England at regular intervals throughout his life. In turn, Gaskell made his considerable resources available to Adams whenever Adams was in need: Gaskell loaned his London townhouse to Henry and Marian Adams on their wedding trip in 1872; Adams sought solace with Gaskell in England after Marian Adams's suicide in 1885; and Gaskell provided Adams emotional refuge during a painful crisis in Adams's relationship with Elizabeth Sherman Cameron, in 1891. Adams's letters reflect the lifelong continuity of his relationship with Gaskell, for in them negotiating parity evolved steadily into a process of alliance rather than of resistance; and Adams's commitment to writing letters to Gaskell continued, virtually without interruption, through the last months of his life.[20]

Adams's letters initially sought to ally him to Gaskell by proving Adams's worthiness as an exemplar of a privileged literary and cultural tradition. Adams's eagerness for that validation showed in a shift in how he positioned himself with respect to the eighteenth-century English familiar letter writer Horace Walpole: while, for example, Adams had claimed, however disingenuously, in a letter to his older brother that he had "no ambition nor hope to become a Horace Walpole," he explicitly identified himself with Walpole and his circle in his correspondence with Gaskell. "Do you know," he wrote to Gaskell from Washington in November 1869, after the Adamses had returned to the United States,

> I have taken up the ever youthful Horace Walpole again, and make him my dinner companion. What surprises me most is that he is so extremely like ourselves; not so clever of course, but otherwise he might be a letter-writer of today. I perpetually catch myself thinking of it all as something I have myself known, until I trip over a sword, or discover there were no railways then, or reflect that Lord Salisbury and not Lord Carteret lives over the way. But all seems astonishingly natural to me; strangely in contrast to what it once seemed. If we didn't know those people—Primoministerio Palmerstonis— then we knew some one for all the world like them. (II, 52)

As this letter suggests, demonstrating his compliance with established standards for the familiar letter felt crucial to Adams as a strategy of class iden-tification, meant to locate him among others "so extremely like ourselves," the elite beneficiaries of those standards. The imperative of achieving what the familiar letter writer John Hoskins called "a kind of diligent negligence" was never simply an aesthetic one.[21] On one hand, the conventions of the familiar letter were rooted in a privileged fiction of informality and privacy. A good familiar letter tried to convey the ease and naturalness of a conversation, emphasizing the process of engagement rather than either information or a finished product.[22] On the other hand, the familiar letter's allegiance to informality was sustained by amply articulated, formal rules and assumed the eventual presence of a public audience.[23] The conceit of spontaneity and ease reflected among men of leisure an assured superiority to quotidian pressures and concerns, a lack of obligation to accomplishing tasks; at the same time, their shared understanding of the conceit reflected confidence in the public resonance of their personal concerns. The familiar letter tradition spoke eloquently for the writer's privileged denial of the potential for conflict between private voice and public world.[24]

Henry Adams built in his early letters to Charles Milnes Gaskell on the confidence as a writer which he had earned in his letters to Charles Francis, Jr. But while literary virtuosity had earned Adams autonomy in his letters to his older brother, from the start it served in Adams's letters to Gaskell as a strategy of reciprocity instead. When, for example, Gaskell invited his help with a satiric essay on a paleontological expedition, Adams responded, from London in March of 1867, by inviting Gaskell to engage in rhetorical play very much in the familiar letter tradition:

> It is easy enough to write on the subject without any acquaintance with it, but a dash of truth would add a certain base to the dish. Could you not hammer out a few couplets in the style of Heine or some other fellow, on the Bos primigenius? Or any other subject? There is nothing like an experiment. Catch an idea, and then hammer out the rhymes. Or omit the rhymes and do it in classic style; Horace, Catullus, Tibullus, Propertius, or some other blessed antique. You send me one verse and I will try to cap it. (I, 526)

Much as he had seen his early letters to Charles Francis Adams, Jr., as "good practice, this fencing with each other," Adams recognized in his early letters to Gaskell the chance to use friendly competition to build rhetorical agility and range: "You send me one verse and I will try to cap it." But from the start Adams entered the ring with Gaskell as an aspiring equal, emulating the examples of literary predecessors rather than the model of his correspondent.

The strain which shows in many of Adams's early letters to Gaskell dramatizes the transitional status of Adams's attempt to acquire the authoritative voice of the "man of the world," above the ordinary fray of events, that he must have thought would appeal to Gaskell's ear. In many of these letters, Adams's efforts to impress and win over his new friend with his sophistication

seem almost laughably affected, signs at least as much of Adams's youth and
naiveté as of his sophistication. From Italy in March 1865, for example, Adams
wrote to Gaskell:

> Sorrento is empty or nearly so, except for a stray American or two
> whom we do not know. I don't think it a good winter place. Amalfi would
> be better, with equally good hotels. But the air is soft and the orange and
> lemon groves full of fruit. I can contrive to drag on a burdensome existence,
> even though it does rain today; especially as the cuisine is good. I could
> wish that the weather was a little steadier and that there was some medium
> between a rainy Sirocco, and a howling Tramontana, but if one must be a
> victim to weather, one suffers as little at Sorrento as at most places. (I, 480–81)

In this letter Adams cultivated for Gaskell a voice born to "good hotels," decent
"cuisine," and hired servants, a voice which belonged much more to the milieu
of British country squires like the Gaskells than to the American Adamses.
Parading his expertise about the landscape of elite leisure, about the quality
of life in Amalfi, and about Mediterranean wind conditions like the "rainy
Sirocco" and the "howling Tramontana" in predictable detail, above either
surprise or naive delight, Adams proclaimed his indifference to the "burdensome existence" which he claimed to be "suffering" on holiday in Italy. Two
years later, from Baden-Baden in August 1867, Adams was still sighing to
Gaskell, equally predictably, of his ennui, this time with a Paris which he took
superior pleasure in seeing crowds of ordinary tourists gawk at:

> Life has been a burden to me for the last fortnight so that I have not been
> able to put pen to paper since I left England. We crossed to Paris on the 10th
> and in that infernal city we remained till the 20th, waiting for ladies' dresses
> and the milliners' bills. You should run over to Paris by all means. Otherwise
> you will be deprived of the precious privilege of abusing it; a privilege which
> I value so highly that I have done little else but exercise it since I arrived there.
> I do not hesitate to say that at present it is a God-forsaken hole, and my party
> unanimously agreed that their greatest pleasure since arriving, was in quitting
> it. . . . (I, 546–47)

If Adams's weariness with the "burdens" of female whim and of the "infer-
nal," "God-forsaken hole" of Paris rings rather false in the mouth of a man not
yet thirty years old, that very pretension attests to these letters' commitment
to mastering a voice whose experience of surfeit was not genuinely Adams's
own but which represented to him a means of gaining access to Gaskell and
of engaging Gaskell as a correspondent. The fact that Adams eventually outgrew the mannered pretensions of these early letters to Gaskell suggests how
secure he came to feel about his status as Gaskell's peer. When Adams wrote

to Gaskell in July of 1870 from his sister's bedside in Italy, where Louisa Adams Kuhn was slowly and gruesomely dying from lockjaw, he directly confronted an experience at the very edge of human endurance and comprehension in moving, skillful language, and refused to take refuge in the detached, predictable voice that he had earlier affected in his letters to Gaskell:

> One night my sister, reduced to the last extremity, gasped farewell to us all, gave all her dying orders, and for two hours we thought every gasp was to be the end. Her breath stopped, her pulse ceased beating, her struggles ended, a dozen people at her bedside went down on their knees, and my brother-in-law and I dropped our hands and drew a long breath of relief to think that the poor child's agony was over even at the cost of suffocation. But after nearly half a minute of absolute silence, the pulse started again, the rattling in the throat recommenced, and presently she waved her arm as though she were ordering death away, and to our utter astonishment commanded us to bring her some nourishment. (II, 73–74)

Such letters proved Adams's ability to cope with, and to express, emotional trauma from which he could count on neither his family nor literary convention to shield him, and positioned him in an increasingly adult posture in his letters to Gaskell.

Like his letters to Charles Francis Adams, Jr., Henry Adams's letters to Charles Milnes Gaskell used Adams's increasing sense of literary professionalism to create transition in his correspondence, to alter his relationship to his correspondent. But while his assertion of literary maturity had posed a challenge to Adams's bond with his older brother, it made it possible for Adams to appeal to Gaskell as a potential ally, outside the sphere of family. Articulating for Gaskell his satisfaction with his success as a political journalist, as editor of the *North American Review*, and as a history professor at Harvard simultaneously displayed Adams's worthiness of Gaskell's friendship and made Adams insistent about his family's receding importance. Writing to Gaskell from Washington in April 1869, for example, Adams took keen pleasure in his independence as a reform journalist—"I rather like all this, for no one can touch me and I have asked nothing of any living person. I express pretty energetic opinions all round, and I wait till the cards are played out"—and went on in the same letter to confide, "Of my family I know almost as little as you do" (II, 25). While his claims of access to an audience wider than the private circle of their correspondence had helped to open a breach between Adams and his older brother, Adams used the same claims to ally himself to Gaskell as a worldly adult in whom he could confide his impatience with the limits of family. In writing to Gaskell, Adams described with pride, yet without competitiveness, his rise to notoriety as a political writer: returning to Washington from a European trip, in September 1870, Adams wrote,

> I found myself growing in consequence. My last article had not only been reprinted entire by several newspapers, but the party press had thought it necessary to answer it. . . . What is more, I am told that the democratic national committee reprinted it in pamphlet form and mean to circulate two hundred and fifty thousand copies of it. If I get a copy I will send it to you as a curiosity. You see I have a tolerably large audience at least. (II, 81)

Summarizing his first year's work at Harvard and on the *North American Review*, from Cambridge in March 1871, Adams wrote to Gaskell with similarly plain pleasure at having successfully met a series of difficult professional challenges on his own:

> My labors are drawing to a close for this year. I have brought my youths so far that I can now see the end. My heavy reading is pretty much finished. My April number of the N.[orth] A.[merican] R.[eview] will be out on the 30th and my work on it is over. So I am ready to enjoy the Spring and to grumble that I have not enough to do. The fact is, I like being overworked. There is a pleasing excitement in having to lecture tomorrow on a period of history which I have not even heard of till today. (II, 103)

At the same time as he made such possessive, territorial claims for himself, Adams emphasized to Gaskell the sense of frustration and claustrophobia that he felt when he was surrounded by his family: "my family retains its Bostonian stupidity. I go into town nearly every day to dine with them, and come out again after dinner" (II, 104).

Perhaps the most sharply defined transition which Adams's letters to Gaskell negotiated was the accommodation of women within an exchange system which had previously been exclusively male and which had been shaped by the notion of "men of the world." In his letters to Gaskell during the years just preceding and following his 1872 marriage, Adams made defusing the threat of change and protecting threatened parity between two male correspondents a central priority of writing.

Before his engagement, Adams's letters to Gaskell struck a pose of beleaguered resistance, positioning both correspondents defensively against the social and sexual pressures which Adams felt as an eligible bachelor of his class coming of age. Adams's complaints about the marriage plans of their mutual friend Sir Robert Cunliffe, for example, adopted, tongue in cheek, a rhetoric of threatened loyalty and of betrayal. "My wrath at the baronet is considerable for having dared to write me a long letter five days before his engagement was announced, and never hinting at it to me," he wrote to Gaskell from Quincy in July 1869, going on later in the same letter; "Would to God that I too could find a mate, but I despair of that. So, as it is good that there should always be a few unmarried men to maintain society and the social bond, I devote myself to this noble task" (II, 40–41). Similarly, in a letter from Washington in April 1870, Adams took Gaskell aside to poke aloof fun at their comrades' social ambitions and to close ranks with Gaskell in resisting obligation, and vulnerability, to the rites of passage looming just ahead of them:

> I propose to be as tender as an angel to all the young women. I propose—
> God have mercy on my soul—to talk with all the rising young men. And I
> propose that you shall carry me about everywhere and do the same things,
> else how can we laugh at them together. (II, 69–70)

On one hand, the posturing visible in such letters—the thin veneer of "noble" arrogance over layers of anxiety and wariness—was clearly a strategy of male bonding, intended to appeal to Gaskell as a fellow sufferer. On the other hand, while Adams committed himself in his letters to Gaskell to the "noble task" of evading the fated routines of courtship, he also seemed shyly eager to be validated in conventional terms as a young man-about-town. From Cambridge in February of 1872, for example, he confided to Gaskell with evident enjoyment the story of one of his flirtatious escapades:

> From a retired and dignified Professor I have come out again as a social
> butterfly. . . . Only last Saturday I made a sensation by giving a luncheon in
> my rooms here, at which I had the principal beauty of the season and three
> other buds, with my sister to preside; a party of eleven, and awfully fashion-
> able and larky. They came out in the middle of a fearful snowstorm, and I
> administered a mellifluous mixture known as champagne cocktails to the
> young women before sitting down to lunch. (II, 130)

Self-conscious, self-ironic, and self-dramatizing, these letters to Gaskell speak audibly to the difficulties of transition which Adams tried to manage by reinforcing a familiar, gendered bond with Gaskell.

Adams's marriage posed an obvious challenge to the protectively male status of this bond, and Adams's letters to Gaskell tried to locate a language which could both preserve its gendered prerogatives and usher exchange between them into the presence of a woman. From Cambridge in March of 1872 Adams wrote to Gaskell, working hard to find an appropriate voice, and announced his engagement to Marian (Clover) Hooper:

> I start on another letter to tell you all I did not tell you before. Imprimus
> and to begin with, the young woman calls herself Marian Hooper and
> belongs to a sort of clan, as all Bostonians do. Through her mother, who is
> not living, she is half Sturgis, and Russell Sturgis of the Barings is a fourth
> cousin or thereabouts. Socially the match is supposed to be unexception-
> able. One of my congratulatory letters further describes my "fiancée" to me

as "a charming blue." She is certainly not handsome; nor would she be quite called plain, I think. She is twenty-eight years old. She knows her own mind uncommon well. She does not talk *very* American. Her manners are quiet. She reads German—also Latin—also, I fear, a little Greek, but very little. She talks garrulously, but on the whole pretty sensibly. She is very open to instruction. *We* shall improve her. She dresses badly. She decidedly has humor and will appreciate *our* wit. She has enough money to be quite independent. She rules me as only American women rule men, and I cower before her. Lord! how she would lash me if she read the above description of her! (II, 133–34)

Bemused, dispassionate, this letter's description of "the young woman" in terms of family pedigree was clearly meant as a caricature of the rhetoric of elite privilege which Adams had earlier affected in his letters to Gaskell. Yet even in irony the letter remained committed to defending the integrity of the male bond between Adams and Gaskell. Simultaneously ticking off his fiancée's most attractive features and "cowering" before her, both gloating and worrying, only half in underscored jest, over "his" woman's looks and her social and intellectual prowess, Adams strained, simultaneously, to initiate and to control change. This letter's thoroughly mixed message served as both a sign and an agent of transition. Eager to display his acquisition, Adams paraded before Gaskell the attributes which he hoped would make up for Clover Hooper's physical plainness. At the same time, Adams tried to contain the threat—"I fear"— to male authority and comradeship which such a gifted, independent woman might pose, even to two sophisticated young men who quite likely prided themselves on knowing better, by sarcastically assuring Gaskell that his fiancée read only "a little" Greek and that "She is very open to instruction. *We* shall improve her."

Two months later, in May 1872, Adams again tried to defuse Clover Hooper's hovering threat to male hegemony by making Gaskell privy to private speculation about her and thus shutting her out of the confidences which these two men shared:

it *is* rather droll to examine women's minds. They are a queer mixture of odds and ends, poorly mastered and utterly unconnected. But to a man they are perhaps all the more attractive on that account. My young female has a very active and quick mind and has run over many things, but she really knows nothing well, and laughs at the idea of being thought a blue. She commissions me to tell you that she would add a few lines to this letter, but unfortunately she is unable to spell. I think you will like her, not for beauty, for she is certainly not beautiful, and her features are much too prominent; but for intelligence and sympathy, which are what hold me. She is quite ready to like you indefinitely, and as she is fond of society and amusement, I do not fear her separating me from my friends. (II, 137)

Clearly Henry Adams saw through his own posturing here: poised between
dismissing "women's minds" and poking fun at the tired language in which
men guard a sense of their own intellectual superiority; between making "his"
woman manageably ignorant and making her an accessory to the joke of her
illiteracy; between judging and dismissing the importance of her physical "features," this letter adopted an ironic stance toward its own patronizing voice.
In fact, it was in large part his own ironic stance toward convention, his ability to transcend the ordinary, which Adams was displaying for Gaskell here;
for Adams both recognized and took pride in his attraction to Marian Hooper's
unconventional qualities, in his secure ability to enjoy these strengths in his
future wife. Yet the conceit of shared male authority which Adams employed
ironically here was, nonetheless, a highly gendered strategy of territoriality,
a means of allaying any anxieties Gaskell might have had about discontinuity in their relationship: "I do not fear her separating me from my friends."

Ultimately, Adams's letters to Gaskell in the years surrounding his marriage brokered transition by controlling the conditions of alliance and by
controlling access to shared territory. The fact that Adams opened up his
relationship with Gaskell to Marian Hooper by making her privy to their correspondence and by validating her as a reader of their letters decisively demonstrates the degree to which parity remained at issue in Adams's early letters.
In the very first letter which followed his engagement announcement, Adams
informed Gaskell that he was sharing Gaskell's letters with his fiancée—"I gave
your's to my young woman who was greatly pleased by it, and I hope you will
soon find out that she is worthy of our society" (April 1872, from Harvard,
II, 134)—at the same time as he used the pronouns "my" and "our" to sustain
the possessive priority of male bonding. Adams opened his next letter to
Gaskell, from Beverly Farms in May of 1872, by confirming Clover's worthiness as a reader of letters: "Your's of May 13th came quickly. I handed it over
to my fiancée who now appropriates my correspondence, and who is quite as
appreciative a reader as I am" (II, 136). In turn, after his marriage Adams relayed
messages from his wife through his own letters to Gaskell. "My wife sends all
sorts of pleasant remembrances and encloses a note to forward" (II, 149), Adams
concluded a letter from Berne on his honeymoon in August 1872. And within
a few months Adams was reporting his wife's reciprocal expectations of letters
from Gaskell. "My wife is indignant with you," Adams coaxed Gaskell from
Boston in December 1873, "because you have never written to her as you said
you should . . ." (II, 183–84).

Henry Adams's early letters, to his older brother Charles Francis Adams,
Jr., and to his friend Charles Milnes Gaskell, expose the transitional status
of authority and the tenuousness of parity for Adams. The letters which Adams
wrote during these early years both documented and acted on a changing set

of needs for autonomy, control, and validation. Their consistent territoriality reveals how deeply the form itself was tied for Adams from the start to a process of claiming and defending authority; their frequent strain reveals how often letter writing was burdened for Adams by the difficulties of sustaining an authoritative voice.

In both these early sets of letters, Adams made a series of fundamentally political moves which challenged inequalities in his relationship to his correspondent. The status of "us" constantly shifted from sanctuary to insufficiency in these letters, as Adams emerged into an increasingly complex social arena—and the form participated directly in this process of transition. Not only records of events but events in their own right, these letters provided Adams occasions for mastering the language by which he could claim and command authority; and they made it possible, in turn, for Adams to construct alliances in his letters which would work, from the start, from the assumption of parity between correspondents.[25]

2   Claiming Allies

In the letters which he wrote during the thirty years following his marriage Henry Adams steadily adjusted the priority of achieving parity between himself and his correspondents, in favor of allying both correspondents in common opposition to public discourse. Returning from Washington in March of 1901 after a six-month stay in Europe, for example, Adams described himself to Charles Milnes Gaskell as helplessly disoriented in modern America:

> Certainly, when I return here after six months in Europe, my poor old senile brain whirls and whizzes for weeks. I do not any longer keep up a pretence of knowing where I am. My country in 1900 is something totally different from my own country of 1860. I am wholly a stranger in it. (V, 225)

Such letters responded to cultural change by consigning Adams irrefutably—"totally," "wholly"—to isolation. But naming the threat of change in these terms also heightened the imperative of alliance by assigning shared responsibility for preserving a set of threatened values. Confiding to Gaskell his alienation invited Gaskell to serve as Adams's collaborator in preserving allegiance to those values and in preserving, in private, a community loyal to them.

In the prefatory letter which he enclosed with copies of his 1909 "Rule of Phase as Applied to History," Adams acknowledged the extent to which the confidentiality of letter writing felt conspiratorial to him:

> This volume sent you was meant as a letter; garrulous, intimate, confidential, as permitted in order to serve a social purpose, but would sound a false note for the public ear. In truth, for the occasion, I am frankly a conspirator; I want to invite private confidence, and the public is my worst enemy.[1]

The letters of Adams's middle years, especially those which he wrote to his male friends Charles Milnes Gaskell, Henry James, and John Hay, dramatize the ways in which privately, even secretly, shared mission—"private confidence"—shaped correspondence for Adams. These letters played an active role in creating the rhetorical conditions under which the imperative of alliance became central; in turn, alliance emerged in these letters as a subversive device, intended to reallocate rhetorical power and control.

The Letter as Agent of Exclusion

His letters of this period served Henry Adams, most plainly, as weapons of exclusion, by erecting a set of rhetorical boundaries which resisted penetration by outsiders. At the same time, in marking boundaries these letters became agents not only of exclusion and resistance but also of community. Adams's anti-Semitism and his stance of public silence provide important examples of the ways in which Adams's letters enclosed a territory of privileged speech whose insularity created commonality as well as difference.

Adams's virulent anti-Semitism made exclusion a precondition of alliance. In locating "the Jew" as a symbol of the corrupting power of money, of the rise of the city, and of the loss of Western European Protestant hegemony, Henry Adams joined a chorus of late-nineteenth-century American voices whose range suggests some of the complexity of his alienation, as well as the broadly disruptive status of cultural transition.[2] On one hand, Adams's anti-Semitism spoke for patrician resentment, both of the growing visibility of a generation of nouveau riche capitalists whose power felt alien to many inheritors of the republican tradition, and of the immigrant workers whom many Anglo-Saxons, like Theodore Roosevelt, saw in extreme terms, as the harbingers of "race suicide."[3] On the other hand, Adams shared his anti-Semitism with the grassroots Populist movement, which identified Jews with problems of tightening financial credit and "the international gold ring."[4] Like both the patricians and the Populists, Adams made the Jews serve a reality which was his rather than theirs. "If the Jew did not exist," Sartre observed, "the anti-Semite would have to invent him": Adams invented his "Jew" as a symbolic locus of blame for the sense of disempowerment whose real sources felt inaccessible to him or were difficult for him to accept.[5] Equally important, like all scapegoating, Adams's was also a rhetorical gesture which sought to rally a set of allies in opposition to a common enemy. Adams's anti-Semitism aggressively named alien a people who figured his own fears of being rendered alien and, at the same time, summoned an audience whose presence validated him as a member of a resisting constituency.

Adams's letters simultaneously released him from his obligation to a world which felt isolating to him and constructed an audience bound by their own oppositional stance. Adams made "Jew" stand in his letters for materialistic display, over which he and his correspondents could gloat together in superior pride rooted in a common store of social expertise. "The house is poor,— and Jew!" he dismissed Coutances, for example, in a June 1907 letter to his close friend Elizabeth Sherman Cameron from Paris, exposing violations of etiquette and emphasizing his recognition of the distinction between money and taste; "The bric-à-brac—boiseries, tapestries and singeries,—excessively rare and fine; costly to a fault; styles to despair; but a large Louis XIII house without an entrance or a stair-case; and in every guest-bed-room a bath *beside the bed*" (VI, 74). Adams turned phrases with intentional, ironic cruelty in order to appeal to his reader's appreciation of his calculated casualness and sophistication: "I stroll down the Avenue of the Bois every morning before breakfast to look at the Jewesses and the horses, as though the season were May" (IV, 519), Adams wrote to Cameron from Paris in January 1898; and, again to Cameron, from Warsaw in August of 1901, "we had the pleasure of seeing at last the Polish Jew, and he was a startling revelation even to me, who have seen *pas mal de Jew*" (V, 276). If his anti-Semitism absolved Adams of responsibility for his own sense of powerlessness, it also constructed a community within which he remained allied to familiar sources of power. In February 1914, for example, Adams sighed to Charles Milnes Gaskell from Washington:

> The winter is nearly over, I am seventysix years old, and nearly over too. As I go, my thoughts turn towards you and I want to know how you are. Of myself, I have almost nothing to tell. It is quite astonishing how the circle narrows. I think that in reality as many people pass by, and I hear as much talk as I ever did, but it is no longer a part of me. I am inclined to think it not wholly my fault. The atmosphere really has become a Jew atmosphere. It is curious and evidently good for some people, but it isolates me. I do not know the language, and my friends are as ignorant as I. (VI, 635)

On one hand, this letter blamed Adams's disempowerment on the "Jew atmosphere" that was paralyzing and even aging him, and "isolating" him from the public of which he was "no longer a part," whose "language" he no longer knew. On the other hand, Adams exploited the threat of otherness which he himself had raised, by identifying privately with "my friends [who] are as ignorant as I," by dramatizing the necessity of turning "towards you," and by consolidating a set of increasingly insular ties: "the circle narrows."

Adams's frequently articulated stance of public silence used the imperative of exclusion as a similar strategy for forging subversive ties. Adams dramatized his silence as a stance of protest, as a refusal of complicity with mass values and with the dominant mode of action and speech.[6] While Adams's aggressive withdrawal did not, like his anti-Semitism, lash out at objects of hatred on whom he laid the onus of his own frustration, it remained similarly poised between rhetorical defensiveness and rhetorical aggression. "My first rule of self-preservation . . . is to hold my tongue . . . ," Adams informed his brother Brooks from Paris in November 1910; "Truth is poison. . . . Yet silence is a sort of truth, and equally virulent,—sometimes, I think, more so" (VI, 381). In choosing public silence Adams claimed simply to be protecting his obligation to a set of "truer," threatened values. Yet Adams's confidentiality with his correspondents actively drew a line between a public world in which he refused to speak and a world within which he maintained control over speech. "I have deliberately put about the story that I am quite ga-ga, to protect myself from people who talk" (VI, 708), he wrote to Gaskell from Washington in December 1915, confirming his control over that line.[7] Similarly, Adams concluded his November 1901 letter to Brooks Adams, from Paris:

> It is imbecile! I can think of nothing but silence and seclusion to escape the dilemma. Action of any kind whatever only hastens the acceleration. All I can do is to assure my getting out of it within five years, but my tail-feathers are caught already. The mess is all about me. . . . (VI, 381)

Adams characterized himself and his correspondents as collaborators against the looming possibility of compromise. To refuse to participate publicly in a culture which was at the brink of disorder constituted for Adams not only self-denial but, equally, self-dramatization. "I look on our society as a balloon," he explained to Brooks from Washington in June 1895,

> liable to momentary collapse, and I see nothing to be gained by sticking pins through the oil-canvas. I do not care to monkey with a dynamo. . . . My destiny—or at least my will, as an element of the social mass in movement—lies in silence, which I hold to be alone sense. (IV, 284)

Declaring silence to be an act of "will" salvaged for Adams, from a situation which he claimed to be helpless to alter, a sense of his own ability to hold chaos at bay.[8] Yet, at the same time, it was Adams's own rhetoric of disaster which made that stance essential and thus legitimated his withdrawal and his construction of private alliance as imperative.

In a frustrating sense, the alliances forged by Henry Adams's letters constituted a kind of self-strangulation, a perpetuation of alienation. There is a fatiguing inevitability in Adams's steady withdrawal behind the boundaries that he drew; and even Adams recognized the fact that he had imprisoned himself within them. From Quincy in June 1887, less than two years after his wife's suicide, for example, he wrote to his friend John Hay with self-defeated irony:

In the entire horizon that bounds my cell . . . I write history as though it were serious, five hours a day; and when my hand and head get tired, I step out into the rose-beds and watch my favorite roses. For lack of thought, I have taken to learning roses, and talk of them as though I had the slightest acquaintance with the subject. (III, 66)

Both Adams's anti-Semitism and his posture of public silence elevated defensiveness and elitism to the unimpeachable status of guardianship. It is this stance apart which has called forth from readers the most impatient accusations that Henry Adams lacked the courage to engage directly a changing America, that he was simply a petulant aristocrat who refused to give up a privileged set of cultural prerogatives: "Adams ran from reality. . . . All that did not harmonize with the hierarchical beauty of the older medieval synthesis was repugnant . . ."; "Adams was incapacitated not by his education, his background, or his intellect, but by his lack of the qualities necessary to political success in a democracy."[9] Yet as Carolyn Porter has pointed out about The Education, Adams used his claims of public disempowerment strategically; for his pose of detachment made possible a different kind of commitment, as a writer.[10] In closing off public responsibility, Adams also generated a set of allies, whose confirming presence legitimated his public silence. In doing so, Adams established a set of rhetorical conditions under which speech remained safe for him and created the possibility of writing an alternative to his own alienation.

The Letter as Agent of Collaboration

If their appeal to a like-minded audience validated the exclusionary gestures which Adams's letters made, those exclusionary strategies also played an active role in creating a set of collaborative relationships by reinforcing a sense of disparity between his correspondents and the world outside their correspondence. "We or our friends have canvassed creation," Adams wrote to John Hay, in October of 1882 from his country house at Beverly Farms, Massachusetts, "and there are but a dozen or two companions in it;—men and women, I mean, whom you like to have about you, and whose society is an active pleasure" (II, 473–74).[11] Such letters simultaneously separated the members of a small, select community, "whose society is an active pleasure" to one another, from the wide "creation" which Adams had "canvassed," and emphasized a unique mutuality among "we," "our friends." Adams made the form itself serve as a token of privileged alliance by locating it at the boundary between public and private discourse which he was struggling to control. "I was grateful for your letter, and for Mrs. Hay's," Adams wrote, again to Hay, from Paris in September of 1900, "because the newspapers were beginning to bother me, and although I am tolerably free from the newspaper habit, I could not altogether disregard their clack" (V, 148). One of the primary functions of these letters was to create an insular rhetorical environment, within which meaning acquired a private status and exchange assumed the status of partisanship.[12] By positioning correspondents in shared opposition to public discourse, these letters invited subversive intimacy; and, ultimately, they rendered intimacy subversive.

Henry Adams's reliance on the letter as an instrument of social differentiation directly reflected the fact that a great deal of his life went on within narrowing circles of privilege.[13] As a student at Harvard, Adams was active in literary clubs, and his own dining club table became a center of "the most select society."[14] As Charles Francis Adams's son, Henry Adams had easy access to an inner circle of political power in Boston and in Washington.[15] During his father's term in London as ambassador, Adams penetrated English society by earning membership in highly selective groups like the St. James Club and the Social Science Society.[16] Later it would be the Cosmos Club, which Adams and some of his friends founded in Washington in 1878, to "promote . . . a social tie and . . . solidarity among men of scientific interests," or New York's Century Club.[17] During the winter of 1880–81, Henry and Marian Adams, John and Clara Hay, and Clarence King formed their tiny private club, the "Five of Hearts," which even went to the trouble of printing its own special stationery.[18] And the Adamses' home in Washington became, during the last years of Marian Adams's life, a salon whose character and vitality were defined by its exclusivity, as an Adams family biographer would later stress with pride: "Mere celebrity or the meretricious fame due to money or office was no passport to the house on Lafayette Square."[19]

Adams's letters did not simply echo the exclusive stance of such groups. They participated actively in creating the rhetorical conditions under which that stance could be sustained. Patricia Meyer Spacks has suggested that the dichotomy between "*we* who talk" and "*them* who listen" in Horace Walpole's letters served as a strategy for creating between writer and reader "a seductive interpretive alliance."[20] A letter from Adams to Gaskell, from Washington in December of 1869, suggests how aggressively Adams used his correspondence to "seduce" mutually corroborating allies:

> Last evening I went with Gen. Badeau to call for the first time on the President [Ulysses S. Grant] and his wife. We were admitted to the room where Gen. Grant and half a dozen of his intimates sat in a circle, the General smoking as usual. There was some round conversation, rather dull. At last Mrs. Grant strolled in. She squints like an isosceles triangle, but is not much more vulgar than some Duchesses. Her sense of dignity did not allow her to talk to me, but occasionally she condescended to throw me a con-

strained remark. I chattered, however, with that blandness for which I am so justly distinguished, and I flatter myself it was I who showed them how they ought to behave. One feels such an irresistible desire, as you know, to tell this kind of individual to put themselves at their ease and talk just as though they were at home. (II, 56)

This passage is infused with Adams's pleasure in his ability to wield language as a conspiratorial weapon by setting up author and reader, on one hand, and subject, on the other, in tension with one another. Slyly using words to render his subject "dull" and ordinary, Adams undermined the officially authorized status of the President of the United States; by adopting a pose of studied casualness, Adams deflated the First Lady's "sense of dignity" and "condescension," ironically relegating both, in a passing reference, to the "vulgar" status of royalty. Staging this scene in a letter to Gaskell committed Adams to an audience—"as you know"—who would recognize the socially coded signals that he sent. The sense of proprietorship which this passage demonstrated in a thirty-one-year-old, ready to insinuate that he had more right to feel "at home" in the White House than its current occupants did, was for Henry Adams a matter of inheritance, belonging in significant part to his family. "As for the White House," Adams recalled his first visit there in 1850, in *The Education*, "all the boy's family had lived there, and, barring the eight years of Andrew Jackson's reign, had been more or less at home there ever since it was built. The boy half thought he owned it. . . ."[21] Yet appealing to Gaskell as "the kind of individual" who would share Adams's pleasure in polishing his scorn for democratically elected officialdom was also a rhetorical strategy, meant to construct a bond based on a privileged reading of this event.

Similarly, Adams reasserted control over meaning which was at risk of being democratized by erecting in his letters a set of rhetorical hurdles for writer and reader to cross together. Appealing to a reader who shared his elite understanding of the world, Adams described, for example, a steamer trip on the Mediterranean, in a March 1898 letter from Beirut to Elizabeth Sherman Cameron:

When I returned on board I found a Mr & Mrs Paton, who call themselves Virginians, but who distil Philadelphia like attar of roses. Paton is—well! you know what a Philadelphian is! Mrs. Paton is—well! as for me I like the female of the species well enough. As Dick Taylor used to say; they are like their own Buck's County chickens. I won't kick at the Patons, although I'd like to; but that evening, at seven, arrived from Cairo fifty more Cookies, all worse than everybody else, mostly American. . . . (IV, 547)

This letter drew a line between Adams and Cameron, on one hand, and the common "species" on the other, by exulting in understanding about "the

Patons" what the Patons did not understand about themselves: although "*they*
call[ed] themselves Virginians," *Adams* knew better, since they "distil[led]
Philadelphia." Adams saw through the Patons' urban pretensions—"well"; "like
their own Buck's County chickens"—and exposed the ignorant simplicity
which they shared with herds of Cook's tourists, "Cookies" to the arrogant
Adams, "all worse than everybody else." In confirming Cameron's ability to
match his own sophisticated assumptions about "what a Philadelphian is!"
Adams allied the two of them against competing, and inferior, interpretations
of social reality.

Adams's correspondence resembled a secret society in holding so close to
the surface its confidential status, in constantly reenacting its own privately
understood significance.[22] His wife's weekly letters to her father suggest how
fully Adams's commitment to private "interpretive" territory was shared by
other members of his circle and sustained in their correspondence. "No good
pictures," Marian Adams pronounced, for example, in an 1881 description of
the house of a "successful public man" where she had dined,

> but plenty of cheap stuff which in the charitable evening light looks well
> enough. An English butler and liveried flunkies add a glamour of magnifi-
> cence calculated to dazzle and charm the simple Congressional guests, and
> the newspaper correspondents think it "magnificent."[23]

Like her husband, Clover Adams drew aggressive boundaries in her letters
around elite standards of "success." She took evident pleasure in subverting
the publicly legitimated authority of elected officials and members of the press,
confirming between writer and reader a sense of confidence in their ability
to see through the pretentious deception of "cheap stuff" and the "glamour
of magnificence calculated to dazzle and charm" the less worldly.[24] Marian
Adams was well aware of her letters' status as performances for a select audience, for she knew that her father often read them aloud in Boston to relatives and friends, and in fact she worried, when her own words sometimes came
back to her in Washington, about the possibility of the letters' reaching the
wrong ears.[25]

Henry Adams openly invoked the image of a wide public world narrowing and yielding to the insular sufficiency of a private community in his October 1882 letter to Hay from Beverly Farms: "The universe hitherto has existed
in order to produce a dozen people to amuse the five of hearts [the Adamses'
private club]. Among us, we know all mankind" (II, 473). Adams's letters
served as the symbolic currency of that community.[26] In them meaning con-
sciously hoarded as private became coded in terms to which only members
had access and was exchanged as shared property. Adams's use of nicknames
in his letters provides the simplest example of such coding. Adams opened a

succession of letters to John Hay from 1882 to 1883, for instance: "Sweet heart" (II, 455); "Dear Sonny" (II, 458); "Dear Pike County Heart" (II, 459); "Cher Coeur" (II, 467); and "My dear Heart" (II, 487), referring repeatedly to the Five of Hearts. Adams also engaged Elizabeth Sherman Cameron's daughter Martha—and her mother, who was reading along—in an ongoing game in which he assigned both of them imaginary names and playfully reversed their roles: he addressed her as his "Dear Aunt Priscilla" (December 1897), and he often signed his letters with the nickname "Dordy" which she had given him when she was very young (July 1892, January 1895, November 1897); sometimes Elizabeth Sherman Cameron also picked up the salutation "Dear Dor" in her letters to Adams.[27] References to specific events familiar to only a few people, perhaps only the two correspondents, all these nicknames reinforced the simultaneity of privacy and connection.

In more complex ways, Adams's letters created an insular linguistic environment similar to that of the seventeenth-century French salon and one of its successors, the eighteenth- and nineteenth-century Anglo-American club, within which members attended to wit and skill in conversation with the same kind of socially and politically coded self-consciousness. Adams's affinity with the elite territory of French epistolary tradition—both with sixteenth- and seventeenth-century court and salon letter writing and with private letter writing of the seventeenth and eighteenth centuries, epitomized by the famous correspondence of Madame de Sévigné—was reflected in his commitment to a similar set of epistolary conventions.[28] Letter writing among the members of the French aristocracy, "l'écho des bavardages des gens du monde," carried a burden of performance which was rooted in salon conversation and inspired rituals of mutual flattery which were similarly charged: "Que vous écrivez bien . . . ," Madame de Sévigné's cousin wrote to her in 1657, "Votre lettre est fort agréable. . . . Qu'on est heureux d'avoir une bonne amie qui ait autant d'esprit que vous!"[29] Demonstrating the proper "spirit" of artful spontaneity in conversation and letters would earn for speakers coveted status as "gens du monde." Similarly, lively conversation was a source of mutual pride within the clubs to which Adams belonged, an equally ritualized sign of social authority: "You will get more live talk about first principles in either our Boston or your New York club in an hour," a fellow member of the Cosmos and Century Clubs once boasted, for example, "than from any gathering of London clergy in a year."[30]

In his letters, Adams made connoisseurship not only a prized condition of alliance but also a prized commodity to be circulated among allies. Linguistic sophistication came in Adams's letters to have an exchange value which was, paradoxically, quite primitive. Like the objects within preindustrial societies whose value inhered in their power to reinforce a sense of mutuality, rather than in their ability to call up a price on an economic market, the words which called attention to Adams's taste and skill had a systemic function, for they honored ritually a commitment to values held in common.[31] Adams's letters drew, for example, on a social lexicon which could be fully unpacked only by readers familiar with a particular elite's experience. "Of course the air up here, near two miles high," Adams wrote to Elizabeth Sherman Cameron in July 1894 from a camping trip in the Rockies, "is rather more stimulating than brandy, and the sky is of that blue which, for my own taste, is a little too keen and merciless, but, at least, like the American mind, has not a shadow or a purple hole to be picked in it" (IV, 206). The stolid impenetrability of "the American mind" and the sharpness of "brandy" served in this letter as coded figures whose knowing exchange would validate between Adams and Cameron both a sense of privileged difference and a sense of privileged commonality. "Winter has come down on us this time," Adams wrote to her again, from Washington in November of 1898, "like a howling herd of office-seekers" (IV, 625), counting for proper metaphorical effect on Cameron's appreciation of the distaste which he felt for mass politics.

Adams's letters carved out a territory of elite speech by confirming his correspondents' and his own virtuosity in a variety of languages requisite of the cosmopolitan "citizen of the world," to whom no corner of the globe would be foreign. Writing to Cameron from a ship returning from Europe in July 1893, for example, that he had been "pavoneggiarcing myself at Lucerne like a Prince" (IV, 115), Adams simultaneously displayed his own linguistic dexterity and cultural fluency and appealed to Cameron as a reader who would be able to appreciate his skill. Similarly, Adams used sudden juxtapositions of vernacular and formal diction to affirm between his readers and himself a connoisseur's sensitivity to innuendo: "The canal was busted and running like an insane mule. The river was quite superb" (III, 179), he wrote, also to Cameron, from Washington in June 1889. Adams used dialect as an ironic device, in order to generate a sense of connection by exploiting a shared recognition of difference. "Ain't I just important?" he teased Cameron from Washington in January 1889; "All the same, important or impertinent . . . do not think I am proud and 'aughty!" (IV, 675). While Adams's early letters, to Charles Francis Adams, Jr., and to Charles Milnes Gaskell, had used foreign languages to emulate the experienced voice to which he aspired, his later letters appropriated the same languages and high-flown diction in order to dramatize his mature recognition of pretension and to ally himself to readers whose ears would be equally subtle: "Even Edith Wharton cannot help me," he wrote wryly to Gaskell from Paris in May of 1909, "though she abides among the high-lights and talks only with *gens-d'esprit à la Louis Quatorze, chez Ritz*" (VI, 247).

Events of ordinary narrative status were converted in Adams's letters into opportunities for displaying his attentiveness to language and his confidence in his correspondents' ability to recognize that care and proficiency: "The spring is here, young and beautiful as ever, and absolutely shocking in its display of reckless maternity" (V, 376), he wrote to Cameron from Washington in April 1902; and again, in February 1904, from Washington, "The winter keeps up its character to the end. Gloom and frost have hung on like heaven. Society seems to feel it. I try to track gossip for you, but it is frozen and damp" (V, 554). Their transcendence of obligation to the mundane necessity of transmitting information reflected these letters' loyalty to the priority of providing pleasure.[32] Adams derived evident satisfaction, for example, from spinning out intricate sentences—crafted, maze-like, to be untangled and admired—out of small, embedded kernels of material. "Did you, or not, leave any plants in my greenhouse?" Adams demanded of Cameron, from Quincy, in August 1888;

> The question is one which I would gladly have answered in the negative, for, ten days ago, I received a series of telegrams and letters from Washington, from which, among a mass of incoherent details about contractors, storms, plants and Mrs. Durkin's bonnet, we eliminated the central idea that, in the process of rebuilding the greenhouse, the contractor had removed the sides while he loaded the top, and one morning, while Mrs. Durkin was putting on her bonnet, he had come in to announce that the whole greenhouse roof was flat on the ground, with the plants and Durkin under it. (III, 135)

The luxury of dawdling together over prose which was more animated than the characters and the events on which it was, ostensibly, reporting would give reader and writer shared enjoyment and validate their leisured status. Similarly, the sharp endings with which Adams sealed off many of his letters, like machines which had been designed to demonstrate the perfection of their own operation, reinforced the letters' commitment to the primacy of style. Adams concluded such letters as decisively as he released his correspondents from the necessity of attending to the ordinary workings of the world around them: "Well! we are all very peaceful now, and out of office. Our songs are lovely" (VI, 595), he sarcastically closed a letter to Cameron from Washington in March 1913. And with equally crisp—and mannered—finality he dropped the curtain on another performance, in a letter to her from Washington in January 1916: "Yet I do not think that here, in America, true thought can ever exist. We never felt it" (VI, 715).

Thus Henry Adams used his letters strategically, to position himself with respect to his correspondents in a stance whose privacy and intimacy constituted, in tandem, a form of alliance against a world which Adams's own prose rendered alien. Like gossip, Adams's letters undermined the authority of public discourse by constructing a private alternative to it.[33]

Adams's letters located themselves both as a point of entry into a rhetorical system over which Adams maintained authoritative control and as the medium of exchange and connection within that system.[34] In constructing their own privilege as publicly threatened, Adams's letters reinforced the private imperative of sustaining that privilege as a source of mutuality and legitimacy.

Private Allegiances: Henry Adams's Letters to Charles Milnes Gaskell, to Henry James, and to John Hay

Henry Adams's letters to three male contemporaries—Charles Milnes Gaskell, Henry James, and John Hay—dramatize more directly the ways in which Adams exploited his own defensive posture in order to claim allies. In his letters to each of these men, Adams referred frequently to a generation of contemporaries which he characterized as besieged. This "generation" served Adams in his letters not only as the central figure in a narrative of public alienation but, equally important, as an agent of private consensus.[35] Adams's rhetoric intensified and validated the imperative of private allegiance, for to engage the threat of a losing battle and a common enemy was, at the same time, to construct a bond of common cause. These letters' emphasis on the tension between public and private discourse posed an ironic challenge to mass democratic values, for consensus itself was transformed in these letters into a prerogative of privilege. The elite models of friendship which this rhetoric characterized as at risk constituted a source of disparity between those whom Adams defined as "his" generation and the rest of Adams's contemporaries; and the threat of change heightened among members of that generation the significance of continuity.[36]

Three passages from Adams's letters to Gaskell, James, and Hay, from Paris in November 1903, dramatize the ways in which Adams made alliance essential by writing his correspondents into a narrative of beleaguerment.[37] In each of these letters, Adams's response to a recently published biography enclosed a territory of private understanding and commitment. In all three cases, Adams distinguished between public knowledge and knowledge shared privately among correspondents, by mourning the public exposure of matters in which the reader and the writer were mutually invested.

Adams wrote first to Gaskell, after reading John Morley's *Life of William Ewart Gladstone*, stressing the distinction between the understanding which he imagined "the world" deriving from Morley's text and the quite different understanding of the same text which he anticipated sharing with Gaskell:

> I feel as though a kind of pious duty required my writing you a letter of sympathy about Morley's murder of Gladstone. Not that the world will ever

know the deed! On the contrary, the world will no doubt regard Morley as giving, rather than taking, life; but to you the double view must be serious. Gladstone was a very decisive element in your life, and came near being so in mine. (V, 521)

A few days later, in response to Henry James's *William Wetmore Story and His Friends*, Adams wrote to James, again emphasizing the narrowness of the community to which the text's full meaning would be accessible:

> So you have written not Story's life, but your own and mine,—pure autobiography,—the more keen for what is beneath, implied, intelligible only to me, and half a dozen other people still living . . . who knew our Boston, London and Rome in the fifties and sixties. You make me curl up, like a trodden-on worm. . . . You strip us, gently and kindly, like a surgeon, and I feel your knife in my ribs. (V, 524)

And a few days after writing to James, Adams wrote to Hay, focusing on the ways in which reading biographies of prominent figures reminded him of the vulnerability to misunderstanding to which he felt both he and Hay were also subject:

> Please read Harry James's Life of Story! Also Morley's Gladstone! And reflect—wretched man!—that now you have knowingly forced yourself to be biographised! You cannot escape the biographer. When I read—standing behind the curtain—these repetitions of life, flabby and foolish as I am;—when I try to glug-glug down my snuffling mucous membrane these lumps of cold calves'-head and boiled pork-fat, then I know what you will suffer for your sins. . . . When I think how all my friends are skewered, and how dreary poor Lowell and Story and Monckton Milnes and Motley and Sumner and Lincoln and Seward and I look in our cages with pins stuck through us to keep the lively attitude of nature, I smile grimly and see you turn ghastly green. (V, 526)

In each of these passages, alliance was actually constituted by Adams's identification of common points of vulnerability; in turn, collaboration was made imperative as a means of mutual protection. Adams bound the writer and the reader of each of these letters by the privileged status which made them objects of public interest and which made them susceptible to public abuse; in doing so, Adams located his correspondents and himself in shared isolation, surrounded by encroaching, uncomprehending readers. Adams reminded Gaskell that "the world" would cooperate in Morley's corruption of Gladstone's memory because it would never know Gladstone as the two of them had, from the unique vantage point of their "double view"; similarly, he stressed to James the fact that only the precious few, "me, and half a dozen other people still

living" who were sensitive enough to feel its probing like "a knife," would recognize the "autobiography" of "our Boston, London and Rome" hidden beneath
"Story's life"; and he warned Hay of the risk that they both ran of being
"skewered" by a crudely "biographising" public, raising before Hay the specter of being exposed publicly, "in our cages with pins stuck through us."

In more extended ways, "us" emerged in Henry Adams's letters to Charles
Milnes Gaskell, Henry James, and John Hay as a rhetorical rallying point,
simultaneously offering a locus of conflict with "them" and naming a locus
of consensus. In these letters, the threat of loss served as a strategic device for
marshaling allies; in them, Adams converted virtually all public events into
occasions for inviting private collaboration among correspondents.

If, for example, in his early letters to Charles Milnes Gaskell alliance had
represented Adams's first achievement of parity with a correspondent, in succeeding letters it invoked Adams's growing sense of disparity with the world
surrounding his correspondence with Gaskell. Within a year of his wife's suicide, Adams had settled in his letters to Charles Milnes Gaskell into a defensive stance, adopted around the imminence of loss. "I have become an old man
in a twelvemonth," he complained to Gaskell from Washington in April 1886;

> The future no longer belongs to us. I care not a silver dollar, even at its
> future value of eighty cents, what kind of society the world is to have; but I
> feel sure that it will be so different from ours that our generation will find it
> a bore. As you know, this settles it. We become *ganaches* [old fogies]. . . .
> (III, 9)

Such letters participated actively in constructing between Gaskell and Adams
the sense of generational continuity which they claimed simply to be defending, by barricading that bond behind a rhetoric of beleaguerment; in turn,
they initiated a collaborative relationship between writer and reader, by naming
the external threat of alienation—"them"—in opposition to "our generation,"
to "us," to a world of "ours." Adams made Gaskell his ally, in other words, by
erecting a defense in both their names. In January of 1894 Adams wrote, similarly, to Gaskell from Beaufort, South Carolina:

> I am myself more than ever at odds with my time. I detest it, and everything
> that belongs to it, and live only in the wish to see the end of it, with all its
> infernal Jewry. I want to put every money-lender to death, and to sink Lom-
> bard Street and Wall Street under the ocean. Then, perhaps, men of our
> kind might have some chance of being honorably killed in battle, and eaten
> by our enemies. (IV, 157)

By setting himself so bitterly "at odds" with the world around him—a world
which his own anti-Semitism had named alien—Adams created a podium from

which he could address Gaskell as his counterpart among "men of our kind." From that position of elevated difference, Adams appealed to Gaskell as a fellow survivor of a threatened class. "I am nothing if not a courtier and a man of fashion;" he wrote slyly to Gaskell from Paris in July 1896, allying himself to Gaskell through their shared patrician skepticism about changing popular taste, "and although I gather that Homburg and his Royal Highness are rather rococo, and not very rigolo, nowadays; and in short that we are all bores together, it will amuse me to see what variety of bore has taken the place of the old types" (IV, 400).

Thus shared difference justified and shaped Adams's bond to Charles Milnes Gaskell in his letters. Equally important, Adams constructed the imperative and the legitimacy of alliance in these letters around the theme of continuity. Adams adopted in his letters to Gaskell a strategy of simplification, distilling a set of frequently repeated concerns which anchored the position from which he spoke.[38] Many of Adams's letters to Gaskell had a formulaic structure, as though they sought simply to make contact by raising a series of professional, political, and social issues of mutual concern. "We are in summer again; I go on with my grind at history; the world chatters louder than ever about its affairs, but it is the same old story," Adams sighed to Gaskell from Washington in May 1884, ticking off a succession of topics as he moved from paragraph to paragraph: "My immediate interest is in a house which I am about to build"—"My second interest is politics"—"You have noticed that we have had another general liquidation which the newspapers call a financial crisis"—"You seem in England to have gone off your heads about Egypt"—"Socially I have little to say" (II, 539–40). In such letters, Adams fixed his position vis-à-vis Gaskell by writing both of them into "the same old story," into a constantly reenacted narrative which stood at a safe distance from change and which did not need explication. Adams expressed little interest in Gaskell's daily life in his letters. "It is a long time since I heard from you, and your winter-fortunes, whatever they were, are still unknown to me. . . ," Adams opened an April 1882 letter to Gaskell from Washington, going on to observe with casual patience, "None of my English correspondents have told me that . . . you have gone into the cabinet or taken an earldom or written an epic poem or done anything senile" (II, 453). For his part, Adams made little effort to provide Gaskell with quotidian detail from his own life. Rather than trying to render for Gaskell his involvement in specific events, for example, Adams surveyed in a transparently generalized way the changes taking place in the United States at the end of the nineteenth century. "So far as I can see, we are all right here. The country is at last filled out; railways all round and through it, and everyone satisfied" (II, 496), he wrote to Gaskell from Washington in March 1883.

Across the Atlantic, Charles Milnes Gaskell became over the years, inevitably, an increasingly less immediate presence in Henry Adams's life. But in his letters to Gaskell, Adams's reinforcement of broadly shared loyalties constantly worked at sustaining continuity between them—and reinforced for Adams, in turn, the imperative of writing letters to Gaskell. Both during and after his marriage Adams held onto the priority of these letters, pushing himself to write to Gaskell even when he had little news to convey. "Our correspondence, for the first time has flagged of late, and indeed it is a wonder to me that it does not expire, for I have literally nothing to write that can possibly be of more than a very vague interest to you" (II, 274–75), he admitted to Gaskell from Beverly Farms in June of 1876; "I drag on, from day to day, and blow my nose and mop my eyes and go to sleep over the oldest books on my shelves" (IV, 360), he yawned from Washington in January 1896, in effect asking Gaskell simply to listen for the regular sound of his voice, for the constant rather than the particular. Letter writing played an active part in holding Adams's connection to Gaskell beyond the reach of time, in binding Gaskell to Adams in ways which resisted change; and Gaskell himself seems to have returned Adams's commitment to that enduring epistolary bond. Anguished in the years following his wife's 1885 suicide, Adams sorted through his effects and tried to shed a past of painful memories and to protect his pain from public exposure. In April of 1890, he wrote to Gaskell from Washington, and offered to return all the letters, spanning twenty-five years, which Gaskell had written to him:

> In anticipation of a long absence, I have gone through all my papers lately, and destroyed everything I should have wished an executor to destroy. Among the rest I have saved a large bundle of your letters, going back five-and-twenty years. I have not had the courage to read them over, but I thought you might like to have them, either to preserve or to destroy . . . . (III, 234)

But Gaskell rejected Adams's offer, refusing to abandon their common memories and affirming his loyalty to the private, even silent, fiction of unchanging continuity which the letters had created: "My poor old letters! I shall not open them and I shall not burn them, as I should look upon the latter act as a sort of burial of the past, and it has given me too many pleasures and enjoyments to be so badly treated. . . ."[39]

Similarly, Adams's letters allied him to Henry James by emphasizing tension between his correspondence with James and the world outside it. In particular, Adams stressed a set of common links to a past which was at odds with the present. Recovering in May of 1913 from a stroke which he had suffered the previous year, Adams wrote to James from Paris,

> Your letter reminds me that it is just a year since I again woke up, after an eternity of unconsciousness, to this queer mad world, ten times queerer

and madder than ever, and what a vast gulf opened to me between the queerness of the past and the total inconsequence of the present. The gulf has not closed: it is rather wider today than a year ago; but I wake up every morning and I go to sleep every night with a stronger sense that each day is an isolated fact, to be taken by itself and looked at as a dance. . . . I take all the help I can get, and hang on to it with a grip that really does me credit. . . .

As for me, I care only for my friends. Write again soon. (VI, 602-603)

Straining to maintain his "grip" on some kind of stability, Adams insisted to James that he turned to letters for constancy, in order to mend the "gaps," in order to close a "gulf" between "queer" past and "inconsequential" present, and between the "isolated" days. Such letters forged an alliance between James and Adams that superseded both human power and the destructive power of time, defining that bond in terms of its difference from "this queer mad world" and insisting, "As for me, I care only for my friends." In the process, Adams's letters to James created their own imperative—by making continuity depend on correspondence and by constructing correspondence as a medium of partisanship: "Your letter reminds me . . . ," Adams opened, and he closed, "Write again soon." James was well connected to the same world of aristocratic Boston as Adams, and James had known Marian Hooper before her marriage to Henry Adams and remained an enthusiastic admirer of hers.[40] James and the Adamses moved in the same international orbit, which brought them together at intervals throughout the 1870s as part of the American expatriate community in Rome, in London, and in Paris; when James visited Washington, first in 1882 and later in 1905, Henry and Clover Adams, and then Henry Adams alone, made living arrangements for him and provided James with a social center; and Adams sought James out in London in 1891 for comfort after his wife's death.[41] Yet despite a passionate final meeting in London in 1914 and despite Adams's considerable sense of loss at James's death, Adams and James were never truly close friends: James found Adams more dry than sympathetic; Adams never read James's work very enthusiastically or shared James's more catholic literary taste; in many ways, Leon Edel concludes, "they made each other uncomfortable."[42] It seems to have been what James represented to him as a fellow survivor and as a surviving connection to his wife which Adams cherished in James; the two shared, as Robert Sayre has put it, "a kind of comraderie, a mutual respect of veterans."[43] It was, therefore, the rhetorical possibility of transcendent loyalty to a common past—rather than intimacy—to which Henry Adams committed his letters to Henry James.

Adams's letters to James invested considerable energy in creating and reinforcing the illusion of unbreakable connection between correspondents. Hovering ambiguously between frustration and pride, Adams named the two of them reluctant exemplars of an outmoded type; "I believe we are all now social luxuries," he wrote to James from Paris in September of 1909, "and, as

for myself, I am much flattered if regarded as bric-à-brac of a style,—dixhuitième
by preference, rather than early Victorian" (VI, 269). Adams appealed to James
as a comrade who could understand the subtle conflicts which cultural change
had imposed on young men reared to the conventional expectations of their
class. "The painful truth," he admitted to James from Paris in his November
1903 response to James's *William Wetmore Story and His Friends*,

> is that all of my New England generation, counting the half-century,
> 1820–1870, were in actual fact only one mind and nature; the individual
> was a facet of Boston. We knew each other to the last nervous centre, and
> feared each other's knowledge. We looked through each other like micro-
> scopes. There was absolutely nothing in us that we did not understand
> merely by looking in the eye. There was hardly a difference even in depth,
> for Harvard College and Unitarianism kept us shallow. We knew nothing—
> no! but really nothing! of the world. . . .
>   Type bourgeois-bostonien! A type quite as good as another, but more
> uniform. (V, 524)

On one hand, Adams lauded the opportunity which James provided him to
identify with a recognizable tradition; on the other hand, Adams seemed to
squirm under the restrictions that accompanied that tradition and reduced
its inheritors to a predictable type, "bourgeois-bostonien." "Your letters, few
as they are, have always the charm of saying something that carries one over
the gaps. . . ," he opened his September 1909 letter to James from Paris, appreciatively, and then went on to insist sarcastically, "Nothing matters much! Only
our proper labels! Please stick mine on, in your wonderfully perfect way, and
I will sit quiet on the shelf, contented among the rest" (VI, 269). In both cases,
Adams constructed a bond between him and James around a past which felt
on the verge of being consigned to irrelevance. If this bond was ambivalent,
that very ambivalence was a sign of shared experience.

Like the artful artlessness of eighteenth-century English epistolary language, the fiction of inheritance rather than of choice was in Adams's letters
to James a made thing. Significantly, although Adams claimed in his 1903 letter to John Hay to feel "caged" by Henry James's characterization of their generation in *William Wetmore Story*, he admitted to James that his loyalty to the
old order of the *dixhuitième* was a "preference." In fact, James responded with
surprise to the introverted sense of finality with which Adams read *William
Wetmore Story*. "*Of course*," he wrote to Adams, "we are lone survivors . . . of
course, too, there's no use talking unless one particularly *wants* to. But the purpose, almost of my printed divagations was to show you that one *can*, strange
to say, still want to—or at least behave as if one did."[44] James claimed that "old
Boston" still had "a golden glow" for him; but Adams committed himself to
an image of James which was painted in the light of his own restlessness, calling

James in a January 1892 letter to Cameron from London, "only a figure in the same old wallpaper" (III, 603).

Perhaps most important, Adams forged alliance by creating in his letters to Henry James special conditions for speech, shaped by the disparity between his need to maintain communication with James and his vow to "sit quiet" among strangers. Adams drew an aggressive boundary in his letters to James between the uncomprehending outsiders whose invasive expectations of "talk" he resented and the insiders whose common understanding of loss he counted on. "Nearly all are gone," he moaned, for example, to James from Washington in January of 1911, feeling in William James's death the loss of an entire generation of male comrades:

> [Henry Hobson] Richardson and [Augustus] St. Gaudens; [John] La Farge; Alex Agassiz, Clarence King, John Hay, and at the last, your brother William; and with each, a limb of our lives cut off. Exactly why we should be expected to talk about it, I don't know. (VI, 407)

In such letters, the posture of speechlessness—"Exactly why we should be expected to talk about it, I don't know"; "There was absolutely nothing in us that we did not understand merely by looking in the eye"—assigned words a ritualistic function, as tokens of shared knowledge and experience rather than as sources of information. If Adams's claim to confidentiality intensified his claustrophobic sense of obligation to fellow exemplars of the "type bourgeois-bostonien," it also conjoined James and Adams as witnesses to a silently respected mutuality.

Finally, like his letters to Charles Milnes Gaskell and Henry James, Henry Adams's letters to John Hay emphasized disparity between the private, insular understanding which the letters reinforced and reality as it was understood by the public outside the correspondence. In particular, Adams used the travel letters which he wrote to Hay as he circled the globe in the years after Marian Adams's death as opportunities to cement old alliances by rendering alien his experience of the new. From Japan, for example, Adams wrote to Hay in July of 1886:

> The temples and Tokugawas are, I admit, a trifle baroque. For sticking a decisive bit of infamous taste into the middle of a seriously planned, and minutely elaborated mass of refined magnificence, I have seen no people—except perhaps our own—to compare with the Japs. . . . Positively everything in Japan laughs. The jinrickshaw men laugh while running at full speed five miles with a sun that visibly sizzles their drenched clothes. The women all laugh, but they are obviously wooden dolls, badly made, and can only cackle, clatter in pattens over asphalt pavements in railway stations, and hop or slide in heelless straw sandals across floors. (III, 15)

Like his anti-Semitism, Adams's racism created distance which he could exploit as a tactic of alliance. Adams's mannered performance claimed its own court: for Hay's corroborating pleasure Adams made the Japanese into jesters, "wooden dolls," "cackling," "clattering," "hopping," and "sliding"; Adams reveled with Hay in his appreciation of the difference between "refined magnificence" and "infamous taste." Like his letters to Gaskell and to James, Adams's letters to Hay read public occasions in terms which allied both correspondents as members of an increasingly isolated "generation." "It is a new century, and what we used to call electricity is its God," Adams intoned to Hay from the Paris International Exposition in November 1900, emphasizing the tenuousness with which their own language for the physical world resonated in a suddenly unfamiliar public arena: "I can already see that the scientific theories and laws of our generation will, to the next, appear as antiquated as the Ptolemaic system . . ." (V, 169).

If his letters to John Hay evince the consistency with which Adams built collaborative relationships around shared class background and past, they also demonstrate Adams's ability to buttress the alliances which he constructed in his letters by taking advantage of differences among them. Adams did not share a common background with John Hay as he did with Charles Milnes Gaskell and with Henry James. The son of a country doctor in an Illinois Mississippi River town, Hay came to most of his money through marriage, and his rise to political power, from service as assistant secretary to Abraham Lincoln to the positions of ambassador to the Court of St. James and secretary of state under McKinley and Theodore Roosevelt, took place through the diplomatic ranks.[45] Perhaps most important, unlike Gaskell and James, Hay became a daily presence in Henry Adams's life in Washington, a fact which the Hays and the Adamses consecrated by commissioning together from H. H. Richardson a double house which was being completed, across from the White House, when Marian Adams committed suicide in 1885.[46] Adams's letters to all three of these men allied correspondents around a privileged continuity; but Adams's letters to Hay constructed a bond around the quotidian intimacy which his letters to Gaskell and James resisted. Adams waited, for example, until he had returned to the United States to send Gaskell news of his 1886 trip to Japan with John La Farge, summing up the entire experience to fit it to a consistent characterization of the man of the world, superior to the local: "My journey to Japan," he wrote to Gaskell from Washington in December, "had at least the advantage of consuming five months, and of doing it in a very amusing way" (III, 48). But Adams regularly dispatched from Japan detailed comments which invited Hay into the daily, viscerally felt experience of the trip: "Japan," he informed Hay from Nikko in August, "is the place to perspire" (III, 32).

Adams's letters to Hay were unique in assigning as much importance to both correspondents' status as individuals, bound by explicitly articulated emotional commitment, as to their status as exemplars of a type. These letters enclosed a zone of intimacy by employing a rhetoric of retreat to an island, where private jokes and indulgences served as signs of mutual loyalty. "You will take me in too, and give me something to do," Adams coaxed Hay, who was working to establish Western Reserve University in Cleveland, from Beverly Farms in October of 1882; "I don't know any history, but I know a little of everything else worth knowing, and can teach just as well without any knowledge at all" (II, 475). "I thought you had forgotten me, so long is it since my last letter was written;" he opened a September 1885 letter to Hay from Beverly Farms during his wife's difficult final months, "but if you have set up an island, I admit the excuse. Please appoint me governor" (II, 626). Adams's letters to Hay intensified, rather than transcended, immediacy, by holding close to the surface Adams's need for Hay, in a ritualistically repeated refrain: "If you and [Clarence] King were with us, we would capture the ship, turn pirate, and run off to a cocoa-nut island" (III, 13), he teased Hay, from San Francisco in June of 1886, before he had even stepped off the American continent on his trip to Japan with La Farge. Less than a month later, on the heels of his arrival in Japan, Adams needled Hay again, from Yokohama in July, "We have been here a week. Between the wish that you were with us, and the conviction that you would probably by this time be broken up if you had come, I am distraught" (III, 14). And two and a half weeks later, from Nikko, he confided to Hay, tongue in cheek, his frustration with the pretensions of the American art collector Ernest Fenollosa, "My historical indifference to everything but facts, and my delight at studying what is hopefully debased and degraded, shock his moral sense. I wish you were here to help us trample on him" (III, 24). While the boundaries which these letters drew spoke, without question, to Henry Adams's elitism, they spoke as well to his sense of vulnerability, and revealed the extent to which trust and emotional safety were at issue in this correspondence. Writing to Hay from Bayreuth in July of 1901, in the wake of the tragic death of Hay's twenty-four-year-old son, Del, Adams allowed himself to be movingly reminded, by a performance of the *Götterdämmerung*, of the sadness with which his wife's 1885 suicide continued to burden him:

> I have done the Ulysses and the Waring rôle for fifteen years; am still doing it, and shall grow imbecile in it. . . . I must still have symptoms of life in me. It is strange to have pulled through every emotion, and to have buried them all, and, millions of aeons afterwards, to find oneself rolling on one's own grave. Every time I hear the Götterdämmerung, I am twisting like a trod worm, for a week.
>
> Happily, no one knows, except perhaps a few other twisters, like you. . . . (V, 269)

Adams's letters to John Hay epitomize the ways in which his letters to all three of these male peers rendered intimacy subversive, by undermining the authority of the world outside the correspondence and by enlisting as allies correspondents—the fellow "twisters" on whose sympathy he counted—whose exchange of letters insulated them from obligation to public discourse. In creating the sense that intimacy was uniquely viable within the boundaries that they drew, Adams's letters to Hay made the world outside those boundaries serve the act of bonding within them: his racist condescension belonged to a rhetorical agenda whose priorities had nothing to do with either Japan or "Japs" but served, rather, as a point of opposition against which Adams could ally both correspondents. The private consensus which these letters not only defended but to a significant degree constructed served Adams's own need to resist dependence on public validation as well as his need to sustain under pressure both privilege and alliance.[47]

Sustaining Alliance

Ultimately, then, the stance of loss which Henry Adams's letters adopted was a strategic device, which initiated for Adams the process of claiming allies. Establishing disparity was an essential precondition to Adams's realignment of those allies in such a way as to constitute collaboration. "As I see the entire world today," Adams complained to his younger brother Brooks from Washington in January 1910,

> it has already reached its lower level, and is likely to stay there. It cannot get much flatter. You may cut off the heads of every rich man living,—of every statesman,—every literary, and every scientific authority, without in the least changing the social situation. Artists, of course, disappeared long ago as social forces. So did the church. Corporations are not elevators, but levellers, as I see them. I cannot see, for example, how France, which is the best type of future society, would be changed by changing anything more. It is resolved into individuals without tie. (VI, 302–3)

Here Adams summarized a great deal of his quarrel with a modern world in which the sources of authority and meaning—statesmanship; literature; science; art; religion—in which he felt invested had been rendered superfluous by anonymous political, social, and technological forces. Significantly, Adams claimed to experience these cultural changes as a breakdown of community: "It is resolved into individuals without tie." The personalized sense of dispossession into which he translated cultural transition was strategically essential in Adams's letters, for it provided both the condition against which the letters defended him and the rhetorical center around which the letters drafted collaborators.

By constructing a shared sense of loss, Adams's letters constructed a shared sense of commitment; by insisting on their own necessity his letters insisted, as well, on the presence of mutual need. As Adams confided to John Hay's wife, Clara Stone Hay, from the Gaskell family estate in September 1902, the existence of friends whose experience corroborated his own challenged the alienation which they shared: "The Gaskells are alone, and with them I don't feel out of date, for we all belong more or less to the year 1000" (V, 406). Equally, such letters' insistence on the continuing viability of exchange sustained for Adams the ability to resist their own narrative of loss. Mark Twain's dramatic confession of being stymied by the task of writing his autobiography until he hit on the idea of imagining that he was writing letters usefully echoes and illuminates the commitment to alliance as a means of marshaling rhetorical resources which Henry Adams made in his letters.[48] Ultimately, the boundaries which Adams's letters drew created the alliances that they claimed simply to be protecting; by constructing disparity in his letters, Adams claimed a set of allies whose presence converted difference from a condition of loss to a condition of power.

3   Authoring Alliance

The Letter Writer as Author

The tension between private and public discourse which formed the basis of a collaborative stance in Henry Adams's letters also formed the basis of an authorial posture there. The letters which Adams wrote during the several decades following his wife's 1885 suicide ceased to rely so heavily on a world outside their own boundaries either for validation or for opposition. Adams's earlier letters had constructed a condition of difference in order, first, in his correspondence with Charles Francis Adams, Jr., and with Charles Milnes Gaskell, to earn parity; and then, in his correspondence with Gaskell, with Henry James, and with John Hay, in order to exploit disparity for the purposes of alliance. Increasingly, proving difference became less necessary in Adams's letters; and in assuming difference and capitalizing on it rhetorically, in his letters to his younger brother Brooks Adams, to his friend Elizabeth Sherman Cameron, and to Cameron's daughter Martha, Adams was able to assume a substantial degree of authorial autonomy. In each of these correspondences, the letter emerged unmistakably as an authored text: by reducing the priority of a world outside themselves, either as model or as antagonist, each of these correspondences moved beyond the problem of parity and invested language with the ability to define the "true" and the "real" in terms advantageous to the writer.[1]

These letters make it possible to speak credibly and usefully of an "epistolary construction of reality." Thus these letters move the form into a quite central position with respect to the political problems surrounding authorship which realism also addressed, especially the question of authority over the constitution of social "truth."[2] At the same time, these correspondences' rhetorical insularity exposes the falseness for letters of the dichotomy between imaginative text and historical document—between a world independent of the writer and a world made by the writer—which has marginalized the form critically.[3] As other readers are increasingly pointing out, letters do not simply mirror context but, instead, participate actively in its creation; if the condition of absence gives epistolary language a uniquely *"real weight,"* absence also invites fiction making.[4] The events on which Marian Adams's letters reported, for example, became raw material to be worked over and converted into what R. P. Blackmur has called "a long serial fiction."[5] Committed to making Washington social and political life serve her own need to write, rather than to doing faithful service to those events, Clover Adams refused to yield her credibility as a "correspondent" to the journalists who determined "truth" in the public sphere: "My facts are facts, too, which all the special correspondents' are not," she insisted to her father from Washington in 1881.[6] Equally, Henry Adams's letters to Brooks Adams, to Lizzie Cameron, and to Martha Cameron did not simply respond to or interpret "reality" outside themselves; they worked, instead, from the inside. To call these letters "autonomous" or "insular" is not, clearly, to make the claim that they operated in a vacuum. Yet each of these sets of letters did have a rhetorical agenda of its own. These letters were emphatically not simply extensions or agents of an existing relationship between the two correspondents, nor were they simply substitutes, in absence, for conversation; and in fact the actual workings of the relationship outside the correspondence sometimes had an intrusive effect on the letters. These letters' fictionality not only remained visible but served as a visible sign of loyalty to the primacy of private rather than of public exchange.

Not all of Adams's letters initiated exchange in equally autonomous terms; like virtually every letter writer, Adams did not have complete control over the duties to which his letters were accountable. Yet even in correspondences in which his letters owed such public obligations, Adams often made a committed effort to protect the letters' loyalty to a set of private "facts." Adams's letters to John Hay during the period from 1898 through 1905 provide an instructive example of this crucial point. Hay's rise to political eminence coincided with the emergence of the United States as a major international power, and had direct effects both on Hay's relationship to Henry Adams and on Adams's letters to Hay.[7] The 1895 outbreak of the Cuban Revolution and the succeeding Spanish-American War of 1898, in which Adams was actively engaged in behind-the-scenes negotiations, framed John Hay's ambassadorship to England, from April 1897 through August 1898. During the following five years, as U.S. secretary of state, first under William McKinley and then under Theodore Roosevelt, Hay helped to extend radically U.S. authority in the Caribbean, the Pacific, the Far East, and Latin America. Hay was involved in American annexation of the Philippines and Puerto Rico; he was the author of the September 1899 "Open Door" policy, which legitimated U.S. commercial expansion in China; Hay played a major role in establishing U.S. hegemony over the Panama Canal Zone; and when he died in 1905 he was at work on the treaties which would eventually end the Russo-Japanese conflict and confirm the United States as a central arbiter of international relations. As decisively as these events altered the role of the United States on an international stage, they transformed Adams's relationship to Hay: on one hand, the two men's intimacy, as close friends and as neighbors sharing the same house, gave Adams direct access to international diplomacy; on the other hand, it provided Hay with trusted counsel on which he relied virtually daily when Adams was in Washington. Clearly the political collaboration which took place between Adams and Hay established an important set of concerns for Adams's letters; and in part, Adams's letters were accessories to the role of "stable-companion to statesmen" which he played outside the correspondence.[8] Yet, just as clearly, Adams remained reluctant to concede correspondence to these political tasks, and he often acted to maintain the letters' insularity.

Adams's earliest letters to Hay during this period illustrate the ways in which he directed exchange with Hay outside the correspondence by offering counsel on political events. In May 1898, soon after Hay had assumed the ambassadorship to England, and after the mysterious sinking of the U.S. Battleship *Maine* in Havana harbor, Adams wrote to Hay from Brighton, offering him help in avoiding war with Spain over Cuba:

> As soon as I can get my teeth sharpened, and a new false set made, I shall come over to take care of you. . . . our first step should be to notify Goluchowski [the Austrian foreign minister] that we are as anxious as Austria is to save the dynasty in Spain, and that we will make any reasonable concession which will tend that way. (IV, 590)

His emphatic shift from reporting to Hay on his dental problems to defining "our first step" in diplomacy signaled Adams's commitment to turning private exchange to the wheel of public, diplomatic discourse. A week later, Adams was yet more emphatic about the priority of state diplomacy. In a series of succinct paragraphs, Adams presented to Hay a peace plan complete with a set of explicit instructions on Hay's own role:

> What we shall want now is to settle our own ideas. . . . I would propose an armistice based on liberal terms like these:
> Spain recognises the independence of Cuba. She grants complete autonomy to Porto Rico. . . . In consideration of these concessions, the United States will not exact a war indemnity. . . .

> If we can get these points admitted by Russia and France, I've little
> doubt that Austria would jump at them, and all the powers would press
> Spain to accept them. . . .
> What we need most is to get our government as quickly as possible to
> formulate its terms of peace. You ought to do that, since your position re-
> quires you to know what language you are to hold. No one except you, on
> this side the water, can speak with so much authority. . . . (IV, 594–95)

As decisively as Adams laid out his scheme and the wide array of countries
involved, he located the meaning of this letter outside the correspondence,
where the major impact of exchange between Adams and Hay would be on
players other than themselves. Equally, Hay's role as a public figure often determined the subject matter of Adams's private letters to him: "why give it up?
You will find life dull, in the reaction, and I cannot see that you will gain anything" (V, 15), Adams advised Hay, for example, from Paris in August 1899,
when Hay's fatigue and frustration with the post of secretary of state made him
consider resigning from it.

However, if some of Adams's letters to Hay were ready to cede the territory of correspondence to obligations outside it, others presented the entry
of Hay's political life into the correspondence as an unwelcome intrusion. The
political collaboration which took place between Henry Adams and John Hay
was not consistently central in Adams's letters to Hay. In part, this is explained
by the simple fact that face-to-face exchange between the two next-door neighbors made the exchange of letters between them superfluous. Adams's letters
to other correspondents during the part of each year that he spent in Washington tell the story of daily walks and consultation that Adams had no reason to recount to Hay himself. "As the world goes, a Boer peace on Boer terms
is inevitable. . . . Then England will have to take Russia by the throat. . . .
Discussing these matters Hay and I ramble our regular afternoon tramp"
(V, 219), Adams wrote to Elizabeth Sherman Cameron from Washington in
March 1901, telling her what Hay obviously did not need to be told. Yet Adams's
letters to Hay also engaged in much more complex rhetorical posturing, which
actively resisted the incursion of Hay's diplomatic imbroglios into the domain
of correspondence. "You are getting on my nerves. I thought that here, buried
in the twelfth century, I should escape the jimjams of your politics" (V, 128),
Adams opened a June 1900 letter to Hay from Paris, following the news of the
Boxer rebellion against the foreign interests in China whom Hay's Open Door
policy represented; "Your open door is already off it's hinges, not six months
old. What kind of a door can you rig up?" (V, 129), Adams continued sarcastically. At the same time as he mocked Hay's diplomatic achievement, Adams
himself retreated to an isolated rhetorical position in the same letter, and left
Hay to swing alone in the wind:

The fun of it is that it should be just you who have got to decide the thing, supposing that it comes to a decision anyhow, and we are not all wrecked first. As one who belongs wholly to the past, and whose traditional sympathies are with all the forces that resist concentration, and love what used to be called liberty, but has now become anarchy, or resistance to civilisation, I who am a worm . . . would I shut down, or put on steam? . . .

God bless you, my son! I will go back to my cloister and pray to the Virgin for you. . . . above all, you need to know the values of at least two fixed elements. I wish you may find 'em. (V, 129–30)

The emergence here of Adams's "twelfth-century" persona, the retiring, insignificant "worm," marked Adams's growing commitment to a set of primarily rhetorical priorities in his letters to Hay, at odds with Adams's commitment to providing helpful counsel to Hay in his struggles outside the correspondence. That "cloistered" narrator, insisting on his "liberty" to resist the tug of Hay's political responsibilities, challenged Adams's own responsibility as an actor in the political arena. Clearly Adams knew that Hay was not having "fun"; but he reinforced his own posturing by employing the transparent conceit of prayer to the Virgin and by closing, "It amuses *me*" (V, 130). Adams's glee at discovering that a government bureaucrat named King had passed this last letter on to Hay with the alarmed note, "We generally put these things in the 'crank box'—but I thought I would ask if you know the handwriting. It's anonymous, and very abusive" (V, 139), dramatically reinforces the rhetorical status which writing letters had assumed for him. "Why did you tell me that there wasn't a single really great man in the Department?" he crowed to Hay from Paris in July 1900; "Your Mr King is the most intelligent person I've yet struck. No one else has ever understood and appreciated me" (V, 138).

Very possibly Henry Adams's withdrawal from political engagement in his letters to John Hay was as much a result of his disappointment with that engagement, especially after his hopes of succeeding Hay in the ambassadorship to England had been dashed, as it was of his commitment to rhetorical autonomy. Adams remained reluctant to give up the input into international diplomacy which correspondence with Hay provided him: "For Forty Centuries I have bitten my tongue off, and babbled only on the stump. I mean to throttle it still; but—but—but—but—hum!—you are going to send a British treaty to the Senate?" he queried Hay, from Paris in November 1901, with heavily dramatized hesitation about interfering in Hay's negotiations for the Panama Canal (V, 303). Yet if Adams appreciated the excitement which politics brought to his friendship with Hay, he also resented the ways in which politics threatened that friendship, by demanding Hay's attention and dominating their time together, and even by making Hay a less responsive companion.[9] More important, Adams came to appreciate the satisfaction of preserving correspondence as a domain of private exchange, where he could choose not to exploit Hay's public influence. "Having no personal animosity to you, more than to the rest of the visible universe, I have thought it best to spare you any remarks I might have had the folly to make about nothing since last May," he wrote to Hay from Paris in September 1903, resisting the temptation to advise Hay on his handling of U.S. involvement in negotiations for the Panama Canal; "I have made them to [Senator Henry] Cabot [Lodge] and Wayne [MacVeagh, chief counsel for the United States in Venezuela negotiations] instead. They bore it with simulated patience" (V, 511). The gap between political involvement and rhetorical autonomy in Adams's letters to John Hay suggests Adams's growing aloofness and also the range of quite different functions which letter writing served for Adams. Even more, it dramatizes the crucial fact that the business which they transacted outside the correspondence may have intensified Adams's commitment to letter writing as an instrument of a worldview—and of an alliance—within which private loyalty could viably compete with public power.

The Autonomy of Correspondences

The autonomous qualities of Adams's letters emerge most visibly in important differences among various correspondences; for Adams assumed rhetorical control over each, as a text, in quite distinct ways. One way to see how independently Adams authored "reality" in these correspondences is to compare the ways in which he treated the same event in each of them. Early in 1898, Adams joined the Hays on a trip to Egypt and the Mediterranean countries (Hay's first leave from his post as U.S. ambassador to England). That trip served, predictably, as an important occasion for letter writing; the substantially different texts which Adams wrote for Gaskell, for Brooks Adams, for Elizabeth Cameron, and for Martha Cameron illustrate in less predictable ways Adams's aggressiveness as an author of letters.

In each of these four letters, the Nile emerged as a different setting for a different narrative with a different cast of characters. First, from Smyrna at the end of the trip, on March 30, Adams wrote to Gaskell:

> Of myself I can only tell you much the old story. I had a month on the Nile with the Hays. It was pleasant. Honestly I am obliged to admit that the Nile itself, all things considered, is still there. It has not essentially changed. Perhaps Cheops might say as much. Cairo has lost color. The Cook tourist is occasionally conspicuous. But from the point of view of Cheops, Herodotus was probably undistinguishable from a Cook's tourist. On the whole, the Nile keeps its local color better than most things.[10]

Several days later, on April 2, Adams wrote to Brooks Adams from Athens:

> Apropos to our—or rather, your—garden! Reflecting at Cairo, Thebes, Baalbek, Damascus, Smyrna and Ephesus—alas, I did not get to Antioch or Aleppo—on your wording of your Law, it seemed to me to come out, in its first equation thus, in the fewest possible words:
> All Civilisation is Centralisation.
> All Centralisation is Economy.
> Therefore all Civilisation is the survival
>   of the most economical (cheapest.) (IV, 557)

In his letter to Gaskell, Adams cast himself as a familiar, conventionalized type, the weary man of the world, who played the protagonist in "much the old story"—and the Nile served him as a stage on which the steady blur of time and human events confirmed the unchanging narrative of constancy around which he had already been allying himself to Gaskell for many years in his letters. But in writing to his younger brother Adams adopted the role, instead, of a historian. For this letter, Egypt provided raw material, the first of the data which Adams would collect throughout the entire trip, for testing the theories about historical change whose exchange shaped this quite separate correspondence and created a quite separate narrative in it.

It was only in the letter which he wrote to Elizabeth Sherman Cameron, on February 3, from a boat anchored off Memphis that Henry Adams emerged as directly responsive, and vulnerable, to the quotidian "reality" of his environment. As a result, it was only in this letter that "the Nile" emerged as immediate, personal, and emotionally penetrating:

> Under this sky, and in the noon-day sun, Washington does not look to me quite so inevitable as it did from Paris. The East certainly has charm, and makes the West seem gray and dreary. Even a steam-dahabiah and a Cook's Tour do not take away all the color and the resistance of Egypt. Indeed, the sudden return to the boat came near knocking me quite off my perch. I knew it would be a risky thing, but it came so suddenly that before I could catch myself, I was unconsciously wringing my hands and the tears rolled down in the old way, and I had to get off by myself for a few minutes to prevent Helen [the Hays' daughter], who was with me, from thinking me more mad than usual. She could hardly know what it meant, in any case, and it would not have been worth while to tell her. A few hours wore off the nervous effect, and now I can stand anything, although of course there is hardly a moment when some memory of twentyfive years ago is not brought to my mind. (IV, 530)

To Cameron, rather than to Charles Milnes Gaskell or Brooks Adams, Adams acknowledged the risk he had taken in returning to Egypt, where Marian

Adams had nearly suffered a nervous breakdown on their honeymoon twenty-five years before, in retrospect an ominous foreshadowing of the suicide about which Adams still made it a firm rule not to speak. Adams's language narrowed his emotional range for Gaskell, summing up and unifying in retrospect—"All things considered"; "not essentially"; "perhaps", "occasionally"; "on the whole"—in order to hold Gaskell as a steadying contact outside the daily disruptions of his life. In his letter to his younger brother, Adams generalized the discrete in order to position himself as an intellectual comrade, committed to creating historical order. But for Elizabeth Sherman Cameron, Adams made the irregularities of time and geography viscerally accessible, stripping away "inevitable" expectations in order to portray himself, unprotected, at the very brink of disorder. If his letters to Gaskell and to Brooks Adams constructed reality around the needs for continuity and for control which those alliances served, Adams's letters to Elizabeth Sherman Cameron constructed reality around a need for intimacy which his embarrassment in front of Helen Hay demonstrated he could not share with anyone else. To sustain that familiar immediacy, Adams tried to keep Cameron in nearly daily touch with him, writing letters to her regularly from this trip and collecting them in groups for mailing: he added another portion as he neared Cairo on the twenty-sixth of February (IV, 537–39); others from Cairo on the twenty-eighth (IV, 539–40) and on the fifth (IV, 541–42) and sixth (IV, 543–44) of March; from Beirut on the twelfth (IV, 545–49), from Baalbek on the sixteenth (IV, 549–50), from Damascus on the nineteenth (IV, 550–52), and then from Beirut again on the twenty-fourth (IV, 552-54); and, the last, from Smyrna on March 28 (IV, 554–55).

Finally, from Cairo on the fifth of March, Adams wrote the following, dramatically different version of the same trip for Cameron's twelve-year-old daughter, Martha:

> My dear Priscilla
>
> Here is your own dear nephew Dordy alone in Cairo, dreadfully homesick for his aunt Priscilla, and with no little girls to play with. Helen and Alice Hay went off yesterday to London. We had a fine time on the river, and rode donkeys and camels all over the country. You know Egypt is something like Mexico. It is very dusty, very hot, very cold and full of ruins and fleas, but it is only a mile or two wide, so one rides across it on a donkey in half an hour or so, and when one reaches the hills where the sand and the desert begins, one gets off, and goes down a hole into a tomb which is all carved and painted to make a nice house for gentlemen to live in when they are dead. They are nicely packed up in mummies, and the ladies have all their jewels and clothes and servants, and I do suppose they're all there, running about and making fun of us foreign fools, now, when we come to

visit them. They are mostly about five thousand years old, but there are younger ones only three or four thousand years old; and they are all a great deal more alive than we are who come and go for an hour in the morning. Indeed, every day, as we went down the river, I thought I could see the owners at the doors of their tombs along the cliffs, nodding to us good-bye, and saying that perhaps we would learn sense when we got to be old enough to stand up.

Next week I expect to go to Jerusalem and see where the Jews lived, and talk with a prophet or two. But I want you very much to tell me the stories and lead me about the shops to buy things.

Your loving child   Dordy (IV, 540–41)

This letter converted Egypt into Henry Adams's and Martha Cameron's playhouse. Within that fantasy, "your own dear nephew Dordy" invited his "dear Priscilla" to play a set of roles whose transparently privatized status narrowed discourse to exchange between a precious "us" of two. Expressly to appeal to his young correspondent, Adams shifted into the language of comparison and simplification which adults often use to convey the foreign and remote for children ("Egypt is something like Mexico"; "a nice house for gentlemen to live in"), and gave himself up to the simple primacy of a child's sensory responses ("very dusty, very hot, very cold") and the random order of a child's vision ("full of ruins and fleas"). In the almost visible process of writing the Nile once again, Adams emerged as yet a different character, renamed "Your loving child"—at the age of sixty, in a letter to a twelve-year-old.

If each of these scenes originated in the same "historical" moment, each of these fictions shaped time differently: in his letter to Gaskell, Adams transcended the irregularities of time; in his letter to Brooks Adams, he converted time into historical patterns. In his letter to Elizabeth Sherman Cameron, in sharp contrast, Adams committed himself to the intimate, uncontrollable moment. And, most radically, in his letter to Martha Cameron Adams made time plastic, weaving back and forth between Helen and Alice Hay's departure for London and his own plan to go to Jerusalem "and talk with a prophet or two" as though the present and the past were equally accessible destinations, and equally subject to invention. In all four of these letters—to Charles Milnes Gaskell; to Brooks Adams; to Elizabeth Sherman Cameron; and to Martha Cameron—one correspondence became the world, constructed around the author's need.

Henry Adams's Letters to Brooks Adams: Authoring Order

Henry Adams's letters to his younger brother Brooks retrace in microcosm the process by which his correspondence assumed the prerogatives of authorship. In these letters Adams steadily mastered writing's controlling potential: first, over the power economy of exchange with his younger brother, and then over the relationship between private and public discourse, as an agent of alliance and as an agent of order. In these letters, "reality" assumed an increasingly rhetorical status, as Adams grew increasingly aggressive about giving history a form and a language which he had generated, to a substantial degree, within the correspondence.

Initially Adams's letters to Brooks spoke for "I" rather than for "we," engaging his younger brother in the struggle for autonomy and authority as a writer which would earn Henry parity within the Adams family. These letters exploited an unequal power relationship: if his earliest letters to Charles Francis Adams, Jr., looked up to the sibling ahead of him for validation from above, Adams's earliest letters to Brooks Adams provided him a podium from which Adams could speak with superior authority to the sibling ten years behind him and claim validation from below. In his very first letter to Brooks, Adams patronized his younger brother by adopting toward him the role of expert letter writer. "You must write a few words of thanks to Mr. Theodore Reichenbach who gave me the old stamps for you as well as a few more which I will send presently," he lectured his twelve-year-old brother from Germany in March of 1860, laying out instructions on epistolary protocol: "Tack on to mamma's next letter a few words to him, saying that you thank him very much and will keep his present with the greatest care" (I, 99). Twelve years later, writing in March 1872 from Cambridge to announce his engagement to Marian Hooper, Adams was still using the tone of an elder to fix Brooks in a static position, even as he himself advanced into marriage: "I shall expect you to be very kind to Clover, and not rough, for that is not her style" (II, 132). In each of these letters, Henry Adams tried to maintain control over exchange by overseeing his brother's writing and by setting limits on Brooks's access to him. In each of them Adams claimed over his younger brother precisely the same kind of authority—"You must write"; "I shall expect you"—for which he had competed in his letters to his older brother, Charles Francis, Jr. Control remained central in Henry Adams's letters to Brooks Adams even after Adams had proven his independence from his older brother by taking on the sibling with whom Charles Francis Adams, Jr., had the most trouble; even after his collaboration with Brooks Adams had helped validate the professional authority which opened up a way for Henry Adams out of the closed system of family—long after Adams's younger brother had reached adulthood.[11] As late as 1895, Adams still felt the need to set decisive limits on his involvement in his younger brother's work, even as he moved aggressively to edit Brooks's prose. "Allow me, first, to strike out the dedication," he wrote from Washington in June 1895, responding to the manuscript of Brooks Adams's *Law of Civilization and Decay* and still claiming an older brother's prerogatives of certainty, dogmatism, and distance;

For me, the dedication is an embarrassment. The book is wholly, absolutely, and exclusively yours. Not a thought in it has any parentage of mine. . . .
    . . . Further, if my opinion has any value, you will find it only in my general rule of correction: to strike out remorselessly every superfluous word, syllable and letter. Every omission improves. I have suggested possible condensations by pencil-marks on the text. (IV, 284)

While such letters reinforced the imperative of autonomy, in other letters to his younger brother Adams worked on a collaborative posture. Like the letters which allied him to peers by articulating a set of shared losses, these letters allied Henry and Brooks Adams by writing both of them into a narrative in which they faced, together, the threat of imminent cultural change. Many of Henry Adams's letters to Brooks Adams told and retold essentially the same story of shifting, anonymous forces rendering irrelevant the sources of power with which he identified both Adams brothers. "I do not believe it matters greatly who is President," he wrote from Washington in February 1896;

A little sooner or a little later, all must follow the drift of human society. The sole interest I feel is that of ascertaining which way the drift is. I feel confident that the world turned a corner in 1870. The siege of Paris was the division between the old and new. Since then, while the world-centre—London, Berlin, Paris—has grown denser and harder, the world's circumference has tended to disintegration and dispersion. (IV, 374)

Against this backdrop of isolation, Adams dramatized the cultural inheritance which he shared with his younger brother: "of all these familiar haunts the one that moved me most with a sense of personal identity with myself, was Coutances," he wrote to Brooks from Paris in September of 1895, going on, "A great age it was, and a great people our Norman ancestors" (IV, 321). As such letters positioned Henry and Brooks Adams in a common stance of vulnerability and opposition, "I" shifted into "we," and the letters to his younger brother evolved from agents of parity into agents of alliance. In the controversy over the gold standard, for example, Adams insisted to his younger brother from Washington in June 1895, "The drift of exchange is stronger than ever against us . . ." (IV, 283); and again from Washington in December of the same year, "The administration seems to be still wabbling between the Jews and the Gentiles, and the only advantage we have gained as yet is the irritation of the President" (IV, 350). In a certain sense, these letters cast themselves as a retreat from public authority: "The ego may pass in a letter or a diary," Adams continued his June 1895 critique of his younger brother's *Law of Civilization and Decay*, "but not in a serious book" (IV, 284). Yet Adams's letters to his younger brother also reallocated power, by validating alliance as a source of private resistance.

Finally, his letters to his younger brother dramatize the ways in which alliance served Henry Adams as a condition of authorship. In these letters, Adams's experiments with models from the physical and natural sciences transformed the language in which he had fixed his disempowerment into a language of empowerment.[12] Writing, for example, to Brooks from Paris in June 1897, Adams used the occasion of correspondence to try out a new, systemic way of expressing power relations:

> As far as I can see, the various forces are now fairly well defined. The disruption of '93 has definitely rearranged society, and we need not fret about new disturbances because we cannot any longer either increase or diminish the forces. . . . For the last generation, since 1865, Germany has been the great disturbing element of the world, and until its expansive force is decidedly exhausted, I see neither political nor economical equilibrium possible. . . . Germany is immensely strong and concentrated. . . . (IV, 476–77)

This letter paralleled Adams's letter to his younger brother from Egypt in locating in the new sciences a new language for human history, a language of "forces"—"disrupted," "disturbed," "rearranged," "readjusted," "equilibrium"—and of "concentration" of "energy." By speaking of history itself in these new terms of relation, Adams converted a passive "I," victimized, narrator of disaster, into an active "we," writing and thus creating order. Eventually, these letters converted two siblings competing for power within a small familial environment into co-conspirators plotting together for subversive power on a much larger scale. "I understand that your book [*The Law of Civilization and Decay*] has been exhausted in New York for some time, and that Macmillan is waiting for more copies," Adams confided in Brooks Adams, from Paris in January of 1896;

> The longer we can keep it working under ground the better. If it once gets notorious, as it well may, under the blessed pressure of the gold standard which turns even defeats into victories for us, I want you to print it in a cheap form for popular reading. (IV, 365–66)

The language which he generated in these letters resisted Adams's own narrative of powerlessness, of silence, and of isolation, by exploiting narrative's ability to set its own ordering priorities. In August 1902, for example, Adams wrote to Brooks Adams from Scotland, insisting on the failure of science to challenge credibly the inevitability of chaos and, at the same time, formulating a prediction which challenged his own claim that he understood nothing.

> I apprehend for the next hundred years an ultimate, colossal, cosmic collapse; but not on any of our old lines. My belief is that science is to wreck

us, and that we are like monkeys monkeying with a loaded shell; we
don't in the least know or care where our practically infinite ener-
gies come from or will bring us to. For myself, it is true; I know nor
care at all. But the faintest disturbance of equilibrium is felt throughout the solar system, and I feel sure that our power over energy has
now reached a point where it must sensibly affect the old adjust-
ment. It is mathematically certain to me that another thirty years of
energy-development at the rate of the last century, must reach an
impasse. (V, 400)

Generating models which promised to see beyond the "old lines" of power to
new patterns of "energy-development" confirmed for Adams rhetorical authority which transcended the limits of the personal voice that he himself had fixed;
at the same time, speaking for "us" confirmed rhetorical prerogatives over the
world which neither "I," "you," nor "they" could claim alone. His letters to
his younger brother fundamentally radicalized language for Adams, for they
claimed the power to author the world in terms which met his own need for
order.

Henry Adams's Letters to Elizabeth Sherman Cameron: Authoring Intimacy

Like his letters to Brooks Adams, Henry Adams's letters to Elizabeth Sherman Cameron invested correspondence with the power to construct and sustain its own insular discourse. These letters became so self-sufficient that contact with Cameron herself often registered in them as intrusive. Tautly bal-
anced between maximizing emotional intensity and minimizing emotional
danger, highly susceptible to external disruption, these letters mark in especially moving ways the epistolary status of the "real" in Adams's correspondence as a whole.

Henry Adams's letters to Elizabeth Sherman Cameron have frequently
been singled out from the rest of Adams's correspondence for their uniquely
compelling qualities.[13] These letters are so compelling, in large part, because
of the risk that they lived with, in what became for Adams a *liaison dangereuse*.
Born in 1857, Cameron came from a powerful, well-connected family—one
of her uncles was a prominent Civil War general, another sponsored the 1890
Sherman Anti-Trust Act, and her father was an Ohio judge—and she was beautiful and intellectually quick, but she was isolated by her unhappy marriage
to Senator Donald Cameron, a man nearly twice her age. As Lizzie Cameron
became a regular member of the Adams household, after Clover Adams met
her in Washington in January 1881, Henry Adams clearly became attracted

to her: "Don [Cameron] and I stroll round with our arms round each other's necks," he wrote to John Hay from Washington, in January of 1883, going on to confide, "I should prefer to accompany Mrs. Don in that attitude . . ." (II, 488). At first Adams made light of that attraction, assuring James Russell Lowell casually, in a May 1883 letter of introduction for Cameron, "You will fall in love with her, as I have" (II, 501). But in the lonely years following his wife's death, Adams's involvement with Cameron grew increasingly intense and conflicted, as he pursued her after she became estranged from her husband, until she finally rejected his advances and the two of them struggled to establish a less charged relationship.[14]

Adams's letters did not simply chart the progress of his relationship with Cameron; instead, they constructed an alternative, rhetorically heightened, ground of exchange. Adams's letters to Cameron locked both correspondents into rhetorical confinement, rendering explicit language for feeling superfluous and, simultaneously, intensifying the pressure which made explicit language dangerous.[15] From the start, like letters of courtship, Henry Adams's letters to Elizabeth Sherman Cameron called attention to their own advances even as they mocked them. "We did not come to see you off at the station," Adams opened his first letter to Cameron, from Washington in May 1883, for example; "Our feelings overcame us. Will you forgive? The dogs wept all the morning; the puppy positively screamed and has not stopped yet" (II, 501).[16] By holding pretense close to the surface in his early letters to Cameron, Adams was able to neutralize his attentions, to patronize a young woman whom he and his wife were in the process of launching in Washington society even as he flirted with her. "We miss you more than ever, and . . . until you come back we shall never be quite contented," Adams teased Cameron from Washington on Christmas Day of 1883; "Last night Mrs Bonaparte gave a little dance, and I looked earnestly about for some one to fill your place. You may be quite safe. No one was there" (II, 524). When his wife's death made his closeness to Lizzie Cameron both more tempting and more dangerous, Adams tried in his letters to balance intimacy and distance by retreating behind fictionality, by emphasizing the staged quality of his own prose. In response to an invitation which Cameron extended to Adams and his companion Theodore F. Dwight, Adams wrote with exaggerated breathlessness, from Washington in November of 1886, "we—or I—or he—are, am or is delighted to accept any invitation you will send us. We will come to dinner, breakfast, tea, lunch or supper, either in the parlor or the nursery" (III, 46). And from Quincy in August 1887, Adams wrote with equally overdone solicitude to Cameron, who was staying with Martha in his house at Beverly Farms, "Please order anything that you want at Beverly, and send me the bills; or let me know, and I will order it. Ober will build you a new house if you prefer one" (III, 72).

Subsequently, Adams's letters often cushioned the growing intensity of his feelings for Cameron by employing the conceit of his affection for her daughter. "Give Martha my tenderest love," he closed a September 1888 letter to Cameron from Quincy; "Propriety forbids me to send as much to her mamma, so I remain only conventionally hers" (III, 142). "I will love you like a—niece!" (III, 90), he wrote with transparent hesitation in a note to Cameron from Washington in November of 1887. Alone but prevented by propriety from asking Cameron to keep him company, Adams teasingly asked Cameron, instead, to send him her daughter. "I wish I could find somebody pleasant to go with me as far as Los Angeles, El Paso, San Francisco, or the next world," he wrote from Quincy in September of 1887; "I dislike solitude, as few do. Lend me Martha . . ." (III, 81). Adams also used Martha to deflect the self-consciousness and awkwardness which he felt as an older man paying court to the much younger Elizabeth Cameron; in April of 1888 he wrote to Lizzie Cameron from Washington,

> I have just seen your daughter, with a huge banana in her clutches. . . . She smiled graciously on me, but preferred, as was just, the society of younger men. John Hay and I who were all I could offer her, bowed as meekly to her will as we do to that of her mother. After all, the relation is not so very different. (III, 109)

These strategies of displacement both defused and intensified the charged quality of Adams's attentions to Cameron, by simultaneously exposing and heightening their own imperative. At the same time as Adams sought protection in these letters behind the cover of his restlessness—"I hardly know which is worse,—to hear, or not to hear from you; for when I do not hear, I am uneasy, and when I do hear, I am homesick" (III, 135), he moaned to Cameron from Quincy in August 1888—he also made himself vulnerable in them. "The rule that nothing matters much, does not apply to you" (III, 130), he opened a July 1888 letter to Cameron, dramatically relinquishing his cover of numbness and making himself accessible to her.

While Henry Adams's letters to Elizabeth Sherman Cameron certainly drew on preexisting tensions between the two correspondents, the correspondence did not constitute simply a substitute for personal contact or even simply a means of avoiding it. Instead, the letters created a discourse with an integrity of its own, whose balance between intimacy and neutrality could not survive outside the correspondence. His letters to Cameron from the South Seas, where Adams went with John La Farge in 1890 on an extended trip intended to provide Cameron with some relief from Adams's attentions, typify the tautness of this balance, for they called attention both to their own necessity and to their own insufficiency.[17] On one hand, Adams committed himself uncompromisingly to correspondence with Cameron and to the life which it sustained in him. "I am something more than dependent on your writing," he informed her from Honolulu in September 1890; "Now that I am here I find what I expected to find when I came away—that you are my only strong tie to what I suppose I ought to call home. If you should go back on me, I should wholly disappear" (III, 285). On the other hand, Adams acknowledged his frustration with the cryptic silence and the subterfuge which this correspondence helped to perpetuate. "I seal and send this long diary, all about myself when I want to write only about you," he concluded an October 1890 letter to her, from Samoa;

> The rest you must fill in, as you would like to have it, and you cannot make it too strong. As the winter approaches I seem to think more and more about you and Martha, and long more to see you. The contrast between my actual life and my thoughts is fantastic. The double life is almost like one's idea of the next world. (III, 299)

These letters created a precarious equilibrium by simultaneously calling attention to the boundaries which they set around their own language and pushing against those limits. From Samoa in January of 1891, Adams described himself to Cameron as isolated by the "double life" in which their correspondence was engaged: "Meanwhile I read your letters over and over—they are all the letters I have to read,—and look at your photographs; and my spirits sink deeper and deeper as I seem to feel that, like the unfortunate Robinson, I cannot get back to land" (III, 382); and then, more directly, "You must imagine what I cant write, and be sure you imagine it strong as it is" (III, 406), from Tahiti in February 1891; and in May 1891, "I wish one could say with cold white paper what one has to keep to oneself . . . but you must fill in the blanks and supply the colors" (III, 469).

Most important, Adams's letters to Elizabeth Sherman Cameron dramatized the paradoxical fact that closeness was dependent in them on distance, that sustaining a balance between inviting and limiting intimacy depended on sustaining the epistolary status of exchange between them: "I suppose no woman can have the heart to object to being made love to, if the offender remains ten thousand miles away" (III, 423), Adams sighed to Cameron, again from Tahiti, in February 1891.[18] The letters charting Adams's headlong rush to meet Cameron in Paris in the spring of 1891 dramatize with excruciating clarity how close to disruption that balance loomed in this correspondence and how fully it depended on absence. With the prospect of Cameron herself clearly ahead—and feeling so eager that he paid a ship captain an extra $2500 to take a more direct route[19]—Adams abandoned the strategies by which he had controlled speech in his letters to her and began, instead, to reiterate explicitly at every step of the journey his hunger to be reunited with Cameron. "I wish I were at sea," he wrote to her impatiently from Tahiti in May 1891; "My only source of energy is that I am actually starting on a ten-thousand-mile journey to see—you!" (III, 482). "We are straining every nerve to reach Paris by October 1" (III, 489), he assured her the next month from Fiji; and from Australia in August he implored, "When—oh, when do you sail? If you had waited till Nov. 1, I should certainly have caught you. As you are to sail in October, I have the worst fears; . . . I cling to the hope that I shall have at least a few hours with you" (III, 523–24). And when, eventually, Cameron confirmed his worst fears and rejected him, Adams left her in London and unburdened himself to her, directly and bitterly, from Charles Milnes Gaskell's estate in Shropshire, in November 1891:

> an elderly man, when hit over the head by an apocalyptic *Never*, does not sublime to Power; but curls up like Abner Dean of Angels, and for a time does not even squirm; then he tumbles about for a while; seeing the Apocalypse all round him; then he bolts and runs like a mad dog, anywhere—to Samoa, to Tahiti, to Fiji; then he dashes straight round the world, hoping to get to Paris ahead of the Apocalypse; . . . no matter how much I may efface myself or how little I may ask, I must always make more demand on you than you can gratify, and you must always have the consciousness that, whatever I may profess, I want more than I can have. . . . I am not old enough to be a tame cat; you are too old to accept me in any other character. (III, 556–57)

When his acceptance of the limits on his intimacy with Cameron had been exposed as a construction of the letters, the autonomous reality which the letters had constructed began to disintegrate. To admit to being both greedy and acquiescent—"I am not old enough to be a tame cat; you are too old to accept me in any other character"—and to acknowledge the strategies of self-effacement and self-denial that he had been employing was for Adams to unglue the narrative patches which he had laid over his own desire.

Significantly, Adams's sense of being abandoned by Cameron was matched by his sense of losing control over the fictionalizing strategies on which he had relied in his letters to her; his effort to reestablish equilibrium in the letters took shape, in turn, as an effort to reclaim those strategies. When he wrote, still hurt, to Cameron from Bristol, England, in early December of 1891, Adams focused his sense of loss on his lack of access to Cameron's daughter Martha: "I felt and feel ever-so-much worse about it than you do, or than you ever will feel; for you at least have Martha, and I have nothing—" (III, 578). Increasingly, Adams resumed the displacing conceits of his earlier letters to Cameron. A month later, on the first of January, Adams began to repeat his lavish feelings for Martha and his coded, teasing references to her mother: "One word

of Happy New Year to Martha. I hunger and thirst to have her with me. . . .
So wish her a Happy New Year, and tell her that the Champs Elizzie look very
natural . . ." (III, 595). In succeeding letters to Cameron, Adams returned to
exploiting his anxiety over loss and displacement rhetorically, to deploying
fictions within which he could define and control a set of conditions for
exchange between Cameron and himself.[20] From Quincy in June 1889, for
example, Adams responded to Cameron's letter of condolence at his mother's
death by enacting a drama of sexually checked, tense neutrality:

> A million thanks for your kind sympathy with me. The world has some
> slight compensations for its occasional cruelties. I suppose, for instance,
> that in gradually deadening the senses it cuts away the unpleasant as well as
> the pleasant. As I walk in the garden and the fields I recall distinctly the
> acuteness of odors when I was a child, and I remember how greatly they
> added to the impression made by scenes and places. Now I catch only a sort
> of suggestion of the child's smells and lose all the pleasure, but at least do
> not get the disgusts. Life is not worth much when its senses are cut down to
> a kind of dull consciousness, but it is at least painless. As for me, waste no
> sympathy. My capacity for suffering is gone. (III, 183–84)

In this letter, Adams reestablished the equilibrium which he had sustained
earlier in his correspondence with Cameron: the letter set firm boundaries
on intimacy, by maintaining the conceit of "gardens" and "fields," and, at the
same time, it constructed the most sensual "us" of Adams's entire correspondence, through its imagery of gardens and childhood. On one hand, Adams
seemed to be pushing Cameron away with his injunction not to "waste" any
sympathy on him. On the other hand, Adams clearly felt too keenly the
"acuteness" of the senses which he feared losing to make convincing his insistence to Cameron that his ability to suffer was "gone." In admitting Cameron
to the privacy of his sensory disorientation and raising the specter of finality,
in setting up a void which the act of confiding in Cameron enjoined her to
fill, Adams was creating two characters who were mutually engaged by the
demands of correspondence.

"The world" became in Adams's letters to Cameron a world which turned,
increasingly, around the exchange of letters between these two characters. For
years Henry Adams's letters built up the fiction of his daily presence in Elizabeth Sherman Cameron's life, despite the fact that Cameron herself did not
always keep up her end of the correspondence.[21] From his travels during the
years following their Paris quarrel, Adams often wrote to Cameron every few
days, collecting material over several weeks into a long letter. Such letters
forged a continual connection to the present instead of recalling it as past
as Adams had done for Gaskell. They offered Cameron regular physical and

emotional access to Adams, constituting a viscerally felt, almost moment-to-moment denial of the geographical separation which made the letters possible—even as they molded exchange around an "us" who wrote and read letters, rather than an "us" who either felt or avoided passion. From London in January of 1892, for example, Adams collected a two-week series of letters to Cameron, assigning to "now" at each of a succession of points a physical or emotional precision which rendered Adams's life with intimate particularity for Cameron. He fixed for her, on the eleventh of the month, the precise sensory experience of his Channel crossing the previous day, "so cold, cold, cold, and iced fog" (III, 601); the precise moment at which he wrote, "now that breakfast is finished" (III, 602), on the fifteenth; his unnerving sense of having outlived the vitality of the world to which he was returning—"Queer sensation, this coming to life again in a dead world" (III, 603)—on the eighteenth; the complex feel of London to him, "A lovely dark day, black as night, and full of refined feeling" (III, 603), on the twenty-first; and finally, on the twenty-third, his painful sense of the isolation that came with age, "Now I seem to be the oldest inhabitant, and forgotten by time" (III, 604). In offering Cameron access to the cold, darkness, and disorientation of his London, Adams was also casting her in the role of sympathetic, committed participant in his life—but that participation was shaped and confined by the exchange of letters: "Your letter of Jan. 5 arrived before breakfast," he informed Cameron from London in the same long letter, establishing her presence in his world in a scene of daily routine, "and now that breakfast is finished . . . I sit down to read your news . . ." (III, 602). Ernest Samuels has called Adams's daily entries to Cameron a journal form, and clearly Adams did use them to keep track of his past. "Except the letters I wrote home," he told her in a December 1897 letter from Paris, referring to his last trip to the South Seas, "there is no record at all of my part of the journey" (IV, 511).[22] Yet important though record keeping undoubtedly was to a historian like Adams, these letters also played a more active role: they constantly erected and reinforced the fiction of Cameron's waiting responsiveness, as reader, and of Adams's essential presence as letter writer.

Like his letters to his younger brother Brooks, then, Adams's letters to Elizabeth Sherman Cameron constructed reality around the letters themselves and around the needs for alliance which they served. Time moved in these letters to the rhythm of correspondence, and intimacy was managed through correspondence's balance between disruption and continuity, between separation and connection. "Where did I leave off, last Sunday?" (V, 654), Adams queried Cameron from Paris in May 1905, with the casualness and the force of routine sustained by the exchange of letters. Strategically defensive, these letters challenged their own message of vulnerability, loss, and isolation; strategically aggressive, they remade the world to meet Adams's need for safety and for responsiveness.

Henry Adams's Letters to Martha Cameron: The Visibility of Fiction

Of all Henry Adams's letters, the ones which he wrote to Elizabeth Sherman Cameron's daughter, Martha, held their own fictionality closest to the surface. In Adams's letters to Martha Cameron, fictionality served from the start as a strategy of alliance, by heightening the distinction between what was credible or "true" outside the letters and the private "truth" shared exclusively within them. As Adams wrote and rewrote both correspondents into a set of constantly, and openly, reimagined narratives, the world narrowed dramatically around correspondence.

Born in 1886, seven months after the death of Adams's wife, and named in Marian Adams's memory, Martha Cameron almost instantly filled an emotional gap for Henry Adams, and he wrote to her steadily until he died, just a month before her untimely death at the age of thirty-two, in April 1918. Clearly Martha Cameron provided welcome release for Adams in the years after Clover Adams's suicide. In May of 1888, a month before he first wrote to Martha Cameron, Adams offered a glimpse of the pleasure which he took in his relationship with her in his diary:

> I have made love to Martha Cameron and by dint of incessant bribery and attentions have quite won her attachment so that she will come to me from anyone. . . . Her drawer of chocolate drops and gingersnaps; her dolls and picture books, turn my study into a nursery. (III, 113)[23]

Adams initiated his correspondence with Martha, a month later, around the assumption of conceit: just as he had used Martha Cameron as an object of displacement in his letters to Elizabeth Sherman Cameron, at first Adams used the fiction of letters from a fifty-year-old man to a two-year-old child to gain freer access to the child's mother.[24] Clearly it was Elizabeth Sherman Cameron rather than her daughter whom Adams meant to tease when he wrote to Martha, "I am afraid of boring your mother with letters"; and clearly it was Elizabeth Sherman Cameron whom Adams was informing in decidedly adult language at the end of the same letter, "Please tell your mamma that history is getting on. . . . [Theodore] Dwight [Adams's research assistant] arrived this morning from a round of visits to fashionable people, and has begun work as *Archiviste*" (MC, 239–40). That double audience in his early letters to Martha Cameron offered Adams a discreet means of maintaining close contact with

Elizabeth Sherman Cameron. "Give my love to your mamma, and tell her all
about me. . . ," Adams wrote from Quincy in September 1888 to Martha and,
obviously, to her mother, who would recognize herself in Adams's queries: "I
know she must have been in some mischief, because she has not written to
me for a month, and I have always noticed that when ladies do not write to
me, they are in mischief of some kind" (MC, 241). Even as late as February of
1905, when Martha was nearly nineteen and certainly reading her own letters, Adams was still circumventing his hesitation and frustration with
Elizabeth Sherman Cameron by exploiting his correspondence with her daughter: "As for your mamma, I will try to keep her out of mischief," he wrote with
mock earnestness to Martha from Washington in February of 1905, "but these
mammas are very anxious charges . . . I want to have her here as much as she
will consent to come to play with me, but I don't know how to ask her . . ."
(MC, 276).

   Although Adams's letters to Martha Cameron eventually outgrew their
double audience, they consistently made conceit a central condition of
exchange. Adams asked Martha to suspend her allegiance to a world outside
his letters, to enter a world which he had created around the two of them, writer
and reader. Adams opened his second letter to her, for example, from Quincy
in September 1888, by spinning a tale in which he played a character in desperate need of personal attention from Martha Cameron:

> I love you very much, and think of you a great deal, and want you all
> the time. I should have run away from here, and looked for you all over the
> world, long ago, only I've grown too stout for the beautiful clothes I used to
> wear when I was a young prince in the fairy-stories, and I've lost the feath-
> ers out of my hat, and the hat too, and I find that some naughty man has
> stolen my gold sword and silk-stockings and silver knee-buckles. So I can't
> come after you, and feel very sad about it. If you would only come and see
> me, as Princess Beauty came to see Prince Beast, we would go down to the
> beach, and dig holes in the sand; and would walk in the pastures, and find
> mushrooms, which are the tables where the very little fairies take dinner. . . .
> (MC, 240)

Although such a letter clearly drew on elements of a relationship that existed
outside the correspondence—Adams's love for Martha Cameron; his anxiety
about aging; his loneliness—it openly rewrote that relationship, so that time
began to start and stop in accordance with narratives which were located
wholly within the letters. Explicitly for these letters, Adams invented characters like the "young prince," who constantly sought responses from Martha
Cameron, sometimes needing affection and at other times requiring discipline
from her. "Mischief and Dordy have been doing all sorts of things that would
displease you very much. Dr. Dobbitt can't manage them all," Adams opened

a letter from Havana in January of 1895, referring in mock panic to the nick-names which Martha had given Adams and his travel companion Chandler Hale; "I think you had better write to tell them that they must behave them-selves better" (MC, 248). Changing shape as she read, in a December 1897 letter from Paris, Adams transformed both correspondents, simultaneously, into characters in his make-believe drama. "I turned into a dormouse and went to sleep for the winter. . . ," he wrote to Martha, and enticed her onstage with him: "You see, dormice must have little girls to play with. If there are no little girls, the dormouse has to go to sleep and dream about them" (MC, 252). Although they were clearly engineered to provoke appreciative giggles, these letters nevertheless made quite serious demands on their reader, for they made meaning depend on both correspondents' willingness to accept in some, quite possibly imaginative, way the credibility of the world which Adams created in them.

Adams intensified the fictional status of his letters to Martha Cameron by using language which was invented for the special occasion of this corre-spondence. He employed fanciful nicknames for Martha, addressing her vari-ously as "Mrs. Martha Gulliver" (MC, 246), "Dear Purple" (MC, 250), "Dear Aunt Priscilla" (MC, 253), "My Only Peacock (Purple)" (MC, 254), "My Nibby Chow" (MC, 263), and "Dear Duck" (MC, 275). Adams himself became "Your affectionate Dobbitt" (MC, 241), proprietor of "Dr. Dobbitt's school" (MC, 249), and "Your little Dordy" (MC, 254).[25] Adams frequently played with words for Martha's amusement, imitating sounds—"My dear own only daaarl-ing" (MC, 259)—and making up new verb forms and spellings. "Your last postal told me that you had excurted to Frankfurt," he opened a July 1904 letter to her from Paris; "You want to know about my mushine [his new car] . . ." (MC, 271). On occasion Adams would even break into foolish song for his young correspondent: "My dear and only Aunt Priscilla," he wrote, for example, from the Nile in February 1898,

> As I was looking at a magician swallow smoke
> On the porch of Shepherd's Hotel at Cairo,
> I looked up and saw Gladdis Vanderbilt,
> Who was very brown and rather thin,
> And rather frightened. (MC, 255)

The personalization and the high imaginative pitch of Adams's language in his letters to Martha Cameron privatized discourse between the two correspon-dents, whom Adams figured in a fantasy retreat together. "My angel muzzer," he opened a letter to her from Washington in March 1907; "Your sweet song of the mocking-bird calling me to your island makes me wish I were able to fly. What fun the birds must have! Yet we do not seem to fly far from here just now, and I am deeper in mire than ever" (MC, 278).

Adams insulated exchange in his letters to Martha Cameron by rendering relations between these two increasingly fictionalized characters increasingly symbiotic. Especially at first, Adams often addressed young Martha Cameron with the superior authority of a teacher. He evaluated her writing. "Your letter was beautiful," he encouraged her from Quincy in July of 1889; "It told me about your journey; the steamer; and how you drove from Chester; and all about London; and how long the sun stays up at night in Scotland when it ought to be in bed" (MC, 242). And he advised her on reading: "Read all the Leather Stocking series, and the next time you cross the ocean, read the Sea stories" (MC, 262), he wrote enthusiastically from Paris in August of 1899, on hearing that she had begun Cooper. Many of his letters to Martha included brief lectures on topics with which Adams seemed to feel responsible for familiarizing her. "You know how King Agamemnon went off to besiege Troy three thousand years ago and stayed ten years, and after he came back was murdered by his wife Clytemnestra at Mycenae" (MC, 257), he wrote to her, for example, from Athens in April of 1898. But as the correspondence developed (and Martha Cameron grew older), Adams equalized authority between the two correspondents, by initiating a series of role reversals. On one hand, in these transparent fictions Adams assumed the role of Martha Cameron's child. "Don't forget your little Dordy, whatever you do . . ." (MC, 251), he implored her from London in November of 1897, and from Paris, a month later, "Write your little boy what to do" (MC, 253). "Good-bye! from your affectionate nephew Dordy" (MC, 254), he signed another letter, from Paris in January 1898. On the other hand, Adams assigned Martha Cameron the role of parent, on whom he could depend for protection from his sense of vulnerability and his fear of abandonment. "This morning scares your poor little timid Dordy. . . ," he confided to her from Paris in July of 1900, "So your scared infant had every window shut tight" (MC, 264); and a month later from Paris, "I've seen no one since you left, and lie awake nights crying for my dear mother who left me all alone when I was only two years old . . ." (MC, 265). In turn, Adams addressed Martha Cameron extravagantly as "My only dear beautiful lovely affectionate mother" (MC, 260, from Washington, March 1899) and "My dear sweet lovely beautiful low-german angel" (MC, 271, from Paris, July 1903) or more simply, "My dear only Mother" (MC, 271, from Paris, July 1904). And while Adams shrank in these letters, Martha steadily grew: "Anyway you are grown so big now that you won't have anything more to do with children, so I don't quite see what's to become of Dordy, who will be only two-and-a-half next year if he keeps getting younger" (MC, 263), he moaned breathlessly to her from Paris in November 1899; and a year and a half later, from Washington in April 1901, "It is so hard to grow littler and littler every year while one's mother gets bigger and bigger . . ." (MC, 266). Adams must have felt that he had to work hard to keep this correspondence fresh, to hold the attention of a bright young reader who might at any moment lose interest in a didactic, aging man. Even more, constantly renaming himself—"your little Dordy"; "your little boy"; "your affectionate nephew"; "your scared infant"—and shifting back and forth between parental authority and childish innocence must have sustained for Adams a strong sense of his own energy and of playful engagement and mutuality.

As surely as these letters recognized that Martha Cameron would never believe in Henry Adams as, literally, her ageless child, they asked her to give herself to a realm created only for her and Adams, within which she and Adams were responsible, ultimately, only to one another. Like his letters to Elizabeth Sherman Cameron, Henry Adams's letters to Martha Cameron wrote both correspondents into a narrative of mutual dependence which acquired over time considerable self-sufficiency. That self-sufficiency was, however, far less susceptible to disruption in Adams's letters to Martha, which rendered less necessary in them the exclusionary strategies like anti-Semitism and irony to which Adams resorted in his letters to Martha's mother. Although, for example, Adams growled to Elizabeth Sherman Cameron from Beirut in March 1898 that Damascus was a "rascally Syrian town, made of Moslem scoundrels, Christian thieves, and Jew money-lenders" (IV, 553), to Cameron's daughter Martha he had remarked placidly three weeks earlier, from Cairo in March of 1898, without a trace of that scorn and that fear, "Next week I expect to go to Jerusalem and see where the Jews lived, and talk with a prophet or two" (MC, 257). And from Washington in November 1908 on the occasion of her engagement to marry Sir Ronald Lindsay, Adams confided with unusual directness to Martha Cameron (after years of virtual silence on the subject of his marriage), "You have a very nice lover indeed, and I wish that I too were young; for you've got all that is worth having in life, and all that I should care to live it over for" (MC, 281).

Most important, the transparency of fictionality in Adams's letters to Martha Cameron deepened, rather than trivialized, the uniquely mutual status of "reality" in them. Adams constantly repeated his special commitment to Martha Cameron. "I am just as homesick for you as ever. I have all the little children paraded here for inspection but they can't any of them take the place of Dr Dobbit's little girl," he insisted to her from Washington in February 1899, taking her into his confidence and assuring her that none of the other children of his friends could provide him the kind of company that she could; "Corker Blaine is a terror. His mother can't manage him now, and in a year or two he will be awful; but he is a splendid great big fellow. Benjamin Thoron is just the opposite; elderly, and like his father; precocious and not handsome. None of our old friends seem to be here" (MC, 259). Over and over in these letters, Adams reiterated his devotion to Martha Cameron, and over and over he named essential the part that she played in his life. "I miss you awfully, you more than anyone and all the rest" (MC, 251), he insisted to her from London in November 1897; "I wish I were with you today on the ocean" (MC 261), he moaned to her from Paris in July 1899; "I've felt sometimes almost like crying about myself, because I was so far from you" (MC, 268), he wrote plaintively from St. Petersburg in September 1901. Many of Adams's last letters to Martha Cameron had a difficult time sustaining such confidence in his ability as a correspondent. "If you are writing to Hattie Kennard," he wrote mournfully in July of 1912 from his brother's house in South Lincoln, Massachusetts, where he was slowly convalescing from a stroke, "please give her my love, and tell her how sorry I am that I should have been such a complete wreck as to be unable to write to her" (MC, 286); "I should have answered long ago your nice letter of Decb. 4, but that I am no great hand now-a-days at writing . . ." (MC, 288), he apologized to her from Washington in February of 1913. And in a November 1915 letter from Washington, Adams's role reversals acquired a shaky poignancy: "I should have written long ago had I not, after our old habit, grown so young— so very young—that I can't manage a pen without inking all my clothes" (MC, 290). But if Adams's late letters to Martha Cameron suffered, like the rest of his correspondence, from his enveloping sense of fatigue and isolation, they also maintained to the very end a sense of their own special imperative which testifies to the satisfaction which writing them provided him. "I can't write; I can't read; I can't talk; I can swear a good deal, but not nicely," Adams wrote in his very last letter to Martha Cameron, from Washington in January of 1916; "I can't eat, and I can't drink, but I can try to acknowledge your letter, which is more than I do for most" (MC, 291).

The Author's Prerogatives: Correspondence as a Source of Responsiveness and Control

In each of these three sets of letters, to Brooks Adams, to Elizabeth Sherman Cameron, and to Martha Cameron, Henry Adams created a world which did not exist for him elsewhere. In each of these correspondences Adams openly committed himself to authorship, to taking control of the meaning which constituted the "real." In each of them fictionality emerged as both a strategy and a prerogative of alliance, and consensus emerged as a function of authorship.

The silence in his letters surrounding his wife's death suggests how much Adams struggled with the form, how little his commitment to it ought to be taken for granted.[26] During the long autumn of Clover Adams's final depression, Henry Adams's letters made only brief mention of her condition, capitulating to rather than challenging his increasing isolation: "We are still in poor state, and unfit for worldly vanities. I see little or no one, and my doors are tight shut" (II, 634), he informed John Hay from Washington in November 1885; "My wife is unwell . . ." (II, 635), he wrote, simply, to Charles Milnes Gaskell a few days later; and on November 29 he wrote cautiously to his English friend Sir Robert

Cunliffe, "My wife . . . has been, as it were, a good deal off her feed this summer . . ." (II, 639). When Marian Adams committed suicide a week later, Adams found that language had become excruciating for him, and his obligation to letters seems to have become a source of pain rather than a weapon against it: "Don't let *any one* come near me" (II, 640), he implored Rebecca Gilman Dodge on the day of Clover Adams's death, 6 December 1885; "I can endure, but I cannot talk, unless I must (II, 640), he concluded a brief note to George Bancroft, two days later; "To have been able to ask for help would have been a pleasure to me, but there are moments in life when one is beyond all help . . ." (II, 641), he confided to Elizabeth Sherman Cameron on the tenth of December; and to Oliver Wendell Holmes Adams wrote with painful effort at the end of the month, "Your kind letter touches me so closely that I hasten to thank you for it. . . . You will not expect me to say anything. All my energy is now turned to the task of endurance . . ." (II, 645). Coming at a time of such emotional need, this resistance marked the limits of Adams's trust in the form, and in its ability to generate an alternative to the reality outside its own boundaries.

The emotional investment which Adams subsequently made in his letters to Brooks Adams and, especially, to Elizabeth Sherman Cameron and Martha Cameron testifies to the toughness and the endurance of Adams's commitment to letters. Jackson Lears has suggested that Adams's depression following his wife's death and his failure to derive satisfaction from "male" ideals like autonomy constituted a "crisis of generativity"; and, in turn, that his attraction to Elizabeth Sherman Cameron and to Maryolatry represented a groping toward the possibility of regeneration through "female" values like dependence.[27] "Only women are worth cultivating, and I am ready to hand over the whole universe to them if they want it . . ." (VI, 602), Adams wrote, only half in jest, to Henry James from Paris in May of 1913. By this Adams may well have meant that in a world where political, social, and cultural change was unnerving him, the kinds of power held by women—and, one imagines, by younger brothers—posed the least threat for him. Indeed, the "nieces in wish" with whom he surrounded himself in his last years and whom he recruited for his experiments in medieval music helped Adams maintain a protective, timeless shell around himself and constituted for him an audience over which he could maintain largely unchallenged control.[28] More subtly, Adams must also have meant that the kind of alliance which women promised him felt most worth his "cultivation" because the fiction of responsiveness which it enabled him to sustain served exchange in his letters, both as a model and as a source of control. In these letters Adams made "reality," and the correspondents who inhabited it, dependent on his own continuing ability to write. Finally, all three of these correspondences demonstrate how Adams's letters committed him not only to allies but, even more, to his own ability to generate through alliance the kinds of power that he needed most.

4   Authorship and Audience in the Work of Henry Adams

Henry Adams's imaginative works—his two novels, *Democracy* (1880) and *Esther* (1884); *Mont Saint Michel and Chartres* (1904); and *The Education of Henry Adams* (1907)—echo and amplify the rhetorical questions with which Adams's letters were occupied. In these works, the relationship between public and private discourse remains a central source of conflict. Together with the letters, these texts make clear the extent to which Adams's concerns with authority and alliance were writerly concerns, the extent to which they were bound up for him with the problematic status of authorship and audience.[1] Ultimately, in turn, the centrality of these issues in Adams's work makes clear the fundamentally *textual* status of the letters.

Adams's loyalty in these prose works to such "epistolary" priorities as mutuality and privacy illuminates the crucial fact that authorship was for Adams a means of alliance—and that alliance was for Adams a condition of authorship. Adams's interest in readers' access to meaning and in reading and writing as thematic issues dramatizes in these texts a set of political commitments, especially to collaboration and control, which his letters clearly shared. At the same time, the broad presence of such questions in Adams's work as a whole helps to explain the attractiveness to Adams of the letter, with its permeable rhetorical boundaries, as a solution to a set of lifelong problems with authorship and audience.[2]

The Problem of Audience

It is impossible to separate the sense of cultural alienation which shaped Henry Adams as a writer from the problematic status of audience for him, from Adams's sense of isolation in the public arena. In all four of these texts, Adams took aggressive steps to construct his audience in ways which would challenge that loss of community and ensure conditions of responsiveness. As he had in his letters, Adams adopted a set of rhetorical strategies which both restricted the readership of these texts and forged alliances with appropriate readers. Thus in these texts, as in Adams's letters, audience emerged as both a subject and a goal.

Even at its headiest, in his early years as a journalist, publication constituted an occasion of keen vulnerability for Henry Adams. His sense of betrayal at being condescendingly exposed by the *London Times* as the author of the *Boston Courier* article on the Manchester cotton industry was acute, and it made Adams reluctant to take the risk of publishing again: "To my immense astonishment and dismay I found myself this morning sarsed through a whole column of the Times, and am laughed at by all England," he moaned to Charles Francis, Jr., from London in January 1862; ". . . for the present I shall cease my other writings as I am in agonies for fear they should be exposed" (I, 269). Adams enjoyed considerable influence as a reform writer in Washington from 1868 to 1870 and as editor of the *North American Review* from 1870 to 1877; and his 1882 biography of John Randolph could be called a popular success.[3] But Adams tended to focus on the poor reception of his monumental work, the nine-volume *History of the United States during the Administrations of Thomas Jefferson and James Madison* (1889–91), rather than on these achievements, and after the *History* Adams never again opened himself up unprotected to an unfamiliar audience.[4] Neither of Adams's novels appeared under Adams's own name: *Democracy* was published anonymously, and *Esther* was published under the pseudonym "Frances Snow Compton." And the first printings of both *Mont Saint Michel and Chartres* and *The Education of Henry Adams* were private. Significantly, Adams justified his refusal to publish *Mont Saint Michel and Chartres* by referring back to the disappointing reception which his *History* had met with. "Thousands of people exist who think they want to read," he sniffed to his younger brother Brooks from Paris in June of 1905; "Barring a few Jews, they are incapable of reading fifty consecutive pages, or of following the thought if they did. I never yet heard of ten men who had ever read my history . . ." (V, 668). This lack of confidence in a responsive audience for his work endured throughout the rest of Adams's lifetime. Adams wrote bitterly, for example, from Washington in January 1911 to Edward H. Davis, an economics professor at Purdue University,

> Nothing has been so difficult in my experience as the effort to ascertain the state of mind of Americans on any subjects whatever, outside the daily newspapers. I have made many, and almost violent efforts as you know, or have probably seen, in the form of eighteen or twenty volumes on the dusty shelves of libraries, without the smallest articulate response. (VI, 403)

Even the knowledge that he was speaking to an admirer did not relieve Adams's alienation from the reading public. "It is now some five-and-twenty years since I laid down my pen, chiefly because I could not see that any one wanted me to go on holding it . . ." (VI, 617), Adams wrote from Paris in October of 1913 to Lawrence Shaw Mayo, a Harvard historian who had written warmly to Adams about the *History*.

While Adams's retreat from the public in these texts may have cost him a popular reputation, it also tightened his hold over the conditions under which his work reached readers. "The question is one of licensed privacy. Any man who mentions my name in a newspaper without my consent, is a liar" (VI, 62), Adams insisted to Henry Holt, the publisher of *Democracy*, from Washington in April 1907, in response to a request to serialize the novel. *Esther*, modeled in significant part on Adams's wife and on Adams himself, remained an even more private affair, and Adams set especially sharp limits on readers' access to it. Adams insisted that *Esther* be issued without either advertising or publicity, and he kept his authorship of it a secret even from most of his best friends, until after his wife's suicide had converted the lovingly private pleasure of her portrait into excruciatingly private heartache.[5] He admitted painfully to Holt, from Washington in March 1886,

> I am almost amused at the idea of my caring now for anything that so-called critics could say. When the only chapter of one's story for which one cares is closed forever, locked up, and put away, to be kept, as a sort of open secret, between oneself and eternity, one does not think much of newspapers. (III, 5)

The letters which Adams wrote to his closest friends in the years following Marian Hooper Adams's death demonstrate the importance to him of protecting that secret, for they are imbued with Adams's sense of the novel as a private memorial and of other readers' presence as intrusive. "I care more for one chapter, or any dozen pages of Esther than for the whole history, including maps and indexes; so much more, indeed, that I would not let anyone read the story for fear the reader should profane it" (III, 409), he wrote in anguish to Elizabeth Sherman Cameron, from Tahiti in February 1891. Adams's continuing enjoyment in holding a curious public at bay over the authorship of *Democracy* testifies, as well, to the satisfaction which limiting his audience gave him. In July of 1911—over thirty years after the publication of the novel—Adams wrote disingenuously to Mary Cadwalader Jones, from Paris,

> Two years ago a gentleman called on me (sent by Henry Holt) to ask whether I wrote Democracy. I told him I did not. He went off, and wrote a book in which he said that I said I did. . . . If it pleases them to think I wrote Shakespeare and Mother Goose, *tant mieux*! Really, of course Henry James wrote it, in connection with his brother Willy, to illustrate Pragmatism. (VI, 457–58)

In addition to controlling conditions of publication, Adams also limited public access to all his major works after the *History* through the more subtle and enduring strategy of privatizing meaning within the texts themselves. Both *Democracy* and *Esther* were romans à clef. While these novels no doubt appealed to a broader audience than Adams's scholarly *History* and his biographies of Albert Gallatin and of John Randolph, at the same time Adams limited that audience's understanding of both texts by retaining the key to references in them.[6] Only a very select set of readers—the members of the Five of Hearts; Elizabeth Sherman Cameron; Brooks Adams; and Henry Holt—was admitted into the mysteries of *Democracy*. Adams took evident pleasure in other readers' unsuccessful efforts to penetrate the layer of secrecy surrounding his fictional characters. "Mrs. Bigelow Lawrence . . . will die convinced that she was meant as the heroine of that scandalous work. I saw it in her eye . . ." (V, 282), he wrote slyly, for example, to Lizzie Cameron from Moscow in August 1901. Satirizing Washington society and power brokers from behind an impenetrable screen, Adams winked to Cameron and teased her, "If I had only invented it for democracy!" (V, 635, Washington, February 1905), punning on the infighting within Theodore Roosevelt's administration.

Adams also insulated meaning in *Mont Saint Michel and Chartres*, a text which he had especially strong reservations about exposing to a public in which he had little confidence. Private publication helped to allay Adams's worries about the demands which this complex volume, with all its theological, intellectual, and scientific unconventionalities, would place on readers. "I could not publish it if I would," he insisted to Henry Osborn Taylor from Washington in January 1905; "I should bring on my head all the Churches and all the Universities and all the Laboratories at once. They would scorch me alive for an anarchist. That is to say, possibly ten men in America might know enough to see what I am driving at . . ." (V, 624). Adams also protected *Mont Saint Michel and Chartres* from readers by working in it from the premise of restricted understanding. "The volume is not intended for the general public, and you will have to make allowances for a certain degree of intimacy in the relation between author and reader" (VI, 35), he explained, from Washington in December of 1906, to David Duncan Wallace, a history professor at a college in South Carolina. "Intimacy" tightens in Adams's text around a set of privatized assumptions about author and reader, about a common past and shared knowledge. The narrator of *Mont Saint Michel and Chartres* speaks of the text as a bridge between the present and the past, as "the *pons seclorum*, the bridge of ages, between us and our ancestors" (MSMC 11). But at the same time as he offers up his words as a point of entry into a lost world, the narrator also narrows access to that world by positing it as the territory of an exclusively defined readership. The narrator clearly counts on his readers to accept his story as "ours" in more than figurative terms. "Normans were everywhere in

1066, and everywhere in the lead of their age. We were a serious race" (MSMC 10, emphasis mine), he wrote, to introduce the building of the Mount; "*Our own* English ancestors, known as Puritans, held the same opinion" (MSMC 244, emphasis mine), he confirmed, in explaining bourgeois reservations about the Virgin. To define his audience in terms of that specific "us" was for Adams both to extend an invitation and to set a boundary. Just as he referred to the "architectural *Douane* to be passed" between northern and eastern France, where "one's architectural baggage must be opened" (MSMC 57), Adams created a set of checkpoints which readers had to pass in order to enter the text. Adams frequently inserted Latin and French—even medieval French— phrases and technical terms into his prose without providing translation.[7] While Adams claimed to be introducing this material to an uninformed audience of nieces, in fact fully appreciating *Mont Saint Michel and Chartres* depends on a substantial degree of linguistic and architectural sophistication. This apparent inconsistency has sometimes disturbed modern readers; but it also speaks to Adams's intention, as an author, of claiming a particular set of readers.[8]

Again, constructing a readership on whom he could make such per-sonalized demands made it possible for Adams in *The Education* to privatize the text's meaning. Initially Adams was so protective of *The Education* that he refused to relinquish ownership of the physical volumes, requesting that the carefully selected readers to whom he sent his autobiography regard it as a draft and return their copies to him. In the letter which accompanied William James's copy Adams referred directly to the sense of alienation that he had felt in releasing *Mont Saint Michel and Chartres* to the public, and he defended his refusal to take the same risk with *The Education*: "I knew that not a hundred people in America would understand what I meant. . . . I need not publish when no one would read or understand" (VI, 91–92). In the letter which he sent from Paris with Henry James's copy of *The Education*, in May 1908, Adams also asked that his need for privacy be respected, and emphasized the impor-tance of being able to count on James to understand that need without ex-plicit explanation:

> this volume is supposed to be lent out only for correction, suggestion and amendment, so that you are invited to return it, with your marginal com-ments whenever you have done with it. I need hardly tell *you* that my own marginal comment is broader than that of any reader, and precludes publi-cation altogether. (VI, 136)

Such letters suggest how strongly *The Education of Henry Adams* depends upon the private significance of what it does not have to explain to its audi-ence, on the hoarded luxury of a set of unarticulated commonalities. Lacking that experience, many modern readers feel burdened by the density of unfamiliar names in Adams's text. "The world never loved perfect poise," Adams wrote of his tense and difficult admiration for his reserved father;

> What the world does love is commonly absence of poise, for it has to be amused. Napoleons and Andrew Jacksons amuse it, but it is not amused by perfect balance. Had Mr. Adams's nature been cold, he would have followed Mr. Webster, Mr. Everett, Mr. Seward, and Mr. [Robert Charles] Winthrop in the lines of party discipline and self-interest. Had it been less balanced than it was, he would have gone with Mr. [William Lloyd] Garrison, Mr. Wendell Phillips, Mr. Edmund Quincy, and Theodore Parker, into secession.[9]

Assuming the presence of readers who would not require explanation from the author in order to appreciate his quiet deprecation of popular heroes like Andrew Jackson and of the common, shallow taste for "amusement" was for Adams, in *The Education* as well as in his letters, a strategy of exclusion and of alliance. Speaking only to the "everyone" whose experience and knowledge matched his own enabled Adams to anticipate a particular resonance from phrases. "Every year some young person alarmed the parental heart even in Boston" (*Ed* 70), he opened the narrative of his graduation trip to Germany, appealing to the circle of readers, like William and Henry James, who might pause here and share his memories of stolid Boston resistance. Such readers would need only a few details from the author to call up memories of the repressive qualities of a nineteenth-century New England upper-class childhood: "the seeds of a moral education would at that moment have fallen on the stoniest soil in Quincy, which is, as everyone knows, the stoniest glacial and tidal drift known in any Puritan land" (*Ed* 14). The dramatic void of twenty years which surrounds Henry Adams's marriage and Marian Hooper Adams's suicide in *The Education* suggests how deeply Adams counted on the prerogatives of meaningful silence as a strategy for privatizing meaning, and on the presence of an intimately familiar audience as a condition for authorship. This puzzling gap in the text has provided suggestive, and sometimes frustrating, material to readers searching for thematic structure in Adams's autobiography. But it is equally important to think about it in terms of Adams's construction of a readership among whom closeness made words unnecessary, who already knew Adams's pain and would appreciate his reluctance to bare it.[10]

These strategies of exclusion were evidently prompted not only by Adams's belief that he lacked a responsive audience but equally by Adams's conviction that constructing such an audience lay within his own power. In investing an exclusive readership with authorial prerogatives, Adams challenged the formal boundaries between writer and reader, and between his letters and his other prose. Adams's pleasure in the public puzzle of *Democracy* suggests how deeply

the controlled status of audience and the private status of meaning in the letters must have contributed to his commitment to that form, by making it possible for him to win the audience whose loss he claimed to have suffered.
Equally, Adams positioned his other work in an epistolary stance: as in the
alternating, interlocking rhythm of correspondence, Adams assigned to writing
the imperative of exchange and to reading the imperative of collaboration.

Adams engaged his letters directly in challenging his loss of audience, by
using the letters to designate exceptional readers and to extend those readers
privileged access to texts. When, for example, Adams finally revealed to John
Hay his authorship of *Esther*, after Marian Adams's death, his confession allied
Adams to Hay, and to Clarence King, in alienated privacy. "My poor boy,"
Adams wrote to Hay from Japan in August 1886, less than a year after Marian
Adams's death,

> how very strong you do draw your vintage for my melancholy little Esther. . . .
> Perhaps I made a mistake even to tell King about it; but having told him, I
> could not leave you out. Now, let it die! To admit the public to it would be
> almost unendurable to me. I will not pretend that the book is not precious
> to me, but its value has nothing to do with the public who could never under-
> stand that such a book might be written in one's heart's blood. (III, 34)

Spilling his "heart's blood" to Hay about "my melancholy little Esther," Adams
named Hay an essential reader—"I could not leave you out"—of a cherished
text as decisively as he protected the text from the "unendurable" intrusions
of "the public who could never understand." Adams often used seductive
appeals to their singularity in order to obligate specific correspondents as
readers. "I told you that I had but you for an audience" (V, 633), Adams insisted to Margaret Chanler, one of the close women friends with whom he
surrounded himself in the last years of his life, from Washington in February
1905, after she had read *Mont Saint Michel and Chartres*; and he wrote, four
months later, from Paris in June of 1905, in response to his younger brother
Brooks's enthusiastic reading of the same book, "you are, as far as we know,
the only man in America whose opinion on this subject has any value" (V, 668).
And Adams reinforced the privileged status of the readership of *Mont Saint
Michel and Chartres* by referring repeatedly in the letters to his dwindling
supply of copies. "I have now only seven copies left, which I have been keeping for libraries, but will send you one by express today" (VI, 132), he wrote,
for example, to Anne Hooper Lothrop, a cousin of his wife, from Washington
in April of 1908. He also reiterated his refusal to compromise the text by appealing to a broader audience. "Professors of Middle-age art and literature . . . worry
me for copies. I will see them roasted before I will let it be published, for I've
published books enough, and there is hardly anyone now living who is worth

writing for" (VI, 424), he wrote to Gaskell from Washington in March 1911. Such confidences bonded Adams and the readers with whom he shared his texts as members of an elite sect. "I have preserved complete silence about my reprint [of *Mont Saint Michel and Chartres*], in order not to be bothered by requests to turn it into a text-book and guide-book," Adams sniffed to Ward Thoron from Washington in January 1911; "I'll burn Chartres itself before I degrade it to such a fate. Our *culte* is esoteric" (VI, 405).

Adams strengthened bonds with his private audience by extending to some of these readers access to his work before it was printed and by insisting on the texts' permeability to their responses. Adams read aloud manuscript portions of both *Democracy* and *Mont Saint Michel and Chartres* to the Five of Hearts in Washington, and he read sections of *Mont Saint Michel and Chartres* to Elizabeth Sherman Cameron and Martha Cameron in Paris.[11] To Elizabeth Cameron, Adams insisted on the informality of *Mont Saint Michel and Chartres*, from Paris in May 1905: "I deny that it is a book; it is only a running chatter with my nieces and those of us who care for old art" (V, 659–60); and, again from Paris, in June of the same year, "The thing must remain Talk, not history" (V, 681). Adams made good on that promise of casual exchange by addressing the readers of *Mont Saint Michel and Chartres* in the second person, as in a conversation or a letter, and inviting a response: "Here is your first eleventh-century church! how does it affect you?" (MSMC 13). And in *The Education* Adams assigned readers patently letterly prerogatives over his manuscript, particularly by refusing for himself the prerogative of determining closure. Adams referred hesitantly to the manuscript as "The volume—or rather, the sheets of the possible, projected book" (VI, 58), in a letter, from Washington in April 1907, accompanying Henry Lee Higginson's copy of *The Education*, and he elaborated on that hesitation, in a letter to Charles Francis Adams, Jr., from Washington in January 1908, by emphasizing the epistolary qualities of his text: "Although I have no idea of publishing, I have all the stronger idea of consulting. My notion of work is that of work among workers, that is, by comparison, correspondence and conversation" (VI, 105).[12]

In appealing to a limited audience Adams placed unusual demands on his readers.[13] At the same time as he prevented readers outside his circle from fully penetrating the texts, Adams applied pressure to readers within the circle, encouraging in them reciprocal commitment to those texts. In jest, Adams implicated John Hay in the public drama over the authorship of *Democracy*: "I am glad the secret is at last coming out. I was always confident that you wrote that book, or at any rate that you knew who did" (II, 459), he wrote playfully to Hay from Washington in June 1882. Adams also imposed on Martha Cameron partial responsibility for *Mont Saint Michel and Chartres* by releasing her from the convention of thanking him for her copy of the book: "I expected no acknowledgment, because you know it was your book, and I read

most all of it to you as I wrote it" (V, 631). More directly, in acknowledging
to many of the readers of *The Education* his obligation to consult them, Adams
assigned those readers a significant amount of entitlement over his text. "You
have a *right* to the volume" (VI, 91, emphasis mine), he insisted to William
James from Washington in December 1907; "in case you object to any phrase
or expression, will you please draw your pen through it" (VI, 48), he invited
Charles Francis Adams, Jr., from Washington in February 1907; "I have to ask
your permission for certain reminiscences which are taking shape in my mind"
(VI, 48), he wrote to Charles Milnes Gaskell a month later. Adams's promise
to alter his text in response to these readers' wishes offered them the prerogatives of authorship. "If any of them, from the President and [Henry] Cabot
[Lodge] and your husband downwards would hint a wish to be left out, I would
do it gladly" (VI, 52), he promised Elizabeth Cameron, from Washington in
March 1907. At the same time as Adams's request that correspondents return
to him the original copies of *The Education* exerted control over outsiders'
access to the text, the letters' requests for "correction, suggestion and amend-
ment" (to Henry James, from Paris, May 1908, VI, 136) extended authority
and liability to Adams's readers. His letters confirm Adams's success at solic-
iting the active participation of his audience in the writing of *The Education*.
"Thanks for your corrections, which prove that your eyes are better than mine.
All are noted on the margin, and will be food for printers whenever the time
comes" (VI, 69), Adams wrote to Gaskell from Paris in May 1907; "My own
copy of the Education is now wholly defaced by notes" (VI, 219), he wrote to
James Ford Rhodes, from Washington in February 1909.[14]

Finally, Adams engaged author and audience—and the letters and his
other prose works—by writing his readers into the texts themselves.[15] Adams's
deference to the audience of *The Education* reflected the fact that many of his
readers—including Charles Francis Adams, Jr., Elizabeth Sherman Cameron,
Henry Cabot Lodge, William James, Henry James, Whitelaw Reid, and
Theodore Roosevelt—also served as characters in his autobiography. "The volume has been put into type wholly for the purpose of getting it, in advance,
to every friend who is drawn by name into the narrative, so that each one may
correct or strike out anything unpleasant or objectionable" (VI, 50), Adams
wrote to Anna Cabot Mills Lodge from Washington in March 1907, acknowledging the obligation which those readers' presence in the text placed on him
as writer. Clearly Henry Adams's use of third-person narration was a naturalistic stance, suspicious of the individual either as actor (rather than "manikin") or as author. At the same time, Adams's refusal to lay autonomous claim
to the story of *The Education* also enabled him to challenge the autonomy of
his personal narrative.[16] For *The Education of Henry Adams* was in many ways
a tribute to the readers who served in the text as a model audience, exemplary
sources of validation and exchange, as well as a means of bonding with the

members of that audience who read the text. Adams honored, for example, the opening moment of his friendship with Charles Milnes Gaskell: "What affected his whole life was the intimacy then begun with Milnes Gaskell and his circle of undergraduate friends . . ." (Ed 205). And Adams praised his younger brother Brooks for providing precious intellectual companionship: "the two brothers could talk to each other without atmosphere" (Ed 338–39). Not all of Adams's portraits of potential readers in The Education were wholly sympathetic. Adams was especially worried that Charles W. Eliot would be insulted by his portrayal of Harvard during Eliot's tenure as president and Adams's as assistant professor of history there. "Having passed your censorship, and Cabot's, and Speck's, I have a greater than you all to face,—Charles Eliot's! I am still trembling before him as though I were always an undergraduate" (VI, 51), he confessed anxiously to Theodore Roosevelt from Washington in March 1907.[17] Yet Adams's concern with the effect of his narrative on his readers paid continuing respect to a valued audience.

Adams's lavish praise of John Hay in The Education memorialized a member of that audience who did not survive to read Adams's text—and, at the same time, allied his surviving readers around their vulnerability to such losses. Adams remembered Hay as a model statesman. "None could have given the work quite the completeness, the harmony, the perfect ease of Hay" (Ed 363), Adams described Hay's service as U.S. ambassador to London. More important, Adams remembered Hay as a model friend, who never compromised friendship with politics: "nor did Hay care whether his friends agreed or disagreed [with his policies]" (Ed 366). The conclusion of The Education is in substantial part a homage to John Hay and to the crucial role which Hay's memory played for Adams in the process of initiating and sustaining authorship. The pivotal fact that Hay's death signaled closure in Adams's autobiography— "It was time to go" (Ed 505)—suggests the extent to which Adams was concerned with his audience's fragile mutuality, both as a subject and as an object of preservation. Adams ended The Education by framing the text in the narrative of safety and responsiveness which he had shared with Hay and with Clarence King, raising the possibility of alleviating modern alienation by someday adopting that redeeming model:

> Perhaps some day—say 1938, their centenary—they might be allowed to return together for a holiday, to see the mistakes of their own lives made clear in the light of the mistakes of their successors; and perhaps then, for the first time since man began his education among the carnivores, they would find a world that sensitive and timid natures could regard without a shudder. (Ed 505)

Henry Adams's efforts to challenge conventional relations between author and reader speak in these texts to the unwavering centrality of audience as a problem and as a condition of writing for him. They dramatize the danger with which audience was fraught for Adams and the pressure to achieve control over the terms of authorship which the uncertainties of audience imposed on him. Adams's anxiety about controlling the boundary between private and public discourse remained extreme, but that extremity also reinforced Adams's need to locate a responsive readership. If Adams was tempted, especially in the excruciating wake of his wife's death, to protect his privacy with silence—"I have brought from Boston the old volumes of this Diary, and have begun their systematic destruction. I mean to leave no record that can be obliterated" (III, 143), he wrote, for example, in his journal after finishing the History in September 1888—the texts which he continued to write testify to his success in constructing that necessary audience.

The Problem of Authorship

The problematic status of *audience* was for Henry Adams inextricable from the problematic status of *authorship,* from the political issues which literary authority and voice raised for him. *Democracy, Esther, Mont Saint Michel and Chartres,* and *The Education of Henry Adams* are all dominated thematically and structurally by authorial problems representing Adams's concern with the power at stake in writing and reading texts. His restlessness with the limits of genre demonstrates the primacy for Adams of locating an appropriate language and form, his unceasing concern with the process of writing.[18] In addition to his journalism and his letters, between 1877 and 1907 Adams wrote his nine-volume History, two biographies, two novels, a study of medieval art and culture, and an autobiography. If the difficulty of classifying Adams's last works testifies to his virtuosity as a writer and his readiness to experiment, it also evinces Adams's failure to be satisfied by existing conditions of authorship and his ambivalence about seeing himself as the inheritor of a sanctioned literary tradition. In all four of Adams's imaginative works, the erosion of human authority in a naturalistic world of anonymous forces is dramatized in the protagonist's quest for knowledge and for a sustainable stance as author.

Both of Adams's novels use the gendered status of authorship to locate writing in a political arena. In both *Democracy* and *Esther,* the female protagonist's inability to take control of narrative dramatizes Adams's concern with equality of access to writing and with writing's abusive potential.

In *Democracy,* Madeleine Lee's quest takes form in the struggle between authorship and readership in which her relationship with Senator Ratcliffe engages her.[19] Reading looms for Madeleine Lee, immediately, as both essential and elusive, precisely on account of its political implications. Reading a set of authoritative texts helps Mrs. Lee qualify for entrée into a privileged circle: "The Senator found that his neighbour—a fashionable New York woman, exquisitely dressed, and with a voice and manner seductively soft and gentle—had read the speeches of Webster and Calhoun."[20] More important, reading Senator Ratcliffe becomes a major activity within the text, both a source and a test of knowledge, for Mrs. Lee: "She had read with unerring instinct one general characteristic of all Senators, a boundless and guileless thirst for flattery" (Democracy 18). Madeleine Lee quickly grasps the fact that the power and mobility which she seeks through Ratcliffe will be determined by her skill as a reader: "To her eyes he was the high-priest of American politics; he was charged with the meaning of the mysteries, the clue to political hieroglyphics" (Democracy 20). Madeleine Lee realizes that deciphering the "hieroglyphics" of power in Washington depends on her ability to unlock Ratcliffe's "mysteries." Although she is not above flirting with Ratcliffe in order to gain access to him—"I am always at home on Sunday evenings" (Democracy 20), she lets him know—Mrs. Lee does not pursue Ratcliffe primarily as a suitor. Instead, she sees him as a source of encoded meaning, a text to be read.

In turn, Ratcliffe's power over Mrs. Lee is dramatized in Democracy in fundamentally authorial terms. Ratcliffe's ability to control meaning emerges in the novel as a function of rhetorical initiative and display. From early in the text, Madeleine Lee is consigned to the role of reader, and she observes the political process as a spectator:

> The stage was before her, the curtain was rising, the actors were ready to enter; she had only to go quietly on among the supernumeraries and see how the play was acted and the stage effects were produced; how the great tragedians mouthed, and the stage-manager swore. (Democracy 8)

Lee conceives of public institutions in terms of grand staging: "in truth, her notion of legislative bodies was vague, floating between her experience at church and at the opera, so that the idea of a performance of some kind was never out of her head" (Democracy 11). But if Madeleine Lee becomes a connoisseur of that "performance," Senator Ratcliffe remains its master. When Mrs. Lee finally confronts him with Carrington's accusations of vote fraud, Ratcliffe insists on his superior rhetorical authority, on his ability to impose upon her his rewriting of Carrington's text. "True in its leading facts; untrue in some of its details, and in the impression it creates" (Democracy 173), Ratcliffe pronounces, after reading Carrington's letter and casually tossing it into the fire. In listening to Ratcliffe's dense, weaving logic—"I did not consider myself at liberty to persist in a mere private opinion in regard to a measure about which I recognized the extreme likelihood of my being in error" (Democracy 173–74)—Madeleine Lee finds her own ethical scruples overcome by her appreciation of Ratcliffe's skill as a narrator:

Not until this moment had she really felt as though she had got to the
heart of politics. . . . Her interest in the disease overcame her disgust at the
foulness of the revelation. To say that the discovery gave her actual pleasure
would be doing her injustice; but the excitement of the moment swept away
every other sensation. (*Democracy* 174)

Here Adams reveals the rhetorical status of Ratcliffe's power: "had Mr. Ratcliffe's
associates now been present to hear his version of it [his story], they would
have looked at each other with a smile of professional pride . . ." (*Democracy*
175). In *Democracy*, politicians are "professionals" in a quite literary sense:
as Ratcliffe demonstrates, the most effective politician is the most effective
author, the most convincing inventor and manipulator of meaning.

In *Esther*, as well as in *Democracy*, the gendered status of authorship and
of the control which inheres in authorship is continually dramatized. Like
Madeleine Lee's loss of her husband, Esther Dudley's loss of her father frees
her for a personal quest; like Senator Ratcliffe's pursuit of Mrs. Lee, Stephen
Hazard's pursuit of Esther Dudley reveals a set of rhetorical limits, especially
on autonomy, under which the female protagonist of the novel is fated to work.
In *Esther*, these limits are figured in a struggle between Esther Dudley and the
male characters who surround her over the initiatives of authorship.

Esther's tortured wavering over Stephen Hazard's marriage proposal provides the novel's most important example of the dominating potential of
authorship and of gendered limits on access to that potential. When Hazard
interrupts Esther's storytelling in the children's ward at the hospital, both the
initiative and the authority of authorship pass to him. As he takes over in enter-
taining the children, Hazard enthusiastically displays his own rhetorical skill:

He drew so good a monkey on a cocoanut tree that the children shouted
with delight, and Esther complained that his competition would ruin her
market. She rose at last to go, telling him that she was sorry to seem so
harsh, but had she known that his pictures and stories were so much better
than hers, she would never have voted to make him a visitor.[21]

Believing that he was won Esther's attention, Hazard is disappointed when
she does not appear in church the following Sunday, for he has already imagined her listening to his sermon: "He felt a sort of half-conscious hope that
Esther would be again a listener, and that he might talk it over with her. . . .
he resented Esther Dudley's neglect to flatter him by coming to his sermon"
(*Esther* 214). Although Adams undermines Hazard's credibility as a narrator—"ill-natured persons, and there were such in his parish, might say that
he was carrying on a secular flirtation in his church under the pretense of doing
his duty" (*Esther* 231)—he still assigns Hazard the ability to obligate Esther

Dudley as his audience: "He lectured Wharton on the subject of early Christian art until he saw that Wharton would no longer listen, and then he went off to Miss Dudley, and lectured her" (*Esther* 232).

Adams makes it clear that Esther has good reason to feel threatened by Hazard's marriage proposal; significantly, Adams figures that threat in Hazard's readiness to take narrative control of Esther. In considering his motives for pursuing Esther to Buffalo, for example, Hazard produces a suspiciously worked tale in which Esther's autonomy steadily recedes:

> The danger of disappointment and defeat roused in him the instinct of martyrdom. He was sure that all mankind would suffer if he failed to get the particular wife he wanted. "It is not a selfish struggle," he thought. "It is a human soul I am trying to save, and I will do it in the teeth of all the powers of darkness. . . . If I cannot wield this fire from Heaven, I am unfit to touch it. Let it burn me up!" (*Esther* 312)

Hazard uses this inflated language to rewrite his desire for Esther, transposing it into a discourse of religious duty which belongs to him and which legitimates his effort as one to "save" her for her own sake. When Esther resists his calls to faith—" 'I have tried,' said Esther. 'I tried desperately and failed utterly' " (*Esther* 328)—Hazard even more aggressively fixes her in a narrative within which his authority would be difficult for her to challenge:

> "*I know you better than you know yourself!* Do you think that I, whose business it is to witness every day of my life the power of my faith, am going to hesitate before a trifle like your common, daily, matter-of-course fears and doubts, such as have risen, and been laid in every mind that was worth being called one, ever since minds existed?" (*Esther* 329, emphasis mine)

By dismissing Esther's doubts as "common" and by reiterating the superior "power" of his own experience and faith, Hazard justifies his refusal to take seriously Esther's resistance to his plans.

Esther's relations with the constellation of male characters surrounding her—each a competing author of his own truth in ways that Esther cannot manage to emulate—dramatize both her inability, like Madeleine Lee's, to make a transition from reader or character to author, and the failure of her environment to provide conditions under which authorship would be a viable option for her. Thus for Esther, retaining her doubts about marrying Stephen Hazard constitutes an act of resistance to the male prerogatives of authorship: Esther resists being *written* by Hazard, as either his audience or his character. Once Hazard has declared his feelings for Esther, being loved seems to obligate her to a gendered—and closed—narrative: "The instant Esther felt herself really loved, she met her fate as women will when the shock is once over" (*Esther* 270). Yet Esther lacks the authority either to challenge or to take control of Hazard's narrative, and she lacks the confidence to rely on her own feelings for Hazard in making her decision. Even when Strong makes explicit the relationship between faith and submission, Esther cannot accept the legitimacy of her own doubts about submitting "faithfully":

> "If you have faith enough in Hazard to believe in him, you have faith enough to accept his church. Faith means submission. Submit!"
> "I want to submit," cried Esther piteously, rising in her turn and speaking in accents of real distress and passion. "Why can't some of you make me? For a few minutes at a time I think it done, and then I suddenly find myself more defiant than ever." (*Esther* 286)

Her responsiveness to nature at Niagara Falls testifies to Esther's hunger for a narrative in which transcending human limits might be possible for her:

> She fell in love with the cataract and turned to it as a confidant, not because of its beauty or power, but because it seemed to tell her a story which she longed to understand. "I think I do understand it," she said to herself as she looked out. (*Esther* 314)[22]

Placing her confidence in nature's superior authority—"To have Niagara for a rival is no joke" (*Esther* 315), the narrator acknowledges, when Esther confronts Hazard—helps to provide Esther, finally, with the courage to criticize, and thus to resist, the church's institutionalization of male domination: "Why must the church always appeal to my weakness and never to my strength!" (*Esther* 333). Yet Esther's rejection of Hazard on these grounds does not prove so clearly to be a victory for her, for it leaves her without an alternative to her loneliness and lack of fulfillment. Liberating herself from Hazard's narrative deprives Esther Dudley of the only text that she had, and she is unable to author another. "But George, I don't love you, I love him" (*Esther* 335), she mourns in the last line of the novel, in response to George Strong's ardent marriage proposal. Rather than acknowledging her need, Strong's promise of a narrative—"'If you will marry me, I will admire and love you more than ever a woman was loved since the world began.'" (*Esther* 335)—simply extends Hazard's dominating authorship and Esther's silence, her inability to write her own story.

Thus in Adam's novels authorship is portrayed as a source of power which is inequitably distributed and potentially hurtful. Moreover, in each of these novels the alienating conditions of authorship have an air of inevitability which is thematically central to the text and its social critique. In his last two major works, *Mont Saint Michel and Chartres* and *The Education of Henry Adams*, however, Adams experiments with alternatives which challenge both autonomy and opposition between author and audience as conditions of writing.

Adams sets these altered priorities decisively in *Mont Saint Michel and Chartres* by directly engaging reader, writer, and characters with one another. The text opens with a discussion of the loss of intimacy between contemporary authors and readers: "The relationship, between reader and writer, of son and father, may have existed in Queen Elizabeth's time, but is much too close to be true for ours" (MSMC 5). Yet while he claims to lack the prerogative of demanding intimacy from his audience, Adams immediately positions his narrator in an avuncular stance—"The uncle talks" (MSMC 6)—which assumes the presence of familiar readers and which transforms the function of authorship from serving an individual's need to control to serving the need to give mutual pleasure. The "uncle" makes mutuality central, both for the nieces in the text, listening, and for the "nieces" who are outside the text, reading. Facing both the Mount and his audience, he introduces his subject:

> one needs to be eight centuries old to know what this mass of encrusted architecture meant to its builders, and even then one must still learn to feel it. The man who wanders into the twelfth century is lost, unless he can grow prematurely young.
> One can do it, as one can play with children. . . . Our sense is partially atrophied from disuse, but it is still alive, at least in old people, who alone, as a class, have the time to be young. (MSMC 7–8)

The narrator immediately insists on the essential role which his audience plays for him: their responsiveness brings him to words and encourages him to believe in words' restorative power; and it makes him willing to be responsive himself, to risk "feeling" and to "play." Alone, he makes clear, neither the "old" nor the "young" can fully appreciate the commitments which informed twelfth-century architecture; but together, as "we," both gain access to a more creatively and spiritually sustaining tradition.

Thus unity—between writer and reader, author and audience—provides *Mont Saint Michel and Chartres* with both a subject and a method.[23] Adams uses the Middle Ages as a historical model of unity between the individual and a greater order and, more generally, between the human and the divine, between reason and faith; in Thomas Aquinas's thought he sees "that celebrated fusion of the Universal with the Individual, of Unity with Multiplicity, of God and Nature, which had broken the neck of every philosophy ever invented" (MSMC 338). Adams's guidebook to twelfth-century architecture attempts to inspire readers with the possibility of achieving cultural renewal by bridging past and present as more informed, responsive *readers*: "One looks back on it all as a picture; a symbol of unity; an assertion of God and Man in a bolder, stronger, closer union than ever was expressed by other art; and when the idea is absorbed, accepted and perhaps partially understood, one may move on" (MSMC 47). Adams himself claimed that he found reading medieval history restorative. "Nobody seems to have the remotest idea about any subject that breathes," Adams complained in a letter to Ward Thoron from Washington in February 1911;

> Probably you see some newspaper. I see lots of them. Their chief effort is to herd the sheep, especially the lambs. The moment a lamb can be induced to buy a share in any market-security, the Jews jump on him. . . .
> So I turn back to Chartres, and find vast interest in the place and the people. The more I study, the more I want to know. . . . (VI, 415–16)

Such angry and bigoted letters make *Mont Saint Michel and Chartres* seem surprising for its largeness of spirit and its playfulness. Yet they also help to explain the text's appeal for Adams. His commitment to "turning back" to this material speaks to Adams's willingness to be moved and changed by reading and, especially, by access to the community whose loss so much of his other work mourned: "The thirteenth century has few secrets. There are no outsiders. We are one family as we are one church" (MSMC 174).

In this spirit of creating community between author and audience, Adams alters the conditions of reading throughout *Mont Saint Michel and Chartres* by emphasizing and legitimating feeling.[24] The narrator exhorts his readers to become more responsive to texts. "Anyone who will take the trouble to catch the metre. . . ," he promises of *La Chanson de Roland*, "can follow the feeling of the poetry. . . . He will feel the simple force of the words and action, as he feels Homer" (MSMC 28–29); "We are trying only to feel gothic art" (MSMC 105). Adams renders medieval unity in terms of a model readership which he then offers his own readers as an example to emulate. Adams pays appreciative attention to the common stock of experience on which medieval poets could count in their audience:

> Everyone in . . . [Aucassins's] audience was,—and, for that matter, still would be,—familiar with the great forests, the home of half the fairy and nursery tales of Europe. . . . Everyone saw, without an effort, the young damoiseau riding out with his hound or hawk, looking for game. . . .
> (MSMC 224)

Adams's own attraction to the Middle Ages speaks in substantial part for his appreciation (and, perhaps, his jealously) of a time when the relationship between author and audience was not conflicted, when Taillefer, for example, could anticipate a set of listeners with respect for his authority—"No modern

singer ever enjoys such power over an audience . . ." (MSMC 27)—and when
cathedrals could be built all over France and expect a passionate reception:
"they were made for crowds, for thousands and tens of thousands of human
beings; for the whole human race, on its knees, hungry for pardon and love"
(MSMC 344–45). Adams attempts to construct, in turn, a relationship of trust
among narrator, reader, and subject, by insisting on the importance of responding directly to Chartres, of setting aside the mediating authority of the church
and of time in order to achieve a heightened spirituality:

> The churchman is the only true and final judge on his own doctrine, and
> we neither know nor care to know the facts, but we are as good judges as he
> of the feeling, and we are at full liberty to feel that such a Last Judgment as
> this was never seen before or since. . . . Never in all these seven hundred
> years has one of us looked up at this Rose without feeling it to be Our
> Lady's promise of Paradise. (MSMC 138).

Adams's own eloquent response to Thomas Aquinas's thought and to its successful authorship of unity testifies to the meaningful effects which he believes
making intimacy a condition of reading could have: "The theology turns always
into art at the last, and ends in aspiration. . . . All they saw was the soul van-
ishing into the skies" (MSMC 355–56).

The extraordinary epiphany which comes in Chartres, at the end of chapter 10, serves in *Mont Saint Michel and Chartres* as a model of this altered condition of reading. The passage's blossoming crescendo of insight bears quoting
in entirety:

> Sitting here any Sunday afternoon, while the voices of the children of the
> *maîtrise* are chanting in the choir,—your mind held in the grasp of the
> strong lines and shadows of the architecture; your eyes flooded with the
> autumn tones of the glass; your ears drowned with the purity of the voices;
> one sense reacting upon another until sensation reaches the limit of its
> range;—you or any other lost soul, could, if you cared to look and listen,
> feel a sense beyond the human ready to reveal a sense divine that would
> make that world once more intelligible, and would bring the Virgin to life
> again, in all the depth of feeling which she shows here,—in lines, vaults,
> chapels, colors, legends, chants,—more eloquent than the prayer-book, and
> more beautiful than the autumn sunlight; and anyone willing to try, could
> feel it like the child, reading new thought without end into the art he has
> studied a hundred times; but what is still more convincing, he could, at
> will, in an instant, shatter the whole art by calling into it a single motive of
> his own. (MSMC 169)

"Anyone willing to try": the narrator makes a promise here whose almost uncontrollably rising pitch—"flooded," "drowned"—challenges the boundary between text and reader with contagious enthusiasm. "If you cared to look and listen," the narrator urges, "you could feel it like the child." Quivering with pleasure in the autumnal afternoon light, at the very edge of wildness, this scene revels in entering "a sense divine" which challenges human isolation in an unknowable, unresponsive universe. Adams's commitment to restoring a condition of creative potential strongly echoes the famous epiphany which Emerson reached as he crossed "a bare common" at twilight, the sense of one-ness with the world embodied in Emerson's figure of the transparent eyeball.[25] Just as Emerson shivered with the inexplicable excitement of that moment of transformation, "glad to the brink of fear," Adams also glories in pushing the boundaries between human and not-human, between Emerson's "me" and "not-me," in gaining access to an empowering consciousness of unity and to the "shattering," generative power of art. But "crossing" is also for Adams a different kind of victory from Emerson's, because Adams is writing at Chartres—looking to the past whose hold over the present Emerson so deeply resented—precisely because he lacks Emerson's confidence in the contempo-rary world as either a safe or an encouraging place for human beings, and because he remains reluctant to assume a public voice. Emerson's epiphany confirmed his own ideological positions and enabled him to provide a national audience with a model of self-reliant authorship, testimony to his own lead-ership and to his conviction that "America" made old, alienating dualisms obsolete. Adams's epiphany gives him the heart to imagine achieving a new condition of authorship—"he could, at will, in an instant, shatter the whole art by calling into it a single motive of his own"—but for Adams holding off alienation, whose possibility remains constant, depends on building respon-siveness rather than autonomy into the text.

Henry Adams's victory—as writer—in Mont Saint Michel and Chartres lies in his ability to build a relationship with his readers which feels neither alien-ating nor threatening. Adams manages, as a writer, to take the cathedral as his model, to take a flying leap and commit himself to constructing the read-ership whose presence might restore his faith in his own ability to express hoarded passions and hopes: "The delight of its aspirations is flung up to the sky," he writes of the cathedral in the concluding lines; "The pathos of its self-distrust and anguish of doubt, is buried in the earth as its last secret. You can read out of it whatever else pleases your youth and confidence; to me, this is all" (MSMC 359). The rhythmic, soaring prose which Adams writes in Mont Saint Michel and Chartres, so radically different from anything that he produced in either novel, wholly and openly moved by his subject, testifies to the con-fidence in his own power which claiming that audience provided Adams as an author:

The Archangel loved heights. Standing on the summit of the tower that crowned his church, wings upspread, sword uplifted, the devil crawling beneath, and the cock, symbol of eternal vigilance, perched on his mailed foot, Saint Michael held a place of his own in heaven and on earth which seems, in the eleventh century, to leave hardly room for the Virgin of the Crypt at Chartres, still less for the Beau Christ of the thirteenth century at Amiens. The Archangel stands for Church and State, and both militant. He is the conqueror of Satan, the mightiest of all created spirits, the nearest to God. His place was where the danger was greatest; therefore you find him here. (MSMC 7)

In *The Education*, Adams claims to be breaking off the quest for knowledge and unity on which he embarked in *Mont Saint Michel and Chartres*, and abandoning it as futile; his frustrated refrain, "The more he was educated, the less he understood" (*Ed* 44), echoes throughout the first half of Adams's text. In the opening chapters of *The Education*, Adams's protagonist claims to be steadily losing touch with the world he inhabits and with the inherited narratives of family and class authority around which he had expected to shape his life: "Always he felt somewhere else. . . . He knew not even where or how to begin" (*Ed* 52–53). A wide gap opens in the text between the narrator and many of the characters, like President Ulysses S. Grant, of whom Adams observes with cynical detachment: "sometimes he made one doubt his good faith; as when he seriously remarked to a particularly bright young woman that Venice would be a fine city if it were drained" (*Ed* 265–66). *The Education of Henry Adams* seems to mark a low point in Adams's confidence as a writer, and to come back to and even deepen the novels' doubts; it seems to speak, even more radically, for the breakdown of authorship. Equally, Adams's autobiography often seems to be resisting readers, by taking pains to dissociate the author from the narrator, by insisting on the third-person point of view and by refusing to provide access to an "I." Benjamin Franklin's *Autobiography* resonates with the pleasure of discovering the plasticity of the world in human hands, with the heady excitement of forging a narrative out of "unlikely beginnings."[26] But the same eighteenth-century victories of human promise which opened up the very possibility of autobiography for Franklin congeal around Henry Adams into a burdensome illusion. Adams's doubts in *The Education* about the autonomous individual express the failure of that eighteenth-century tradition, of human knowledge and ordering power, and cut off Adams's ability to author a text whose narrative would inevitably claim both.[27]

The Education of Henry Adams embodies one of the central paradoxes of literary naturalism: the paradox of writing under the shadow of radical doubt about human power. For Stephen Crane, as well as for Henry Adams, authorship constituted a thematic problem; and the crisis of war in *The Red Badge of Courage* becomes a crisis of narrative, a writer's crisis.[28] Similarly reluctant to impose direction, *The Education of Henry Adams* seems to chronicle the end of narrative: "Drifting in the dead-water of the *fin-de-siècle* . . ." (*Ed* 331), Adams describes himself in the opening line of his chapter on the 1893 Columbian Exposition. Adams claims in his preface to be indebted to Benjamin Franklin's "model . . . of self-teaching" (*Ed* xxix). Yet Franklin's *Autobiography* managed not only to take confident pleasure in speaking in the first person but even to project the revolutionary history of "America" in the author's personal narrative.[29] Adams, in dramatic contrast, creates the figure of the "manikin" in order to build provocative hesitation into the whole project of assigning meaning to and taking control over his own story:

> The manikin, therefore, has the same value as any other geometrical figure of three or more dimensions, which is used for the study of relation. For that purpose it cannot be spared; it is the only measure of motion, of proportion, of human condition; it must have the air of reality; must be taken for real; must be treated as though it had life. Who knows? Possibly it had! (*Ed* xxx)

In challenging ironically the conventional relationship between author and subject, Adams challenges assumptions about the writer's authority to invent and sustain a life of his own.[30] Adams confronts the problematic status of authorship under a set of cultural conditions in which it seems to him—as it emphatically had not to Franklin—impossible to take for granted either the possibility of creating a controlling self or the legitimacy of the self as speaker. At the same time, Adams positions himself ambiguously with respect to his reader, as both passive spectator and active participant in his own narrative.[31] In a sense, Adams faces the prospect of narrative with the wariness of a reader rather than with the conviction of a writer.

Yet it is as writer that Adams emerges in *The Education*; and it is as author that Adams holds himself accountable in the text, both to his own need to express himself and to the task of providing his readers with some kind of coherence. Like *Mont Saint Michel and Chartres*, *The Education* comes to an epiphany that turns on a problem of authorship, after which it becomes impossible for Adams to sustain his stance of detachment. In the scene in which he describes his sister's hideous death from lockjaw, Adams confronts a crisis that moves him too deeply to permit withdrawal. Here Adams simultaneously writes his disappointment with a world in which human suffering does not matter and insists on writing his quite human pain. With cadenced vigilance, Adams renders his sister's death as a taunting drama of contrasts, unlikely and riveting:

> Never had one seen her so winning. The hot Italian summer brooded outside, over the market-place and the picturesque peasants, and, in the singular

color of the Tuscan atmosphere, the hills and vineyards of the Apennines seemed bursting with midsummer blood. The sickroom itself glowed with the Italian joy of life; friends filled it; no harsh northern lights pierced the soft shadows; even the dying woman shared the sense of the Italian summer, the soft, velvet air, the humor, the courage, the sensual fulness of Nature and man. She faced death, as women mostly do, bravely and even gaily, racked slowly to unconsciousness, but yielding only to violence, as a soldier sabred in battle. For many thousands of years, on these hills and plains, Nature had gone on sabring men and women with the same air of sensual pleasure. (*Ed* 288)

Deprived of the quintessentially eighteenth-century props of reason and the senses in which Franklin placed his faith, Adams faces what he fears most, the defenselessness of being human in a world of inhuman forces. "For the first time, the stage-scenery of the senses collapsed; the human mind felt itself stripped naked" (*Ed* 288), he writes, in shock; "For pure blasphemy, it made pure atheism a comfort. God might be, as the Church said, a Substance, but He could not be a Person" (*Ed* 289). This passage transforms Adams's use of third-person narration, breaking down the barrier between an Adams who has passed beyond emotion, and has no reason to seek language for it, and an Adams who comes in need to language, because he is so conscious of his own vulnerability. Adams's juxtaposition of images bursting with life and the droning approach of death sustains his investment in human feeling and words at a moment when both seem radically threatened. Adams's own prose, rocking lushly at the edge between surfeit and deprivation, "bursting with midsummer blood" in "the soft, velvet air," as his sister is "racked slowly to unconsciousness," dramatizes this tension with excruciating effectiveness.

In continuing to write in the face of doubt and disjunction, Adams acts on the basis of considerable confidence in the audience to whom his eventual authorization of publication gave access to the text.[32] Moreover, Adams takes creative advantage of the alienating sense of "doubleness" which vexes him throughout the first chapters of *The Education* and uses it thematically and strategically. Like a letter, *The Education of Henry Adams* challenges the inevitability of alienation, for it commits Adams to authorship as an act of allegiance, not only to his own ability to create an ordering form which might challenge his loss of authority, but also to the potential allies whom the act of writing claimed as Adams's audience: "Chicago asked in 1893 [at the Columbian Exposition] for the first time the question whether the American people knew where they were driving. Adams answered, for one, that he did not know, but would try to find out" (*Ed* 343). Adams's insistence on the failure of history as a forward-moving force of change underlines his own sense of isolation and stasis: "One was almost glad to act the part of horseshoe crab in Quincy Bay, and admit that all was uniform—that nothing ever changed—and that the woman would swim about the ocean of future time, as she had swum in the past, with the gar-fish and the shark, unable to change" (*Ed* 448). But Adams remains committed to his two explaining metaphors, the dynamo and the Virgin, and to his search for language and models which could translate historical narrative's incremental progression of individuals and time into the accelerating motion of forces. That commitment confirms the act of writing as sign and as agent of both personal and communal responsibility. "The Virgin herself never looked so winning—so One—as in this scandalous failure of her Grace," he writes after hearing of the revolutionary assassination of the Russian minister of the interior in 1904 during a visit to the cathedral at Troyes, and then asks his readers, bitterly, "To what purpose had she existed, if, after nineteen hundred years, the world was bloodier than when she was born?" (*Ed* 472). In response, Adams pushes against his own intellectual fatigue, and makes the commitment to engagement in the world around him—by closing the gap between author and audience, writer and subject—which his narrative claims to have abandoned:

> To the tired student, the idea that he must give it up seemed sheer senility. As long as he could whisper, he would go on as he had begun, bluntly refusing to meet his creator with the admission that the creation had taught him nothing except that the square of the hypothenuse of a right-angled triangle might for convenience be taken as equal to something else. Every man with self-respect enough to become effective, if only as a machine, has had to account to himself for himself somehow, and to invent a formula of his own for his universe, if the standard formulas failed. (*Ed* 472)

Writing and the Marketplace: The Alternative of the Letter

The problematic status of audience and authorship in all four of these texts—*Democracy*; *Esther*; *Mont Saint Michel and Chartres*; and *The Education of Henry Adams*—is a sign, finally, not only of the unease which Henry Adams personally felt but, equally, of Adams's reservations about the commercialization and professionalization of writing during his lifetime. Adams recognized in the end of the nineteenth century the end of literary era which had belonged to an elite form of authorship, to the gentleman amateur, the "man of letters."[33] Rapid urban growth, technological innovation, and expanded advertising led, steadily from the 1830s onward, to dramatic increases in the circulation of newspapers and in opportunities for journalists.[34] In the United States, book production rose from about one hundred titles annually in the 1830s to three thousand in the 1870s, and by the turn of the century six thousand new volumes were being issued every year.[35] In England, the census recorded a jump during the three decades from 1881 to 1901 in the number of respondents who identified themselves as "authors," from 3,400 to 6,000 to 11,000.[36] All of these texts dramatize Henry Adams's effort to resist the pressures which a market economy was exerting on writers, and help to locate Adams's letters in the same stance of resistance.[37]

Christopher Wilson has argued that the emergence of a mass literary market both democratized access to writing, previously dominated by a leisured elite, and made writers newly beholden to the commercial demands of the marketplace, where they eventually ran the danger of being reduced to "properties" themselves.[38] In refusing to obligate himself to mass conditions of production, Adams managed to sustain his loyalty to a genteel, preindustrial vision of authorship, to resist the bourgeois ideal of productivity which was reshaping writing at the end of the nineteenth century. "You know that my sympathies have always been small with the Kipling and Dickens, or British cad, school of literary parent, whose only idea of children was the *patria potestas* in its least lovely form,—the right of selling them!" (V, 283), Adams insisted to his publisher, Henry Holt, from Russia in August of 1901. At the same time, these texts also dramatize Adams's awareness of the limitations of resistance to public obligations and his commitment to locating an alternative to withdrawal, a podium from which he could sustain a legitimate voice.

The commodification of values in industrialized society is one of the most frequently expressed thematic concerns in all four of these books. In *Democracy*, Adams satirizes the transactions in which power is bought and sold in the U.S. capital: "the two whited sepulchres at either end of the Avenue reek with the thick atmosphere of bargain and sale. . . . Wealth, office, power are at auction" (*Democracy* 58). Madeleine Lee steadily discovers the extent to which money sets the agenda of national government in Washington: "She felt an atmosphere of bargain and intrigue, but she could only imagine how far it extended" (*Democracy* 80). Even more, the selfish terms of Ratcliffe's marriage proposal demonstrate the extent to which Mrs. Lee herself has become commodified. "I *must* insist upon pressing it," Ratcliffe admits to her; ". . . my future is too deeply involved in your decision to allow of my accepting your answer as final. I need your aid. There is nothing I will not do to obtain it" (*Democracy* 177). In *Esther*, Adams's critique of late-nineteenth-century American materialism focuses on the Protestant church. Stephen Hazard's first sermon at St. John's has to work hopelessly against the fact that services at this Fifth Avenue church are primarily occasions for the conspicuous display of wealth:

> Most of his flock were busied with a kind of speculation so foreign to that
> of metaphysics that they would have been puzzled to explain what was
> meant by Descartes' famous COGITO ERGO SUM, on which the preacher laid
> so much stress. They would have preferred to put the fact of their existence
> on almost any other experience in life, as that "I have five millions," or "I
> am the best-dressed woman in the church,—therefore I am somebody."
> (*Esther* 190)

Clearly this loss of spiritual substance is meant to raise serious questions about
the conditions under which authorship had to take place in the industrializing United States. Such questions inform Adams's retreat in *Mont Saint Michel
and Chartres,* as well, from the bourgeois superficiality which he finds in the
present: "When we get to Chartres, which is largely a twelfth-century work,
you will see that the Cathedral there too is superbly built. . . . The thirteenth
century did not build so. The great cathedrals after 1200 show economy, and
sometimes worse. The world grew cheap, as worlds must" (*MSMC* 14).

For Henry Adams, resisting the pressures of literary commercialism meant
insisting on a set of privileged alternatives to the marketplace, as his defense
of his refusal to publish *Mont Saint Michel and Chartres,* in a June 1905 letter
to Brooks Adams from Paris, makes clear: "This sounds contemptuous to my
fellow men, and perhaps it is so; but I am quite sure that whatever my fellow
men may say about it, or think they ought to say about it, both they and my
fellow-women in their hearts agree with it, and will like me better for not being
on sale" (V, 669). Industrial capitalism was the object of many late-nineteenth-
century American writers' and Progressive reformers' cultural critiques; but
the commercialization of their work had quite different meanings for different
writers. As Michael Anesko has shown, Henry James invested considerable
effort in attempting both to court publishers and to avoid compromising his
art for the sake of achieving commercial appeal.[39] Henry Adams, however,
remained more stubborn in his loyalty to preindustrial literary conditions—to
what felt to him like a human scale—and to a set of insular alliances with readers who did not come to literature as consumers:

> The fateful year 1870 was near at hand, which was to mark the close of the
> literary epoch, when quarterlies gave way to monthlies; letter-press to illus-
> tration; volumes to pages. The outburst was brilliant. Bret Harte led, and
> Robert Louis Stevenson followed. Guy de Maupassant and Rudyard Kipling
> brought up the rear, and dazzled the world. As usual, Adams found himself
> fifty years behind his time, but a number of belated wanderers kept him
> company, and they produced on each other the effect or illusion of a public
> opinion. . . . Adams was not the only relic of the eighteenth century, and
> he could still depend on a certain number of listeners—mostly respectable,
> and some rich. (*Ed* 259)

Adams's refusal of obligation to a literary public was, then, a fundamentally epistolary strategy of alliance as well as of exclusion, which bound him to fellow "relics" who "kept him company" in shared distaste for the mass marketplace. Adams's refusal to pander to popular taste or to market his writing was a means of reinforcing and legitimating his allegiance to the "certain number of listeners" who held themselves above the priority of profit, and of sustaining the viability of that class of writers and readers and their cultural loyalties.

The tension between public and private discourse that remains consistently central throughout Henry Adams's work evokes Adams's anxiety over cultural change which presented elite writers with shifting grounds of control. Adams's efforts to sustain writing as a domain of privilege represent his resistance to the mass culture which emerged in the turn-of-the-century United States, and accompanying pressures to write for a mass audience. The letter was, as a form, uniquely disengaged from market values, and located instead in an essentially preindustrial exchange economy. Similarly, all four of these texts' efforts to distance authorship and audience from a mass-market context speak to Adams's enduring concern with written discourse as an arena of control and validation.

The interpenetration between Adams's letters and his imaginative works evinces, finally, Adams's refusal to abandon either the prerogative of silence or the imperative of speech. Adams's entire career shapes itself to a pattern of privatization: the letters seem, steadily, to retreat from their own transition out of the private context of family and into the public literary arena; and all of Adams's works after the *History* remain reluctant to face a public audience.[40] A convincing case might even be made for calling all these works "letters," both because they so aggressively privatized their original audiences and because they built so much mutuality into the process of reading: *The Education of Henry Adams* might be seen as a letter to a hundred of Adams's best friends, continuous with the actual letters which accompanied the original copies; *Mont Saint Michel and Chartres* might be read as a letter to Martha Cameron and as a love letter to her mother, Elizabeth Sherman Cameron; and *Esther* comes, especially after Marian Hooper Adams's death, to feel like a love letter to Henry Adams's wife. But the feeling for language and its generative possibilities that privacy and mutuality made it safe for Adams to express in these texts seems too passionate, especially in the two culminating works, to allow privacy to be read in them solely as a strategy of exclusion. These texts' creative range testifies movingly to the lengths to which Adams was prepared to go in constructing an audience whose presence would sustain the viability of authorship for him and in locating a stance as author which would legitimate his claims to a responsive audience.

Conclusion:
The Resisting Letter

Correspondence as Resistance:
Henry Adams's Late Letters

The correspondence of the last twenty years of Henry Adams's life provides dramatic concluding evidence of the letter's ability to exploit the very characteristics which have marginalized it as a literary form: its obligation to convention; its lack of metaphorical and narrative unity; and its lack of closure. The letter's permeable rhetorical boundaries were crucial to Adams's deployment of the form in his late, perhaps his neediest, years, because they provided him with strategies for resisting the losses with which old age threatened him. These rhetorical advantages crystallized for Adams around the form's ability to work against its own narrative.

During these final, "posthumous," years of his life, correspondence served Adams as an occasion of resistance rather than of acquiescence. The very odds against which the letters worked sustained their imperative for Adams. "As Christmas comes, I feel restless at the idea of not sending you a word through this long time, and I must try to scratch a line, even if it is like drawing teeth. Not that I have anything to say, beyond sending love" (VI, 708), Adams opened a letter to Charles Milnes Gaskell, from Washington in December of 1915, three years before his death. The tension in such letters between the text's message of "restless" drift and the anchoring act—"even if it is like drawing teeth"—of writing was for Adams a source of endurance rather than of contradiction. His unrelenting commitment to marshaling his letters against loss sustained authority and alliance for Adams at precisely the moment when both seemed out of narrative reach.

In the plainest sense, Adams's late letters sustained his engagement in the world around him, even as they became dominated by the dispiriting narrative of his capitulation to a series of strokes. Paralyzed and isolated by physical trauma, Adams felt robbed of human dignity, as he complained to Gaskell from Washington in April 1912: "I live in a sort of medicated cotton, carefully protected from pin-pricks and aches. Doctors stick things into my eyes, and rub me down like a training horse" (VI, 533). Adams felt especially defeated by the ways in which illness deprived him of language and made speech an occasion of fear. "The only incurable and helpless person is myself," he confessed to Elizabeth Sherman Cameron from Washington in March 1911; "My memory diminishes, and my aphasia increases month by month, till I am afraid to utter a word, for fear of its being a wrong one" (VI, 424). From Paris in September of 1908, Adams described for Cameron one such moment of humiliation:

> one day in July I happened to go into Audrain's place [an antique dealership] to ask a question, and, to my consternation, my French tumbled out all in a heap. The words came without connection. The man looked at me queerly; I mumbled something, and got into the street. . . . (VI, 180)

Yet while his late letters seemed to be abandoning Adams to this narrative of paralysis and silence, they also enabled Adams to contest it. In writing letters, Adams was able to exploit a set of predictable conventions and to observe a prescribed rhythm of exchange that made speech safe for him. Letter writing provided Adams with formal gestures by which he could preserve a semblance of normalcy and self-respect, refuge from the embarrassment of public scenes in this time of vulnerability: "One thinks of life only as a thing to quit," Adams sighed to Charles Francis Adams, Jr., from Washington in January 1908, "and one is quite absorbed by the wish to quit it with an air of a gentleman. . . . If you can help me to a *beau geste*, pray do so" (VI, 102).

More deeply, letter writing summoned from Adams in these final years of his life rhetorical power which countered his claims of depletion. Correspondence brought Adams constantly back to words at the very moments when his confidence in his own resources felt most fragile, and transformed an occasion of obligation into an occasion on which he could reassert his authority as a writer. Despairingly, Adams wrote to Elizabeth Sherman Cameron from the coast of Norway, in September of 1901, of his inability to break through the silence that was both sign and agent of his decline. "I've no one to talk to but you, and I do want to talk about it, though I don't want to talk," he fumbled; "No one understands. I'm only a bore" (V, 294). But Adams went on in the same letter to display considerable control over language:

> The worst of this show is its awful seriousness to the elderly tourist. The show is a good show. It is like the music of the Götterdämmerung; it takes

hold of an elderly person with unfair brutality and suddenness. At first, one
gets off one's balance. One cries. Not on account of its beauty; for its beauty
has nothing much to do. It's a sad kind of beauty at best, and silent. Even
Tahiti is sad, but it is a tropical sadness. This is the sadness of a life that
never knew fun. These long mountains stretching their legs out into the sea
never knew what it was to be a volcano. They lie, one after another, like
corpses, with their toes up, and you pass by them, and look five or ten miles
up the fiords between them, and see their noses, tipped by cloud or snow,
high in behind, with one corpse occasionally lying on another, and a skull
or a thigh-bone chucked about, and hundreds of glaciers and snow-patches
hanging to them, as though it was a winter battle-field; and a weird after-
glow light; and a silent, oily, gleaming sea just lapping them all round, as
though it were tired as they are, and chucked the whole thing. (V, 294)

In this fatigued, deathly landscape, Adams located the geographical figure
which corroborated his sense of emptiness, at the end of "a life that never knew
fun." Yet, at the same time, his evident investment in his own prose confirmed
the survival of an Adams—acute observer; emotional presence; *writer*—who
remained determined to hold off the inevitability of that ending. Just as one
of Adams's earliest letters had resisted its own message of awkwardness by
describing skillfully Adams's debut into Dresden society, this late letter resisted
its message of numb, mute loss by facing Adams's vulnerability, the "unfair brutality and suddenness" with which this scene moved him, and using language
to master it. One after another, Adams's phrases—"high in behind"; "a sad
kind of beauty at best, and silent"; "silent, oily, gleaming"—built up a rhythmic composition sharply at odds with his images of wordless decay. Most of
all, the high metaphoric pitch of the entire passage—a stage strewn with skel-
etal fragments glowing "weirdly" in the aftermath of battle—belies Adams's
submission to his own narrative of rhetorical fatigue and withdrawal.

Adams resisted the narrative of displacement and isolation that dominated
his late letters, as well, by maintaining his commitment to the form as an agent
of alliance. Throughout the long last years of his life, these letters frequently
reiterated Adams's sense of abandonment: returning to Washington from Paris
in March, probably of 1901, Adams wrote to Gaskell, "My country in 1900
is something totally different from my own country of 1860. I am wholly a
stranger in it" (V, 225); over a decade later, when the lease on his Paris apartment was expiring, he wrote to Cameron, from Washington in February of 1912,
"After having my nervous system shocked by being turned into the street in
Paris, I imagine the world in a great conspiracy to turn me out of everything,
and have a nightly nightmare figuring myself ejected from this house" (VI, 512).
Jarring natural imagery signified Adams's alienation in many of these letters.
"I am, like Ruth, a little sick at heart among the alien corn" (VI, 74), Adams
moaned to Cameron from Paris in June 1907, paraphrasing Keats; and from

Washington in March of 1916, two years before his death, Adams lamented to Gaskell, "Many times in my life I have felt myself out of place, but never so much as now, when it is quite clear that I am a grasshopper in October without legs or wings or song" (VI, 726). Yet Adams also used these complaints strategically, to appeal for support. From Washington in February of 1903, for example, Adams queried Cameron bitterly:

> Perhaps you don't want to know that tomorrow is my birth-day? and perhaps you don't feel a little sick when you remember that I am sixtyfive? or do you care a straw anyway? . . . I wish it was over! nothing annoys me more than the sense of preparing to start on a journey; especially paying my bills and catching the train. One hates to disturb one's friends, too! (V, 457–58)

Clearly Adams's eagerness for life to be "over" and his reluctance to "disturb" his friends were barely disguised demands for attention; clearly Adams expected Cameron to respond with sympathy to his angry, self-pitying anxiety. Physical links with the world beyond Adams's insular deterioration, such letters also maintained in more direct ways the hold on a sustaining community which their narrative claimed to be relinquishing. "I was rejoiced to see your handwriting again" (V, 605), Adams opened another letter, to Gaskell from Paris in August 1904; and, five years later, in November 1909, again to Gaskell, "I am glad to see your handwriting again . . ." (VI, 286).

Ultimately, to write letters meant for Henry Adams to keep writing—to resist closure. To continue to write letters in the face of isolation and illness was for Adams an act of faith in the possibility of sustaining both community and continuity. "The past is more alive than ever, and your letter is of it, full of it" (VI, 712), Adams wrote to Cameron from Washington in December 1915. To write letters was for Adams to refuse to surrender either to aloneness or to silence. J. Gerald Kennedy has suggested that Edgar Allan Poe's first letters, to his foster father, constructed a "rhetoric of dread" in order to provide Poe with a saving object of resistance and to draw out of him "a text that would save him from dissolution."[1] Similarly, correspondence gave Henry Adams a formal context—and sanction—to keep writing his need for responsiveness. It also offered him a structure of exchange which lacked a terminus, and thus sustained his unwillingness to write himself into an ending: "Not that I have anything to say, beyond sending love," he had written in his December 1915 letter to Gaskell. Like Poe, Adams produced in his last letters, to the circle of friends and family who survived to old age with him, a set of texts whose resistance to their own rhetoric of loss and to their own narrative movement toward closure constituted for him a strategy of survival, as a writer, as a human being, and as a member of a community.

To appreciate the letter's stance of resistance as a defining feature of genre, it is useful to compare Adams's letters to his autobiography, especially in terms of each form's relationship to narrative and to closure. Letters skirt some of the same literary boundaries as autobiography: on one hand, they share autobiography's debt to a personal voice and to a "real" life, and they depend, as Paul de Man has put it, "on actual and potentially verifiable events in a less ambivalent way than fiction does"; on the other hand, letters share autobiography's creative prerogatives, its license to construct a world around the writer's need.[2] Even Henry Adams's uniquely epistolary autobiography, however, used many standard literary strategies differently than did his letters. While, especially, narrative and metaphor served in *The Education of Henry Adams* as important means of achieving unity, Adams's letters managed to avoid conforming to such expectations.[3] In fact, Adams's letters not only failed to observe many of the conventions which confirm a text's "literary" status, but actually managed to exploit many of the form's structural limitations.

The Education of Henry Adams claims, paradoxically, to chronicle the failure of narrative: the narrator's enduring inability to overcome his sense of alienation in the late-nineteenth-century United States is paralleled and intensified by his discovery of the inadequacies of conventional history. "Chaos was the law of nature; Order was the dream of man" (*Ed* 451), the narrator mourns in frustration. Adams's text seems to record the disintegration of its own central figure, who remains unable to satisfy his craving for either meaning or direction. Yet Adams's investment—as author—in the figures of the extinct Pteraspis and of the Virgin and the Dynamo, in the concept (if not the process) of "education," and in the text's movement toward his "Grammar," "Theory," and "Law" of History testifies to his belief in the possibility of creating narrative alternatives to disorder. Adams's decision to create his manikin-protagonist and to write its story was a fundamentally unifying act, for it provided *The Education* with a metaphorical center around which the task of "running order through chaos" could be directed.[4]

Unlike *The Education*, Adams's letters have neither a decisive beginning nor a coherent story. There *is* metaphor and there is even considerable metaphorical consistency in Adams's depiction of himself in the letters—but meaning in the letters always depends on changing constructions of "us" and "now," and unity always yields to the letter writer's prerogative of interrupting continuity. In defending this prerogative, Adams's correspondence exploited one of the form's apparent limits, its inability to pause and reorder preceding material. From Berlin in November of 1858, for example, Adams described himself in his first letter to his older brother Charles Francis, Jr., as "a gentleman and a man of sense" (I, 5). Here the youthful Adams sought validation from his family by adopting a conventionalized rhetoric of gentility. Later, however, when he had achieved more independence, Adams demonstrated his maturity by using the same rhetoric against itself, exposing the limits of convention by insisting to his younger brother Brooks from Washington in June 1895, during the silver currency scare, "As a man of sense I am a gold-bug and support a gold-bug government and a gold-bug society. As a man of the world, I like confusion, anarchy and war" (IV, 283). Elsewhere in Adams's correspondence, the ideals of connoisseurship which had initially served Adams's discourse of ambition came to serve, instead, a discourse of obsolescence. "I had all sorts of invitations for Sunday; indeed a man of the world is going about Paris just now; it is I . . ." (V, 29), he wrote with emphatic irony to Elizabeth Sherman Cameron from Paris in September of 1899; and he confided to her with equal ambivalence from Nuremberg in August 1901, "As for a lady or a gentleman, the thing has disappeared with the buffalo" (V, 273).

Their resistance to narrative and metaphorical unity suggests for Adams's letters a political model different from that typical of autobiography. Many American autobiographies, and many critics, have identified autobiography with "American" conditions of individuality, since the form fits so well the ideology of self-creation which for many years dominated American literary culture's projection of personal and national destiny.[5] This andocentric bias helps to explain why "autobiography" has constituted both an obstacle and a subversive tactic for many women writing; even *The Education of Henry Adams* is constructed around the centralizing, if self-doubting, figure of a narrator, who assumes the appropriateness of appealing to an audience on his own behalf and the generalizing potential of his own experience.[6] In contrast, in their refusal to impose or to take responsibility for closure Adams's letters might be seen—like the correspondence between anarchists Emma Goldman and Alexander Berkman, from 1919 to 1936—as serving a radical politics of mutuality.[7] Letter writing provided Henry Adams access to an exchange economy in a society aggressively committing itself to capitalist growth, an alternative to autobiography's model of private ownership.[8] In this sense, letter writing constituted a stance of resistance on Adams's part to bourgeois discourses of individualism: his letters' refusal to give up their incomplete status expressed and enacted Adams's reluctance to accept the sufficiency of publicly authorized literary forms.[9]

At the same time, if comparison with Adams's autobiography appears to reveal the letters' unselfish suspicion of centralized narrative authority, their resistance to closure also reveals the letters' hunger for autonomous power. Privatizing discourse in the letters allocated rhetorical authority, ultimately, to Adams himself. Adams's letters subverted their own narrative of marginalization by exploiting the distance with which the letters were ostensibly at odds, in order to convert the recipients of his letters into collaborators and to construct audiences whose presence actively forestalled the possibility of writing in isolation.[10] Adams's letters remained resistant to the pressures of closure which his autobiography accepted as a source of validating unity; and the condition of "exchange" in the letters legitimated Adams's stance of resistance.

The Education of Henry Adams concludes, logically, with the "end" of "education," as John Hay's death locks into the past the last of what Adams claims to "know." In acknowledging his loneliness for a world "that sensitive and timid natures could regard without a shudder" (Ed 505), Adams names his alienation and unifies its story. If Adams's letters never achieved either that unity or that closure, it was in substantial part because they retained their loyalty to private alliances; because their integrity as texts did not depend on their ability to establish their credibility with an audience or to provide an audience with coherence. Although they relied on essentially the same narrative of loss as The Education, Adams's letters converted the structural impossibility of ending into a rhetorical advantage. "The winter is nearly over, I am seventysix years old, and nearly over too. As I go, my thoughts turn towards you and I want to know how you are. Of myself, I have almost nothing to tell. It is quite astonishing how the circle narrows," Adams opened a letter to Gaskell, from Washington in February 1914, closing, "Send me a line about yourself" (VI, 635–36). Undermining the narrative of stasis, silence, and isolation which he himself had invoked, by insisting on the imperative of correspondence, Adams challenged the "narrowing" motion of his own words. Such letters fixed alliance as an act of resistance and located exchange as a ritual of subversion, stronger than any public obligation to narrative consistency that Adams might have owed. It was this commitment to his own need—as much as his loyalty to a particular set of correspondents—which enabled Adams's letters to construct the alternatives to alienation for which his autobiography remained lonely.

Resistance to Narrative in the Letters of Alice James and Walt Whitman

Their resistance to narrative and to closure dramatizes both the fundamentally controlling features of Henry Adams's letters and the centrality of control as an imperative of letter writing for Adams. This imperative and the letter's resisting posture emerge with more clarity and sharpness when they are seen in the context of the letters of two other late-nineteenth-century American writers, Alice James and Walt Whitman. James and Whitman can hardly be aligned politically with Henry Adams, or with one another; and the differences in the claims to authority with which all three writers came to correspondence are quite visible in their letters. Yet, like Adams, both James and Whitman became adept at exploiting the form's permeable rhetorical boundaries. While each writer's political location was quite distinct, for all three that location was determined in important ways by the relationship between private and public—and for all three correspondence served as a medium for negotiating that often tense, or at least unequal, relationship. Given the political differences among these three letter writers, the rhetorical affinities among them confirm a set of defining features common to the form.

This comparison of the letters of Alice James and of Walt Whitman with those of Henry Adams identifies, and even implicates, the form's stance of resistance as an instrument of cultural transition. In all three of these correspondences, the letter was deeply engaged with the negotiation of parity and the assertion of control, especially over the politically charged relationship between private and public discourse. For Whitman and James, as much as for Adams, *narrative* assumptions, especially about the relationship between author and audience, were frequently in conflict with the rhetorical effects of correspondence on the same relationship. Ultimately, this conflict and the stance of resistance which sustained it in all three writers' letters dramatize the crucial fact that it was the writer who emerged as the beneficiary of the form's ambiguous literary status.

Alice James's commitment to letters was in significant part a confirmation of her marginalized status as a woman in late-nineteenth-century bourgeois American society, of her consignment to peripheral literary ground, where she had limited access to public speech. Around images of herself as superfluous, James wove an enervating story of passivity and isolation. "I wish I were where I could be of some service," James admitted to her Aunt Kate from England in November 1887, in response to the news of a cousin's stroke, "but the most I can ever hope to do in this world is to keep out of the way."[11] Yet by converting the status of language in her letters from passive to active and by mastering a set of strategies for assuming rhetorical control, James learned to exploit her consignment to a marginalized form and, ultimately, to subvert its marginalizing effects. By rewriting the narrative which positioned her, helplessly, "out of the way," and making herself central in it, James renegotiated the relationship between author and audience, and thus between private and public, in her correspondence.

James's own conflicted experience made strategies of resistance deeply attractive to her, as her lifelong invalidism demonstrates. The only daughter in a family with four sons, James was both doted on and left out, particularly by her adored father and by her brother William.[12] Outside James's family, ambiguous cultural signals intensified the confusing status of marriage, domesticity, and sexuality: while the increasing availability of leisure for women of James's class in the industrializing United States opened up the possibility of activism outside the home, it also invited refinement of conservative and sometimes contradictory notions of "true womanhood" and "true motherhood," sharpening the gendered separation of private and public spheres.[13] In response, James's invalidism, like that of other "female sufferers" of her time, sent a mixed message of resistance and acquiescence, both challenging and reinforcing her position vis-à-vis the male authority of her father, her brothers, and her doctors.[14] Letter writing located James on literary territory which was equally ambiguous, neither public nor wholly private, both obligation and pre-rogative—but it also provided her with strategies for exploiting that ambigu-ity, by aggressively pitting the language which she claimed for herself against the narrative of dependence to which she seemed fated by gender.

Like Henry Adams, Alice James constructed in her letters a narrative of isolation and stasis. James seems timelessly poised in many of her letters at the edge of her own strength, fighting a losing battle for control over her life. "As always happens as my physical strength increases," she groaned from Lon-don in November of 1885, to Aunt Kate, "my nervous distress & susceptibil-ity grows with it, so that from an inside view it is somewhat of an exchange of evils" (AJ 104). James portrayed herself as destined to a life of loneliness and vulnerability—"It is terrible to be such an unprotected being as I am" (AJ 131), she wrote to her friend Sara Darwin from England in October 1887—in which she was locked into dependence on forces beyond her con-trol. "This has not been a happy winter & I am always at the mercy of what are called the events of life" (AJ 171), she sighed to her friend Fanny Morse, from England in June 1889. Even acknowledging her fatigue with its change-lessness failed to liberate James from that story. Describing for her family at home in Cambridge yet one more doctor's visit, from London in November 1884, James satirized herself as a prisoner of her own case history: "He listened with apparent interest & attention to my oft-repeated tale, which by the way to save breath & general exhaustion I am going to have printed in a small pamphlet . . ." (AJ 97).

Yet if her letters served Alice James as a vehicle for this narrative of marginalization, they also provided her with a set of strategies for interrupt-ing and resisting it. In the letters, James repositioned herself and the sources of authority which dominated her in her own narrative, by subverting the form's obligated status, by appropriating for herself the words in which she was named "in-valid," and by adopting a critical language of her own.

From very early on, James managed in her letters to undermine her obli-gation to the form. Initially James accepted correspondence as a young lady's duty, as a means of achieving and displaying the mastery of literary ritual expected of a woman of her class. Writing her first letter was clearly tied for James to a set of standards of female comportment, to a daughter's responsi-bility to please her father: "I will try and be good and sweet till you come back, and merit the daisy curtains, and get a chance at your dear old pate again" (AJ 49), she wrote plaintively from Geneva in Henry James, Sr.'s, absence, at the age of twelve in March 1860. But by the time she reached young adult-hood, James had begun in her letters to challenge these conventions, and to mock the rhetoric of female propriety which they sustained. "We will have none of that Miss, just you come home after a respectable fortnight, that is quite long enough for a modest woman to stay away from home . . ." (AJ 62), she teased her friend Sara Sedgwick (Darwin) from Cambridge in February 1874, in response to a letter announcing Sedgwick's plans to postpone returning to Boston.

James's use of letters to resist the language with which her doctors enforced her passive status marks a turning point in her deployment of the form. In January 1885, James wrote with knowing frustration to Aunt Kate from Bournemouth:

> My doctor turned out as usual a *fiasco* an unprincipled one too. I could get nothing out of him & he slipped thro' my cramped & clinging grasp as skilfully as if his physical conformation had been that of an eel, instead of a Dutch cheese—The gout he looks upon as a small part of my trouble, "it being complicated with an excessive nervous sensibility," but I could get no suggestions of any sort as to climate, baths or diet from him. The truth was he was entirely puzzled about me & had not the manliness to say so. . . . My legs have been entirely useless for anything more than hobbling about the room for three months & a half & most of the time excessively painfull. I asked the doctor whether it was not unusual for a person to be so ill & have no organic trouble & he said, "yes, very unusual indeed."——I should have thought he would therefore have liked to do some thing for me—but it was only my folly in going to a great man their *only* interest being diagnosis, & having absolutely no conscience in their way of dealing with one. (AJ 101–2)

This letter expressed directly James's resentment at being reduced to a disembodied female problem to be solved by a male expert: "It was only my folly in going to a great man their *only* interest being diagnosis." It was James who was examining her doctor here, rather than the other way around, making it quite clear that she saw through her doctor's evasive tactics. In challenging her doctor's judgment, James challenged his domination. Even more, by appropriating her doctor's language, James resisted the agenda of unthinking collaboration in which that language implicated her. James shrewdly let the doctor's own words expose the emptiness of his claims to authority, quoting verbatim his strained effort to use technical jargon and the weight of his professional experience ("it being complicated with an excessive nervous sensibility"; "yes, very unusual indeed") to hide his failure to relieve the symptoms which she herself had laid out so plainly. Even as they left intact James's resignation to her status as patient and her obligation to consult medical professionals, such passages challenged the power economy of James's relationship with her doctors by claiming words as a weapon which James could wield with subversive confidence and strength.

To challenge the rhetoric of medical omnipotence was for Alice James both to challenge the narrative of powerlessness in which her own silence locked her and to locate in language an empowering set of resources. Such letters demonstrate the extent to which the form provided James with crucial means, unavailable to her elsewhere, for transforming the status of language from passive to active. James took aggressive advantage, for example, of her obligation to write to family members in the United States during her years in England, in order to assert her increasing mastery as a writer: "Nearly all my friends are imbecile [British] Unionist abortions," she complained, sharply and impatiently, to William James from London in April of 1887;

> Their hideous, patronizing, doctrinaire, all-for-Ireland's-good, little measured out globules of remedies make my blood boil so I never speak on the subject. Their *stoop*idity, the impossibility of their ever suspecting that the situation is one to be treated imaginatively makes them on this subject as hopeless intellectually as beasts of the field. (AJ 127–28)

In crafting rhythmic crescendoes of anger against the "imaginative" and "intellectual" limits of the world around her, in naming others "*stoop*id," James made a decisive commitment to language. Letter writing made it possible for James to challenge the privileged status of physical health and of male authority, and to claim for herself the subversive prerogative of independent judgment over an inherited power structure: "When you consider that these men are not the discredited, mushroom politician of the hour, known to us," she wrote to William James of the Liberal Unionists, from London in April 1889, "but the heirs of centuries of education, of noble traditions & honourable birth, with responsibilities not only to the present & the far-reaching future, but to the historic past, what an ignoble picture do they present!" (AJ 169–70).

Finally, James faced her most extreme trial, her fatal diagnosis of breast cancer and impending death, by adopting her most extreme stance of resistance. By refusing to be written into a traditional death narrative, James resisted closure.[15] James's early letters had relied dutifully on the sentimental clichés of the period: when her father died, for example, she described herself, in a letter to her brother Henry from Boston in December 1882, as "thankfull . . . that the weary burden of life is over for him" (AJ 87); and she responded to the news of her friend (and Marian Adams's sister) Ellen Gurney's suicide by writing to her sister-in-law Alice, William James's wife, from Leamington in December 1887, "I am indeed as you say 'triumphant' that her bruised wings are folded, no more desperate flapping to prolong that weary flight" (AJ 140). But as the imminence of her own death became unmistakable, James's letters broke from these conventions of fatigue and burden. From England in July of 1891, Alice James wrote dramatically to her brother William:

[Death] is the most supremely interesting moment in life, the only one in fact, when living seems life, and I count it as the greatest good fortune to have these few months so full of interest & instruction in the knowledge of my approaching death. It is as simple as one's own person as any fact of nature, the fall of a leaf or the blooming of a rose, & I have a delicious consciousness, ever present, of wide spaces close at hand, & whisperings of release in the air.

. . . so when I am gone, pray don't think of me simply as a creature who might have been something else had neurotic science been born; notwithstanding the poverty of my outside experience I have always had a significance for myself, & every chance to stumble along my straight & narrow little path, & to worship at the feet of my Deity, & what more can a human soul ask for? (AJ 186–87)

While her death might appear to fix James as the helpless protagonist in a medical tragedy, James used this climactic moment to free herself from that story: while her death might look to others like a stroke of bad luck, James converted it into "the greatest good fortune"; while others might fear death as the ultimate loss, James derived a sense of fulfillment from the experience, and insisted that "It is the most supremely interesting moment in life, the only one in fact, when living seems life." "Pray don't think of me . . ."—this letter drew a decisive boundary between the public domain, "outside" herself, where James would be named neurotic, and the private domain within which she could name her own "significance for myself." James made a firm choice here between accepting death's approaching finality as an occasion of decline and insisting, with equal finality, on her ability to write her own death as a source of sustaining power. In making that choice, James resisted the authority over her of the culture whose continuity those narrative conventions surrounding death enacted ritually.

Alice James's letters dramatize the subversive status of letter writing for James, even as they dramatize James's dependence on strategies of resistance rather than of autonomy. Clearly Alice James recognized, and suffered for, the alienating split between public powerlessness and private power which has hobbled so many women writing: "I seem perfectly grotesque to myself, a wretched, shriveled alien enclosed between four walls, with such an extraordinary disproportion between what is *felt* & what is heard & seen by her—an emotional volcano within, with the outward reverberation of a mouse & the physical significance of a chip of lead-pencil" (AJ 144), James confided with excruciatingly insightful frustration to Alice and William James from Leamington in August 1888.[16] James's letters were liberating gestures, because they claimed for her a language which she could wield with authority and thus transcended both her "grotesque" silence and the defensive status of resistance. James's letters also marked the limits of that liberation, by accepting her consignment to the private sphere and her dependence on an unauthorized form of speech: for while James did not, certainly, hover uselessly "out of the way" in these letters, she remained wary to the end of making demands in them on the world which was marginalizing her, of directly confronting and challenging the gendered conflict which bound her.[17] Yet if Alice James accepted the privatization of speech which the form imposed, her letters managed to exploit the access to language which privatization extended and to claim the "delicious consciousness" which contesting silence and closure earned her.[18]

Ideologically opposed to the condition of conflict between private and public discourse which both Henry Adams and Alice James accepted, Walt Whitman appears at first to have little in common with either Adams or James as a letter writer. Perhaps most, or at least most loudly, of all late-nineteenth-century American writers, Whitman was committed to a political agenda which would have been repugnant to Adams, which turned on the possibility of enfranchising a new literary constituency.[19] And unlike James, as a man Whitman was in a position to challenge disparity between public and private authority, and to extend parity to correspondents. Yet—like Adams and James—Whitman also employed the letter as a means of resisting his obligation to closure and to narrative (even narrative which he himself had issued publicly) and of consolidating his own authority as a writer. The letter's ambiguous literary status fit perfectly Whitman's program of democratization and enabled Whitman to use the form to broaden access to writing. But the same formal ambiguities also made it possible for Whitman to use language to restrict rather than to enlarge access to him in the letters—and many of Whitman's letters tried to hoard rhetorical control rather than to share it with his readers.

One of the most strongly articulated imperatives of Walt Whitman's letters is the writer's effort to reduce the threat of the "literary" and to break down writing itself as a domain of privilege. By signing his published work "Walt," Whitman challenged the distance between writer and reader, and between private and public discourse, positioning himself at informal, close range.[20] Letter writing offered Whitman even greater opportunity to lift restrictions surrounding authorship. Whitman could make himself available to correspondents in familiar, immediate terms by using colloquial speech and by structuring his sentences in casual, impromptu ways. "Last night was perfect, & only middling cool—I staid crossing till 12 o'clock—felt good—& then got hungry & went and got a dozen nice oysters & a drink (Dont that make your mouth water, Tommy boy?)," he wrote, for example, from Camden in December 1880 to Thomas Nicholson, an attendant in his friend Dr. Richard Maurice Bucke's Canadian asylum.[21] Tangible detail served in these letters to reinforce an image of Whitman as ordinary and approachable rather than to showcase Whitman's virtuosity as a writer. "Well, Pete, dear son, I have just had my dinner (stewed chicken & onions—good,)," he wrote to Peter Doyle from Camden in February 1874, "& here I sit again in the same old chair, in the parlor, writing my weekly screed to you—Nothing to brag of this week" (WW2, 278).[22] In turn, Whitman was able to encourage ease and spontaneity in his correspondents. "My darling boy," he wrote from Washington in August of 1863 to Lewis K. Brown, a soldier whom he had met in a Civil War hospital, "when you write to me, you must write without ceremony . . . you need never care how you write to me, Lewy . . . I never think about literary perfection in letters either, it is the *man* & the *feeling* . . ." (WW1, 134). By freeing letters of the restraints of "ceremony," Whitman made the act of writing them cease to loom as an elite prerogative, requiring either leisure or special expertise: from Washington in November 1868, he urged John Flood, Jr., another ex-soldier, "Jack, you must write often as you can—anything from my loving boy will be welcome—you needn't be particular about the writing—you might write in the car with pencil, when you have any time" (WW2, 70).

Yet while Whitman claimed in his letters to be challenging a highly politicized inequality between private and public speech, his letters often exploited the same disequilibrium. Like the poses that he struck for the many artists who came, fascinated, to him, Whitman's letters made him available to the public in carefully measured doses which seem at odds with the letters' ideology of informality.[23] His letters were far from the careless, rough productions which Whitman assured his correspondents he would welcome from them. As their editor has pointed out, Whitman's letters were actually well-rehearsed performances whose claims to spontaneity are visibly undercut by the many heavily reworked drafts which have survived.[24] While Whitman claimed to be providing in his letters unguarded access to himself, in fact correspondence became for Whitman a source of strategies for limiting that access. In, for example, his famous response to John Addington Symonds's August 1890 inquiry about the homosexual implications of the "Calamus" poems, Whitman constructed a deceptively detailed fiction, which established distance rather than intimacy between him and his reader: "Tho always unmarried I have had six children—two are dead—One living southern grandchild, fine boy, who writes to me occasionally. Circumstances connected with their benefit and fortune have separated me from intimate relations" (WW5, 73).

Most important, while Whitman's letters seemed to extend the privileges of parity to correspondents, parity also remained privileged in them. If Whitman located in the letter strategies for democratizing written discourse, he also located there a set of strategies for disrupting the process of democratization which he himself had initiated. This tension between broadening access and consolidating control can be seen clearly in his letters to three important correspondents, Peter Doyle, Harry Stafford, and Anne Gilchrist. In all three of these correspondences, Whitman responded to conflicts over parity by reasserting authority as a writer which his correspondents could not match.

His letters to Peter Doyle and to Harry Stafford amply demonstrate Whitman's reluctance to make himself accessible to correspondents on equalized terms. These letters had good reason to be watchful, for they were written under conditions of enormous vulnerability.[25] (Whitman's attraction to Doyle became a source of such anxiety to him that even in his journal he resorted to tense strategies of concealment, reverting to code in his references to Doyle.)[26] In both cases, Whitman used his superior mastery of language to fix his much younger and less literate correspondents in positions of limited rhetorical initiative. Although, for example, Whitman's encouragement offered Doyle the gift of written expression, it also served to retain Whitman's authority over Doyle.[27] Despite their claims to the contrary, Whitman's letters to Peter Doyle never seriously challenged the imbalance of power with which they began—with *words*—on Whitman's own turf. The same praise with which Whitman defused the threat of writing for Doyle, in October 1868—"glad enough to hear from you—the oftener the better. Every word is good" (WW2, 56)—also positioned Whitman as Doyle's literary mentor. "You too have done first rate & have sent me as many as I have you, and good letters too" (WW2, 67), Whitman wrote to Doyle in the same month and, five years later, in October 1873, "your latest two letters have *been first rate* . . ." (WW2, 250). When Harry Stafford, an eighteen-year-old errand boy for the Camden printer of *Two Rivulets*, replaced Peter Doyle in Whitman's correspondence, Whitman proved equally reluctant to relinquish rhetorical control.[28] Whitman's early letters to Stafford drew him close, with seductive intensity: "Dear Harry, not a day or night passes but I think of you. . . . Dear son, how I wish you could come in now, even if but for an hour & take off your coat, & sit down on my lap" (WW3, 86), he wrote to Stafford from Philadelphia in June 1877. But, increasingly, Whitman's letters to Stafford exploited disparity between the two correspondents, by adopting the stance of expert reader and by translating Stafford's feelings into timeworn lessons to which Whitman's superior experience made him uniquely privy. From Camden in February 1881, for example, Whitman wrote to Stafford:

> I have just rec'd yours of 26—a little wild & nervous & uncertain some parts, (but I am always glad to get any letters from you, dear boy). . . . Harry, dont be discouraged by any business or other disappointments of the past— It will all turn out right—The main thing, in my opinion, after finding out as much as possible of life, & entering upon it (it is a strange mixed business this life) is to live a good square one. . . . (WW3, 214–15)

Moreover, Whitman refused to respond to Stafford's efforts to break down such barriers between them. In late January of 1882, Whitman sternly diverted an attempt by Stafford to draw out of him an equalizing token of shared vulnerability: "Nothing new with me—I keep well as usual—you say when I have a *blue spell* I must write to you—I don't have any such spells—& seems to me it is time you grew out of them . . ." (WW3, 265). In telling contrast to this aloof and patronizing letter to Stafford, Whitman responded a week later, in early February, to the manuscript of Richard Maurice Bucke's biography by correcting Bucke's cheerful image of him: "The character you give me is not a true one in the main—I am by no means that benevolent, equable, happy creature you pourtray" (WW3, 266).

His responses to the romantic overtures of the English writer Anne Gilchrist provide the most dramatic evidence of the ways in which Whitman retreated in his letters behind the boundaries of rhetorical privilege which he himself had challenged. Anne Gilchrist had reviewed *Leaves of Grass* in 1870 so sympathetically that Whitman commented appreciatively, "I had hitherto received no eulogium so magnificent" (WW2, 91).[29] A year later, in September 1871, Gilchrist wrote directly to Whitman the first in a series of passionate letters, confessing to him the desires which reading *Leaves of Grass* had aroused in her:

> I never before dreamed what love meant: nor what life meant. Never was
> alive before. . . . nothing in life or death can tear out of my heart the pas-
> sionate belief that one day I shall hear that voice say to me, "My Mate. The
> one I so much want. Bride, Wife, indissoluble eternal!" (WW2, 135–36)

Gilchrist's letter challenged Whitman to make good on his poems' promise to break down the writer's autonomous authority and to remove the barrier between public and private speech which that authority sustained. Instead, Whitman's response rerouted Gilchrist's private feelings into channels which he himself had publicly sanctioned. From Washington in November 1871 he wrote, firmly, to Gilchrist:

> My book is my best letter, my response, my truest explanation of all. In it
> I have put my body & spirit. You understand this better & fuller & clearer
> than any one else. And I too fully & clearly understand the loving &
> womanly letter it has evoked. Enough that there surely exists between us
> so beautiful & delicate a relation, accepted by both of us with joy. (WW2, 140)

Such letters demonstrate how effectively Whitman translated Gilchrist's intrusions on his privacy into a conflict over literary authority, which he was in a superior position to broker. Whitman actually imposed closure—"Enough"—on Gilchrist. Immediately upon establishing his claim to "fully & clearly" understanding Gilchrist's love, Whitman assigned that "love" a narrative—"so beautiful & delicate a relation, accepted by both of us with joy"—which regulated it in language of his own. Anne Gilchrist exhibited alarming patience in her pursuit of Whitman: "You might not be able to give me your great love yet—to take me to your breast with joy. But I can wait" (WW2, 142), she wrote to him in November of 1871. In exasperated response, from Brooklyn in March 1872, Whitman warned Gilchrist that she had crossed a forbidden boundary:

> Dear friend, let me warn you somewhat about myself—& yourself also. You must not construct such an unauthorized & imaginary ideal Figure, & call it W.W. and so devotedly invest your loving nature in it. The actual W.W. is a very plain personage, & entirely unworthy such devotion. (WW2, 170)

If Whitman softened his "warning" to Gilchrist—"somewhat"—by professing his "unworthiness," his reassertion of rhetorical command was nonetheless unmistakable. Gilchrist's image of him was, Whitman insisted, "unauthorized": the right to "construct" an idealized image and to "call it W.W." belonged only to Walt Whitman himself—and Whitman's letters moved aggressively to reclaim his hold on that threatened authority.

Conclusion: The Empowering Letter

The correspondences of Henry Adams, of Alice James, and of Walt Whitman demonstrate, together, the extent to which parity—not only between correspondents but, equally important, between private exchange and public speech, between elite and democratic discourse—remains at issue, and subject to negotiation, in letter writing. In all three of these correspondences, resistance to narrative and to closure constituted a controlling stance, capable of adjusting or reinforcing difference.

For each of these writers, the letter's location on essentially private ground had quite different implications, especially in terms of the form's role as an agent of parity. Yet, at the same time, privacy provided all three writers with rhetorical privileges which tension with their own narrative indicates were unavailable to them elsewhere. Privacy was a sign of Henry Adams's failure to act in a public arena, and prolonged his defensive posture; but privacy was also an elite prerogative belonging to the "gentleman amateur," and in protecting it the letters reinforced Adams's lack of obligation to a public audience. Privacy was a sign of Alice James's consignment to marginal literary territory, where there would be no danger of abrogating male authority; but the condition of privacy also provided James with permission to write.[30] And while Walt Whitman treated privacy as an obstacle to democratic consensus, his letters transformed privacy into a privileged source of autonomy. If, in short, disparity between public and private constituted an object of resistance for all three of these letter writers, all three of them also learned to exploit that tension and to use it to their own rhetorical advantage.[31]

In the context of the conflicts over authorship and subject matter in which literary realism was embroiled, the contested status of "legitimacy" in the letter emerges as a struggle over control.[32] To write letters was in a sense to abandon this struggle for public validation and to retreat to turf from which claims to parity would, inevitably, be compromised. It was to accept the limits on control which attend resistance's oppositional stance. Yet the form's marginality also enabled the writer of letters to circumvent some of the limitations of literature and to challenge in more radical ways the conventions to which literature was obligated: in Adams's letters, expression and invention neither exacted the loss of control over audience that comes with publication nor imposed the public responsibility that comes with authorship.[33] Moreover, that marginality located the letter on fluid rhetorical ground—between prerogative and obligation; between fiction and nonfiction—which was both characteristic of and amenable to transition.

Thus the letter's marginal location provided a site from which transition could be effectively brokered. The form seems equally suited to either engaging or defending against shifts in power relations: on one hand, Alice James was able in her letters to claim authority which was denied her in public; on the other hand, Henry Adams could rely on the form as a bulwark against the erosion of his public authority. Walt Whitman managed to transform his duty, as a military nurse, to write letters for soldiers too badly wounded to write on their own and to comfort the parents of soldiers who had died, into an opportunity to assert his expertise as an author. That rhetorical pliancy further dramatizes the political advantages of the form. "You must write to Alfred often," he informed N. M. and John B. Pratt, for example, from Washington in June 1865, instructing them on how to correspond with their own convalescing son, "as it cheers up a boy sick & away from home. Write all about domestic & farm incidents, and as cheerful as may be" (WW1, 264). As Whitman learned to convert letter writing from an occasion of obligation into an occasion for craft, he claimed for himself in the letters, increasingly, prerogatives of literary style. "Poor dear son, though you were not my son, I felt to love you as a son, what short time I saw you sick & dying here" (WW1, 129), he broke into rhythmic, mournful address in a condolence letter to Mr. and Mrs. S. B. Haskell from Washington in August 1863. Similarly, as it did for Whitman and for James, writing letters enabled Henry Adams to make the crucial transition from rhetorical obligation to rhetorical mastery which reshaped his relationship to particular correspondents and to discourse outside the correspondence.

Finally, its marginal location provided a site from which the letter's stance of resistance could be viably adopted and maintained. Henry Adams's incessant complaints and pessimism must have made him difficult company during his last years, a kind of human angel of death. "When I called at his house and he was posing to himself as the old cardinal," Oliver Wendell Holmes, Jr., recalled without much sympathy, in a June 1919 letter to Sir Frederick Pollock, "he would turn everything to dust and ashes."[34] In a January 1912 letter to Elizabeth Sherman Cameron from Washington, Adams himself expressed that mood of disintegration more plainly: "Everything crumbles to the touch" (VI, 494). Many of Adams's late letters are thick with the same relentless resentment of the ways in which his life was emptying out, and with Adams's sense of correspondence as a ritualistic form of resignation to that loss. "I can't drift with the current," he complained to Cameron from Paris in October 1899, "for that is only possible in quiet waters. I can't even run away without cutting myself off from communion. So I linger in Paris, and bask in the warmth of the twelfth century, and write letters about nothing, as much as possible" (V, 50). But these letters also resisted their own obligated status, their proximity to closure, and their own narrative of depletion. "Here, as at Washington, I have no life," Adams claimed to Gaskell from Paris in December 1910—yet he went on to insist on the surviving imperative of letter writing: "This does not prevent my seeing a good many people, and writing a good many letters . . ." (VI, 398).

Threatened with isolation, Adams chose alliance. Threatened with closure, Adams chose resistance. Threatened with silence, Adams chose speech. Faced with each of these threats, Adams also chose letters, because they enabled him to occupy rhetorical ground over which he could retain control. Adams's enduring commitment to "writing a good many letters" testifies to his refusal to abandon either resistance or alliance as weapons against alienation, even as he recognized in alienation an important source of his authority as a writer and of strategies of collaboration.[35] If Henry Adams's letters implicate the form in the consolidation of elite cultural control in the United States at the turn of the century, they also demonstrate the letter's ability to speak with strategic force from the margins, where authority and alliance remain continually negotiable.

Notes
Index

Notes

Introduction: The Letter at the Margins

1. R. W. Stallman and Lillian Gilkes, eds., *Stephen Crane: Letters* (New York: New York University Press, 1960), p. xi. Whitney Balliett, "Raymond Chandler Speaking [review of Columbia University Press edition of *Selected Letters of Raymond Chandler*]," *New Yorker*, 8 March 1982, p. 138.

2. See Barbara Herrnstein Smith, *On the Margins of Discourse: The Relation of Literature to Language* (Chicago: University of Chicago Press, 1978), pp. 19–21, on letters as examples of the "natural" utterances which mark the margins of literature's "fictive" utterances.

3. A number of recent critics have discussed the political implications of women's consignment to such marginal literary forms as the letter and the diary. See, for example, Patricia Meyer Spacks, "Selves in Hiding," in *Women's Autobiography: Essays in Criticism*, ed. Estelle C. Jelinek (Bloomington: Indiana University Press, 1980), p. 112: "Women, for obvious social reasons, have traditionally had more difficulty than men about making public claims of their own importance. They have excelled in the writing of diaries and journals, which require no such claims, more than in the production of total works offering a coherent interpretation of their experience."

4. See, for example, Bruce Redford, *The Converse of the Pen: Acts of Intimacy in the Eighteenth-Century Familiar Letter* (Chicago: University of Chicago Press, 1986), pp. 1–13, for a discussion, in part in response to Smith, of letters' performative functions; James G. Watson, *William Faulkner: Letters and Fictions* (Austin: University of Texas Press, 1987), especially pp. 1–8, on the "proximity" of Faulkner's fiction making in his letters to the imaginative prerogatives of his fiction; Janet Gurkin Altman, *Epistolarity: Approaches to a Form* (Columbus: Ohio State University Press, 1982), pp. 185–88, on the strategic importance of polarities like "portrait/mask, presence/absence, bridge/barrier . . . closure/overture" in epistolary fiction; and Louise K. Horowitz, "The Correspondence of Madame de Sévigné: Letters or Belles-Lettres?"

French Forum, 6 (January 1981), 13–27, especially pp. 18–22, on Madame de Sévigné's use of her letters to her daughter as "a powerful means of transcending a day-to-day life pattern judged unsatisfying"; as a "transformation of life into epistolary tale. . . ."

5. On the Columbian Exposition as a symbol of cultural conflict, see Alan Trachtenberg, *The Incorporation of America: Culture and Society in the Gilded Age* (New York: Hill and Wang, 1982), especially "White City," pp. 208–34; Reid Badger, *The Great American Fair: The World's Columbian Exposition and American Culture* (Chicago: Nelson Hall, 1979), especially "A Confusion of Symbols," pp. 119–23; Larzer Ziff, "Land of Contrasts," in *The American 1890's: Life and Times of a Lost Generation* (New York: Viking, 1966), pp. 3–23; Ray Ginger, "White City in the Muck," in *Altgeld's America: The Lincoln Ideal Versus Changing Realities* (New York: Franklin Watts, 1958); and Robert Rydell, "The Chicago World's Columbian Exposition of 1893: 'And Was Jerusalem Builded Here?'" in *All The World's a Fair* (Chicago: University of Chicago Press, 1984), pp. 38–71.

6. See John F. Kasson, *Amusing the Million: Coney Island at the Turn of the Century* (New York: Hill and Wang, 1978), p. 8: "[Amusements parks'] creators and managers pioneered a new cultural institution that challenged prevailing notions of public conduct and social order, of wholesome amusement, of democratic art—of all the institutions and values of the genteel culture [and] thus shed light on the cultural transition and the struggle for moral, social and aesthetic authority that occurred in the United States at the turn of the century." See Kathy Peiss, *Cheap Amusements: Working Women and Leisure in Turn-of-the-Century New York* (Philadelphia: Temple University Press, 1986), on working-class women's claims to space and apparel for leisure and on middle-class reformers' responses. And on middle-class reformers' class biases, see T. J. Jackson Lears, *No Place of Grace: Antimodernism and the Transformation of American Culture, 1880–1920* (New York: Pantheon, 1981), pp. 7–26.

7. See Lincoln Steffens, *The Shame of the Cities* (New York: Hill and Wang, 1957), p. 6, for one of many examples of Progressive reformers' middle-class assumptions about access to the political process: "We are a free and sovereign people, we govern ourselves and the government is ours. But that is the point. We are responsible, not our leaders, since we follow them. We *let* them . . . boss the party and turn our municipal democracies into autocracies and our republic nation into a plutocracy."

8. Henry F. May, "Custodians of Culture," in *The End of American Innocence: A Study of the First Years of Our Own Time, 1912–1917* (New York: Knopf, 1959), pp. 30–51.

9. In *Chicago: Creating New Traditions* (Chicago: Chicago Historical Society, 1976), pp. 39–68, Perry Duis quotes from Jane Addams on George Pullman, and provides a series of essays on city planning in Chicago and reformers' contributions to it, including reproductions of Graham Taylor's settlement house maps.

10. See William M. Tuttle, Jr., *Race Riot: Chicago in the Red Summer of 1919* (New York: Atheneum, 1970), for an extended discussion of such riots, which took place in 1919 in Chicago.

11. On gender and public amusements, see Peiss (*Cheap Amusements*) and Kasson (*Amusing the Million*). On the department store, see Susan Porter Benson, *Counter Cultures: Saleswomen, Managers, and Customers in American Department Stores, 1890–1940* (Urbana: University of Illinois Press, 1986), pp. 75–123, " 'An Adamless Eden': Managing Department-Store Customers."

12. See Stephen Kern, *The Culture of Time and Space 1880–1918* (Cambridge: Harvard University Press, 1983), p. 7, on the X ray.

13. Ibid., pp. 316–17.

14. For one of many examples of discussions of realism's imperatives, see "American Realism: A Grammar of Motives," in Warner Berthoff, *The Ferment of Realism: American Literature, 1884–1919* (Cambridge: Cambridge University Press, 1981), pp. 1–47.

15. Sandra M. Gilbert and Susan Gubar's discussion, "Infection in the Sentence: The Woman Writer and the Anxiety of Authorship," pp. 45–92, in *The Madwoman in the Attic: The Woman Writer and the Nineteenth-Century Literary Imagination* (New Haven: Yale University Press, 1979), provides exemplary evidence of the political status of "literary" authority. With more specific respect to American realism, see Amy Kaplan's excellent Introduction to *The Social Construction of American Realism* (Chicago: University of Chicago Press, 1988), especially pp. 8–14, in which she discusses American realism as an effort to gain access to and control over a radically changing world which challenged literature's ability to represent it.

16. On the tensions surrounding writing and narrative in Stephen Crane's *The Red Badge of Courage*, see Michael Fried, *Realism, Writing, Disfiguration: On Thomas Eakins and Stephen Crane* (Chicago: University of Chicago Press, 1987), "Stephen Crane's Upturned Faces," pp. 91–161; and Donald Pease, "Fear, Rage, and the Mistrials of Representation in *The Red Badge of Courage*," in *American Realism: New Essays*, ed. Eric J. Sundquist (Baltimore: Johns Hopkins University Press, 1982), pp. 155–75.

17. See Trachtenberg, *Incorporation of America*, pp. 182–207 ("Fictions of the Real").

18. Quoted in Ernest Samuels, *The Young Henry Adams* (Cambridge: Harvard University Press, 1965), p. 60.

19. See Newton Arvin, ed., *Selected Letters of Henry Adams*, p. xi: "Except for Franklin, the best letter-writers of the Revolutionary period were John Adams and his wife, and John Adams himself had even theorized informally on what might pompously be called the aesthetic of the letter." And see Earl N. Harbert, *The Force So Much Closer Home: Henry Adams and the Adams Family* (New York: New York University Press, 1977), p. 14: "by the time of the fourth generation, Henry and his brothers were inducted by their Adams birth and their early training, in school and at home, into a literary tradition that had already proved to be as forceful and compelling as their political heritage."

20. Except where otherwise noted, all citations to Henry Adams's letters will be made in the text, by volume number, to the standard edition of the letters recently published by J. C. Levenson, Ernest Samuels, Charles Vandersee, Viola Hopkins Winner, eds., *The Letters of Henry Adams*, Volumes I [1858–1868], II [1868–1885] and III [1886–1892] (Cambridge: Harvard University Press, 1982) and Volumes IV [1892–1899], V [1899–1905], VI [1906–1918] (Cambridge: Harvard University Press, 1988).

21. Ward Thoron, ed., *The Letters of Mrs. Henry Adams, 1865–1883* (Boston: Little, Brown, 1936), p. 56.

22. See Paul C. Nagel, *Descent from Glory: Four Generations of the John Adams Family* (New York: Oxford University Press, 1983), pp. 240, 248–49, and 309–11, and William Dusinberre, *Henry Adams: The Myth of Failure* (Charlottesville: University

Press of Virginia, 1980), p. 44, on each of the brothers' efforts to destroy or preserve his letters, or to control public access to family documents.

23. See Carolyn Porter, *Seeing and Being: The Plight of the Participant Observer in Emerson, James, Adams, and Faulkner* (Middletown, CT: Wesleyan University Press, 1981), pp. 171–72.

24. See Stow Persons, *The Decline of American Gentility* (New York: Columbia University Press, 1973), pp. 292–97, on the New England gentry's defensiveness with respect to the incursions of immigration.

25. See Cecilia Tichi, *Shifting Gears: Technology, Literature, Culture in Modernist America* (Chapel Hill: University of North Carolina Press, 1987), pp. 137–70, for a discussion of Adams as "an engineer by proxy."

26. Henry Adams, *The Education of Henry Adams*, ed. Ernest Samuels (Boston: Houghton Mifflin, 1973), p. 4.

27. Ibid., pp. 32–33.

28. See Ernest Samuels, *Henry Adams: The Major Phase* (Cambridge: Harvard University Press, 1964), pp. 470–74, on Adams's completion and distribution of the *Letter*. Citations will be made in the text to Henry Adams, *A Letter to American Teachers of History* (Washington, D.C.: private printing, 1910), as *Letter*.

29. See Samuels, *Henry Adams: The Major Phase*, pp. 491–92, on the dated qualities of Adams's speculations.

30. See ibid., pp. 471–72, on the original conditions of publication and the prefatory letter, and pp. 491–93, on Adams's refusal to have the book reviewed and on his younger brother Brooks Adams's posthumous publication of the volume in 1919.

31. See, for example, Louis Auchincloss, " 'Never Leave Me, Never Leave Me,' " *American Heritage*, 21 (February 1970), 20–22 and 69–70, for an account of Adams's daily letter-writing routine by Aileen Tone, one of the "nieces in wish" who kept Adams company in his later years.

32. Arvin, *Selected Letters of Henry Adams*, p. xxx; Viola Hopkins Winner, "Style and Sincerity in the Letters of Henry Adams," in *Essaying Biography: A Celebration for Leon Edel*, ed. Gloria G. Fromm (Honolulu: University of Hawaii Press, 1986), p. 91.

33. Robert Hume, *Runaway Star: An Appreciation of Henry Adams* (Ithaca: Cornell University Press, 1951), p. 150; Louis Kronenberger, "The Letters—and Life—of Henry Adams," *Atlantic*, 219 (April 1967), 80, 89.

34. Worthington Chauncey Ford, ed., *Letters of Henry Adams (1858–1891)* (Boston and New York: Houghton Mifflin, 1930), p. v. As Winner's essay indicates, Adams's current editors have asked more questions: she writes of Adams, "Letter writing was for him a literary activity, less demanding than formal kinds but not essentially different" ("Style and Sincerity," p. 91).

35. Ford, *Letters of Henry Adams*, p. vi; Hume, *Runaway Star*, p. 163.

36. Stewart Mitchell, "*The Letters of Henry Adams (1858–1891)*," *New England Quarterly*, 4 (July 1931), 563.

37. William S. McFeely, "The Letters of a World Watcher [review of Volumes 1–3 of the Harvard edition of Adams's letters]." *New York Times Book Review*, 6 March 1983, p. 24.

38. Arvin, *Selected Letters of Henry Adams*, p. xxv.

Chapter 1. Negotiating Parity

1. In his excellent *Intimacy and Power in the Old South: Ritual in the Lives of the Planters* (Baltimore: Johns Hopkins University Press, 1987), pp. 4–5, Steven M. Stowe also demonstrates how the active status of language in antebellum planter family correspondence made these letters "both about and of a person's experience of culture. . . . Such letters existed as a bond and a commentary on the bond."

2. See Steven M. Stowe, "The Rhetoric of Authority: The Making of Social Values in Planter Family Correspondence," *Journal of American History*, 73 (March 1987), 916–33, for a corroborating discussion of the correspondence of antebellum Southern planter families whose children were educated away from home. Stowe argues that while, initially, "Family bonds and the social order were jointly strengthened by a youth's learning the elements of written self-expression" (p. 917), eventually children's letters to their parents became weapons of autonomy, enabling the writer to "stake out a rhetoric different from his parents'" (p. 932).

3. See Paul C. Nagel, *Descent from Glory: Four Generations of the John Adams Family* (New York: Oxford University Press, 1983), pp. 214–16, 244–50, and 302, on Charles Francis Adams, Jr.'s, efforts to prove himself in these arenas, and p. 312, where Charles is quoted as acknowledging in a late letter to his wife what he saw as his most serious error: "I should have cut clear from the family traditions."

4. Adams's "Two Letters on a Prussian Gymnasium" were eventually published in the *American Historical Review*, 53 (October 1947), 50–74.

5. Dated Palermo, 9 June 1860, signed "H.B.A.," in the *Boston Daily Courier*, reprinted in the *American Historical Review*, 25 (January 1920), 247–48.

6. A list of Henry Adams's publications during the period 1855–77 appears in the appendix of Ernest Samuels, *The Young Henry Adams* (Cambridge: Harvard University Press, 1965), pp. 313–32.

7. See Cruce Stark, "The Development of a Historical Stance: The Civil War Correspondence of Henry and Charles Francis Adams, Jr.," *Clio*, 4 (June 1975), 383–97, for a discussion of Adams's acceptance of his role as a historical observer, in response to his older brother's combat experience in the Civil War.

8. *New York Times*, 7 June 1861.

9. *New York Times*, 8 October 1861.

10. Worthington Chauncey Ford, ed., *A Cycle of Adams Letters* (Boston: Houghton Mifflin, 1920), 1: vii.

11. *New York Times*, 30 December 1861; column dated 14 December.

12. Ford, *Letters of Henry Adams*, 1: 91.

13. Henry Adams, "Diary of a Visit to Manchester," *Boston Daily Courier*, 16 December 1861; reprinted in *American Historical Review*, 25 (October 1945), 74–89; quoted from p. 83.

14. Quoted in ibid., p. 77; the other English newspapers which picked up Adams's article were the *Manchester Daily Examiner and Times* and the *Manchester Guardian*.

15. See William Dusinberre, *Henry Adams: The Myth of Failure* (Charlottesville: University Press of Virginia, 1980), pp. 18–24, on the evolution of Henry and Charles's correspondence from mutuality—providing a place where they could "practice imagery on each other" and serve as each other's "whetstones"—into tense competition.

16. Worthington Chauncey Ford, *Letters of Henry Adams (1858–1891)* (Boston and New York: Houghton Mifflin, 1930), 1: 238.

17. See Stowe, "Rhetoric of Authority," pp. 929–33, on antebellum planter children's letters as agents of rhetorical autonomy and rhetorical distance.

18. See Ernest Samuels, *Henry Adams: The Middle Years* (Cambridge: Harvard University Press, 1958), pp. 64–66.

19. Quoted in Ernest Samuels, *Henry Adams* (Cambridge: Harvard University Press, 1989), p. 143.

20. See Dusinberre, *Henry Adams: The Myth of Failure*, pp. 42–53, for a discussion of the effects on Adams of the "unconstrained companionship" which Gaskell extended to Adams in England and of Gaskell's allegiance to the sociocultural tradition of the English upper class, and Samuels, *Young Henry Adams*, p. 127: "the lively sportiveness of his [Adams's] letters to his new friend reflects how deeply grateful he was for the chance of dropping his diplomatic guard."

21. Quoted in William Henry Irving, *The Providence of Wit in the English Letter Writers* (Durham: Duke University Press, 1955), p. 10.

22. See ibid., pp. 6–9 and 14–16, and Keith Stewart, "Towards Defining an Aesthetic for the Familiar Letter in Eighteenth-Century England," *Prose Studies*, 5 (September 1982), 179–89, for discussions of the familiar letter's loyalty to the immediacy of conversation.

23. See Irving, *Providence of Wit*, pp. 14–20, and Stewart, "Towards Defining an Aesthetic," pp. 182–83.

24. See Bruce Redford, *The Converse of the Pen: Acts of Intimacy in the Eighteenth-Century Familiar Letter* (Chicago: University of Chicago Press, 1986), pp. 3–6, on the eighteenth-century familiar letter's "civilized" assumptions about itself.

25. See Louise K. Horowitz, "The Correspondence of Madame de Sévigné: Letters or Belles-Lettres?" *French Forum*, 6 (January 1981), 24, on Madame de Sévigné's letters as events: "She wrote when events lacked, creating out of her own words a 'happening,' even if it was only letter writing itself."

Chapter 2. Claiming Allies

1. Quoted in Henry Adams, *The Education of Henry Adams*, ed. Ernest Samuels (Boston: Houghton Mifflin, 1973), Appendix A, p. 515.

2. See Edward N. Saveth, "Henry Adams: The Waning of America's Patriciate," *Commentary*, 24 (October 1967), 305–6, on Adams's conflicted patrician loyalties and his flirtation with Populism.

3. See Carey McWilliams, *A Mask for Privilege: Anti-Semitism in America* (Boston: Little, Brown, 1948), pp. 76–77, and T. J. Jackson Lears, *No Place of Grace: Antimodernism and the Transformation of American Culture, 1880–1920* (New York: Pantheon, 1981), p. 30.

4. Richard Hofstadter, *The Age of Reform: From Bryan to F.D.R.* (New York: Random House, 1955), p. 78.

5. Jean-Paul Sartre, *Anti-Semite and Jew* (New York: Schocken, 1948), p. 13; see Hofstadter, *Age of Reform*, pp. 77–81, on the "rhetorical" nature of Populist anti-Semitism.

6. See J. A. Ward, *American Silences: The Realism of James Agee, Walker Evans, and Edward Hopper* (Baton Rouge: Louisiana State University Press, 1985), pp. 11–14, on silence in late-nineteenth- and early-twentieth-century American literature and art as a stance of protest against "the American bias toward power and action"; as "an expression of severe social criticism, a radical rejection of the blatancy and falseness of a society and of a dominant art"; as "a subversive undertaking in a period of history absorbed in the rapid motion of objects and the incoherent noise of machines and persons"; and as an acknowledgment of "a radical discord between private men and public men." See also Marcus Cunliffe, "'What Was the Matter with Henry Adams?'" *Commentary*, 39 (June 1965), 71, where Cunliffe takes a sympathetic stance toward Adams's unsatisfactory "choice between ineffective protest, and capitulation to the major political and commercial interests. . . . Power entailed not only responsibility, but complicity in dubious enterprises."

7. See Sissela Bok, *Secrets: On the Ethics of Concealment and Revelation* (New York: Random House, 1984), p. 38: "To realize that one has the power to remain silent is linked to the understanding that one can exert some control over events. . . . that one need not be entirely transparent, entirely predictable. . . ."

8. See Ward, *American Silences*, p. 204, for a discussion of Adams's effort to earn a "release from . . . directionless acceleration[,] . . . one of the most maddening conditions of recent history."

9. Abraham Blinderman, "Henry Adams and the Jews," *Chicago Jewish Forum*, 25 (Fall 1966), 3–4; Norman Podhoretz, "Henry Adams: The 'Powerless' Intellectual in America," *New Criterion*, June 1983, p. 11.

10. See Carolyn Porter, *Seeing and Being: The Plight of the Participant Observer in Emerson, James, Adams, and Faulkner* (Middletown, CT: Wesleyan University Press, 1981), pp. 165–204 (chap. 6), "Henry Adams: The Posthumous Spectator."

11. See Georg Simmel, *On Individuality and Social Forms*, ed. Donald N. Levine (Chicago: University of Chicago Press, 1971), pp. 199–209, on elite social structures among the "nobility," which sustain their sense of mutuality by reaffirming the power disparity between those inside the social circle and those outside the circle.

12. See Terry Eagleton, *Literary Theory: An Introduction* (Minneapolis: University of Minnesota Press, 1983), pp. 13–14, on the ways in which speech assumes the status of "a coded way of signalling . . . partisanship."

13. See Elizabeth C. Goldsmith, *"Exclusive Conversations": The Art of Interaction in Seventeenth-Century France* (Philadelphia: University of Pennsylvania Press, 1988), pp. 1–15, for a helpful discussion which also locates the correspondence of the seventeenth-century French aristocracy in a larger matrix of similarly ritualized interactions of privilege.

14. See Ernest Samuels, *The Young Henry Adams* (Cambridge: Harvard University Press, 1965), pp. 36–38.

15. See ibid., p. 81.

16. See ibid., pp. 127–33.

17. Quoted in Ernest Samuels, *Henry Adams: The Middle Years* (Cambridge: Harvard University Press, 1958), p. 36.

18. Patricia O'Toole's *The Five of Hearts: An Intimate Portrait of Henry Adams and His Friends* (New York: Clarkson Potter, 1990) deals at length with the "Five of Hearts"

and relations among members of the group. See especially chapter 6, "Infinite Mirth," pp. 61–77, on the origins and the exclusivity of the Hearts.

19.   James Truslow Adams, *The Adams Family* (Boston: Little, Brown, 1930), p. 327.

20.   Patricia Meyer Spacks, *Gossip* (Chicago: University of Chicago Press, 1986), pp. 83–85.

21.   Adams, *Education of Henry Adams*, p. 46.

22.   See Bok, *Secrets*, pp. 48–49: "Initiation into such a society serves as proof that they count. It marks their acceptance into a community of those who *can* keep secrets, and who have important secrets to keep."

23.   Ward Thoron, ed., *The Letters of Mrs. Henry Adams, 1865–1883* (Boston: Little, Brown, 1936), p. 264.

24.   See Spacks, *Gossip*, p. 84, for a discussion of Walpole's sharing of his "mastery" of experience with his readers, and of the centrality of power in that process: "My vocabulary (*controlled, command, submit*) suggests that the relation of writer and reader reiterates the issue of power."

25.   See Eugenia Kaledin, *The Education of Mrs. Henry Adams* (Philadelphia: Temple University Press, 1981), p. 57: "Eventually, the gregarious Dr. Hooper with fatherly pride would read Clover's letters aloud to gathered relatives and friends, making her all the more self-conscious as a writer. Her very own words would sometimes be repeated to her from Boston visitors to Washington, and she would have to urge her father to use discretion concerning special tidbits: 'I wouldn't have my gibes come back to hurt feelings,' she insisted."

26.   See Carroll Smith-Rosenberg, "The Female World of Love and Ritual: Relations between Women in Nineteenth-Century America," *Signs*, 1 (1975), 1–29, for a pioneering discussion of the homosocial networks which developed around ritual events in eighteenth- and nineteenth-century American women's lives; such networks, far from Adams's world of privilege but close in spirit to his world of privacy, depended in important ways on the exchange of letters.

27.   Since not all of Adams's letters to Martha Cameron have been included in the Harvard edition of the letters, for the sake of convenience all citations to them in this discussion will be from Charles Vandersee's earlier edition, "Henry Adams' Education of Martha Cameron: Letters, 1888–1916," *Texas Studies in Literature and Language*, 10 (Summer 1968), 233–293; letters cited here appear on pp. 253, 246, 249, 250. See also Harold Dean Cater, ed., *Henry Adams and His Friends: A Collection of His Unpublished Letters* (Boston: Houghton Mifflin, 1947), p. lxxv.

28.   See Janet Gurkin Altman, "The Letter Book as a Literary Institution, 1539–1789: Toward a Cultural History of Published Correspondences in France," in *Men/Women of Letters*, ed. Charles A. Porter, *Yale French Studies*, 71 (1986), 33 and 34–35: "[seventeenth-century published] anthologies stake out a space for the letter which is essentially uniform, public, and limited to persons of a particular social status"; "epistolary space, even in manuals designed for popular consumption, remains throughout the seventeenth and eighteenth centuries defined by the space of the court and the salon"; and pp. 39 and 41: "officially sanctioned letter books [following the founding of the Académie Française and its institutionalization of a state-approved language in 1635] bear clear traces of the alliance between letters and state leaders, showing

the extent to which the former depend on the latter"; "When private epistolary space exists—as it does for Chapelain and Sévigné—it must be defended *against* publication. Readdressing of truly familiar letters, when it occurs is limited to a known circle of friends and family." And see Goldsmith, *"Exclusive Conversations,"* p. 1, on "ritualized interaction" in seventeenth-century French court society.

29. Roger Duchêne, *Réalité vécue et art épistolaire: Madame de Sévigné et la lettre d'amour* (Paris: Bordas, 1970), p. 36; quoted on p. 103.

30. Phillips Brooks, quoted in Samuels, *Henry Adams: The Middle Years*, pp. 242–43.

31. See Marcel Mauss, *The Gift: Forms and Functions of Exchange in Archaic Societies* (New York: Norton, 1967), especially chap. 2, pp. 17–45, "Distribution of the System: Generosity, Honour and Money," on the symbolic role of rites and obligations of gift exchange within precapitalistic, "archaic" societies: "Everything is tied together; things have personality, and personalities are in the same manner the permanent possession of the clan. Titles, talismans, coppers and spirits of chiefs are homonyms and synonyms, having the same nature and function" (p. 44); "Our feasts are the movement of the needle which sews together the parts of our reed roofs, making of them a single roof, one single word," Mauss quotes the members of a New Caledonian community (p. 19).

32. Duchêne, *Réalité vécue*, p. 110, also stresses the French salon's observance of "la grande règle de plaire."

33. Spacks, *Gossip*, p. 85: "in gossip, talkers affirming the beliefs of unofficial or unnoticed groups may reconstrue their social universe. Inasmuch as readers feel allied with the letters' writer, they share his protected (because private) position as critic of his society, thus duplicating the position of intimate talkers."

34. See Stephen M. Stowe, *Intimacy and Power in the Old South: Ritual in the Lives of the Planters* (Baltimore: Johns Hopkins University Press, 1987), p. 24, on the similar functioning of letters in "affairs of honor" in the antebellum South: "The form and language of letters remain the point of entry into routines of honor."

35. See Bruce Redford, *The Converse of the Pen: Acts of Intimacy in the Eighteenth-Century Familiar Letter* (Chicago: University of Chicago Press, 1986), pp. 5–7, on letter writing as a coded dramatic performance designed to create between writer-actor and reader-audience the illusion of "cultural consensus."

36. See Keith Stewart, "Towards Defining an Aesthetic for the Familiar Letter in Eighteenth-Century England," *Prose Studies*, 5 (September 1982), 187–189, for a discussion of a similar dynamic, of loyalty to a particular notion of "friendship," in the eighteenth-century English familiar letter.

37. See Stowe, *Intimacy and Power*, p. 48, for a related discussion of the ritual of the duel in the antebellum South: "It shaped conflict into a story that interpreted the elite to itself."

38. See Wendy Deutelbaum, "Desolation and Consolation: The Correspondence of Gustave Flaubert and George Sand," *Genre*, 15 (Fall 1982), 281–301, for a discussion of a similar strategy employed by Sand and Flaubert.

39. Quoted in William Dusinberre, *Henry Adams: The Myth of Failure* (Charlottesville: University Press of Virginia, 1980), p. 44.

40. See Elizabeth Stevenson, *Henry Adams: A Biography* (New York: Octagon/ Farrar, Straus and Giroux, 1977), p. 340: "Although they saw each other seldom, for Adams there was something inviolable in the tie that bound him to Henry James. James belonged to Marian Adams's dead past. He had been an acquaintance of the circle which had included, long ago in Cambridge and Boston and Newport, not only Miss Marian Hooper and her sister and brother, but John La Farge, Margaret and Thomas Sergeant Perry, Wendell Holmes, and Henry and William James"; Kaledin, *Education of Mrs. Henry Adams*, p. 77, quotes James as calling the witty Clover Adams "the genius of my beloved country," and Leon Edel, in *Henry James: A Life* (New York: Harper and Row, 1985), p. 241, quotes James as calling her "a perfect Voltaire in petticoats."

41. See Edel, *Henry James: A Life*, pp. 147–51, 240–41, and 249 on James and the Adamses in Europe; pp. 271–74 and 604 on their time together in Washington; pp. 412–13 on Adams and James in London. See O'Toole, *Five of Hearts*, p. 396, on Adams's emotional response to Henry James's death.

42. See Leon Edel, *Henry James, The Master: 1901–1916* (New York: Lippincott, 1972), p. 522, for a description of this last meeting; see Dusinberre, *Henry Adams: The Myth of Failure*, pp. 55–56, on James's feelings for Adams; see Samuels, *Young Henry Adams*, p. 187, on Adams's literary evaluation of James; Edel, *Henry James: A Life*, p. 413.

43. Robert F. Sayre, *The Examined Self: Benjamin Franklin, Henry Adams, Henry James* (Madison: University of Wisconsin Press, 1988; reprint of 1964 Princeton University Press edition), p. 46. Sayre's entire chapter, "Henry Adams and Henry James," pp. 44–89, provides a thoughtful and sensitive evaluation of relations between James and Adams.

44. Quoted in J. C. Levenson, *The Mind and Art of Henry Adams* (Stanford: Stanford University Press, 1957), pp. 384–85 (letter dated 21 March 1914).

45. See Kenton J. Clymer, *John Hay: The Gentleman as Diplomat* (Ann Arbor: University of Michigan Press, 1975), pp. 1–6, for a summary of Hay's rise to social and political prominence.

46. Hay and Adams met and became friends in 1861 in Washington, when Adams was serving as his father's private secretary during Charles Francis Adams, Sr.'s, term in Congress and Hay had come to Washington as assistant private secretary to Abraham Lincoln. When both men and their wives returned to Washington in the late 1870s, their lives became intimately intertwined. See Peter Shaw, "The Success of Henry Adams," *Yale Review*, 59 (Autumn 1969), 77: "Hay was an alter ego who proved, like the ghost of Spencer Brydon in 'The Jolly Corner,' the futility of engaging in American life during the Gilded Age. And so closely did Adams identify with Hay that, at the same time as Hay stood for the early Adams who might have engaged in politics, he also justified the later Adams who had not. . . ."

47. See Donald Pease, "Fear, Rage, and the Mistrials of Representation in *The Red Badge of Courage*," in *American Realism: New Essays*, ed. Eric J. Sundquist (Baltimore: Johns Hopkins University Press, 1982), p. 163, for a discussion of the similar ways in which Henry Fleming, in *The Red Badge of Courage*, "invests fear with enough privilege" to subvert his marginalization in the army.

48. Henry Nash Smith and William M. Gibson, eds., *Mark Twain-Howells Letters* (Cambridge: Harvard University Press, 1960), 2: 844: "My mind's present scheme is a good one. . . . It is this: to write letters & *not send them*."

Chapter 3. Authoring Alliance

1. In *The Converse of the Pen: Acts of Intimacy in the Eighteenth-Century Familiar Letter* (Chicago: University of Chicago Press, 1986), Bruce Redford begins to comment on the authorial prerogatives of correspondence in his brief discussion, pp. 10–11, of the "correspondent-specific" nature of familiar letters. See also Louise K. Horowitz, "The Correspondence of Madame de Sévigné: Letters or Belles-Lettres?" *French Forum*, 6 (January 1981), 24–25, for a corroborating discussion of Madame de Sévigné's naming of the world in accordance with a relationship and its internally defined needs: "those who Mme. de Sévigné *claims* are most deeply involved with Mme. de Grignan's [her daughter's] welfare receive the greatest attention, as if all shared collectively her passion for her daughter. The world is named and described within the confines of the mother's preoccupation."

2. For especially helpful discussions of realism and the power inhering in the authority to define the "real," see Eric J. Sundquist's introductory essay, "The Country of the Blue," in his collection *American Realism: New Essays* (Baltimore: Johns Hopkins University Press, 1982), pp. 3–24, and Amy Kaplan's Introduction to *The Social Construction of American Realism* (Chicago: University of Chicago Press, 1988), pp. 1–14.

3. See Barbara Herrnstein Smith, *On the Margins of Discourse: The Relation of Literature to Language* (Chicago: University of Chicago Press, 1978), pp. 19–24 and 139–44, especially p. 140, on the distinction between the "natural" discourse of the letter—"We would recognize, in short, that if the letter *was* a natural utterance, composed as a historical act and regarded as a historical event, some of its meanings were *historically determinate*, at least theoretically locatable in the historical universe"—and the "fictive" discourse of a poem, in which "All . . . meanings, to the extent that the poem is offered and taken as a fictive utterance, will be understood to be unfixable, unlocatable in the historical universe."

4. See Redford, *Converse of the Pen*, p. 9: "At its most successful, in fact, epistolary discourse . . . fashions a distinctive world at once internally consistent, vital, and self-supporting." And see Mireille Bossis, "Methodological Journeys through Correspondences," in *Men/Women of Letters*, ed. Charles A. Porter, *Yale French Studies*, 71 (Summer 1986), 64 and 68.

5. R. P. Blackmur, "The Letters of Marian Adams," *Virginia Quarterly Review*, 13 (April 1937), 290.

6. Ward Thoron, ed., *The Letters of Mrs. Henry Adams, 1865–1883* (Boston: Little, Brown, 1936), p. 301.

7. In his *Henry Adams* (Cambridge: Harvard University Press, 1989), pp. 317–53, Ernest Samuels provides a clear narrative of these events and their impact on the relationship between Hay and Adams.

8. Henry Adams, *The Education of Henry Adams*, ed. Ernest Samuels (Boston: Houghton Mifflin, 1973), p. 317.

9. See Patricia O'Toole, *The Five of Hearts: An Intimate Portrait of Henry Adams and His Friends, 1880–1918* (New York: Clarkson Potter, 1990), pp. 309–10 and 376–77, and Samuels, *Henry Adams*, p. 353, on the pressures which Hay's political life put on his friendship with Adams.

10. Worthington Chauncey Ford, ed., *Letters of Henry Adams (1892–1918)* (Boston: Houghton Mifflin, 1938), p. 161 (omitted in the Harvard edition).

11. There is ample commentary on Brooks and Henry Adams's relationship as historians. See, for example, R. P. Blackmur, "Henry and Brooks Adams: Parallels to Two Generations," *Southern Review*, 5 (August 1939), 308–34, especially p. 308: "each inseminated the other; their thought along certain lines was coöperative, and it is impossible to deal fairly with the political and energetic ideas which occupied Henry Adams towards the end of his life—from 1893 to the end—without considering them in connection with those of Brooks Adams," and Timothy Paul Donovan, *Henry Adams and Brooks Adams: The Education of Two American Historians* (Norman: University of Oklahoma Press, 1961), especially p. 95: "Both were attempting to provide an absolute synthesis which would illuminate the goal or end toward which history was moving." On the differences between Charles Francis Adams, Jr.'s, and Henry Adams's relationship to Brooks Adams, see Paul C. Nagel, *Descent from Glory: Four Generations of the John Adams Family* (New York: Oxford University Press, 1983), pp. 344–45: "In contrast to Henry's high opinion of Brooks, Charles' evaluation was: 'Poor Brooks. An insatiable ambition, intense egoism, no judgment, and only fair abilities—what a nuisance he is!'" and Abigail Adams Homans, "My Adams Uncles: Charles, Henry, Brooks," *Yale Review*, 55 (March 1966), 332: "where Brooks always irritated Charles, Henry rather affectionately put up with him with a toleration which later grew into genuine admiration and respect."

12. See Mina J. Carson, "The Evolution of Brooks Adams," *Biography*, 6 (Spring 1983), 95–116, especially pp. 98–102, for a discussion of the two brothers' importance to one another in this exchange.

13. See, for example, Robert A. Hume, *Runaway Star: An Appreciation of Henry Adams* (Ithaca: Cornell University Press, 1951), p. 153: "If any one group of [Adams's] letters may be called exceptional, they probably are those written to Elizabeth Cameron."

14. See Arline Boucher Tehan, *Henry Adams in Love: The Pursuit of Elizabeth Sherman Cameron* (New York: Universe Books, 1983), for a detailed chronicle of the relationship between Adams and Cameron: pp. 54–69 describe Cameron's initial years in Washington with Henry and Clover Adams, and pp. 91–146 describe Adams's pursuit of Cameron, her ambiguous behavior toward him, and her eventual rejection of his advances.

15. See Stephen M. Stowe, *Intimacy and Power in the Old South: Ritual in the Lives of the Planters* (Baltimore: Johns Hopkins University Press, 1987), p. 31, for a related discussion of the ways in which antebellum Southern men engaged in the exchange of letters of honor became "locked into language that would surely pull them into a duel."

16. See Ellen Rothman, *Hands and Hearts: A History of Courtship in America* (New York: Basic Books, 1984), p. 9, on nineteenth-century American letters of courtship as both narrative and act: Rothman explains that while these letters provide "a remarkably full record of the ideas and experiences surrounding the transition to marriage," they also "are more than the artifacts of a relationship; in many cases they were, for a time, the relationship itself."

17. See Tehan, *Henry Adams in Love*, pp. 105–6, on Henry Adams's "temporary banishment" from Elizabeth Sherman Cameron.

18. See Bossis, "Methodological Journeys," pp. 68–69, on the ways in which some correspondences rely and even "thrive" on absence.

19. O'Toole, *Five of Hearts*, p. 250.

20. See Horowitz, "Correspondence of Madame de Sévigné," p. 21, for a corroborating discussion of Madame de Sévigné's thematic use of solitude, as a strategy for constructing a world around her own fiction: "The world intrudes into her world, more importantly into her *word*, only insofar as it does not distract from this essential self-characterization—or, more accurately, intrudes only when it is intended to distract by the letter-writer."

21. See Tehan, *Henry Adams in Love*, pp. 166–76, on the first break in Cameron's letters to Adams, in the spring of 1900, during her affair with the poet Joseph Trumbull Stickney.

22. Ernest Samuels, *Henry Adams: The Middle Years* (Cambridge: Harvard University Press, 1958), p. 418.

23. Not all of Adams's letters to Martha Cameron have been included in the Harvard edition of Adams's letters. For the sake of consistency, therefore, subsequent citations in this chapter to Adams's letters to Martha Cameron will be made in the text as "MC," and will come from Vandersee's edition, "Henry Adams' Education of Martha Cameron: Letters, 1888–1916," *Texas Studies in Literature and Language*, 10 (Summer 1968), 233–93.

24. See ibid., p. 235, on the double audience of Adams's early letters to Martha Cameron.

25. See ibid., note, p. 241, on the nicknames which Adams adopted in his games with Martha Cameron.

26. See Carolyn Porter, *Seeing and Being: The Plight of the Participant Observer in Emerson, James, Adams, and Faulkner* (Middletown, CT: Wesleyan University Press, 1981), pp. 180–81, on the ways in which Marian Adams's suicide crystallized for Adams the problem of "his own impotence."

27. See T. J. Jackson Lears, *No Place of Grace: Antimodernism and the Transformation of American Culture, 1880–1920* (New York: Pantheon, 1981), pp. 266–86.

28. See Mabel La Farge, "Henry Adams: A Niece's Memories," *Yale Review*, 9 (January 1920), 271–285, and Louis Auchincloss, "'Never Leave Me, Never Leave Me,'" *American Heritage*, 21 (February 1970), 20–22 and 69–70, for two of the many accounts of Adams and his "nieces."

Chapter 4. Authorship and Audience in the Work of Henry Adams

1. Raymond Carney's Introduction to Adams's *Mont Saint Michel and Chartres* (New York: Viking Penguin, 1986), pp. ix–xxxvii, provides a very helpful discussion of the centrality of authorship as a problem and as a subject in Adams's book. See especially pp. xxvii–xxviii, on the text as "the record of the struggle" between "Adams's ambivalences and uncertainties about the role of an author in the modern world" and "the drama of

Adams's writing, the spectacle of his imagination asserting its simultaneous openness to and mastery over all of these inherited forms and potentially daunting structures of knowledge." Hereafter all citations to this edition of *Mont Saint Michel and Chartres* will be made in the text as *MSMC*.

2. In preparing the final version of this manuscript for publication, I see many similarities in concepts and even in critical language between my argument and William Decker's, in *The Literary Vocation of Henry Adams* (Chapel Hill: University of North Carolina Press, 1990).

3. See Ernest Samuels, *Henry Adams: The Middle Years* (Cambridge: Harvard University Press, 1958), pp. 168–83 ("A Power in the Land"), for a discussion of Adams's successes as a reform writer, and William Dusinberre, *Henry Adams: The Myth of Failure* (Charlottesville: University Press of Virginia, 1980), p. 198, on the popular success of *John Randolph*.

4. See Dusinberre, *Henry Adams: The Myth of Failure*, pp. 195–201, for a discussion of Adams's disappointed hunger for public literary acclaim and, especially, his hurt at the *History*'s lack of public success. Carolyn Porter, *Seeing and Being: The Plight of the Participant Observer in Emerson, James, Adams, and Faulkner* (Middletown, CT: Wesleyan University Press, 1981), pp. 172–79, and Ernest Samuels, *The Young Henry Adams* (Cambridge: Harvard University Press, 1965), pp. 112–20, both discuss the unnerving effects on Adams of being exposed to ridicule by the *London Times*.

5. Patricia O'Toole, *The Five of Hearts: An Intimate Portrait of Henry Adams and His Friends, 1880–1918* (New York: Clarkson Potter, 1990), p. 140, discusses Adams's "experimenting" in persuading Henry Holt to publish *Esther* without advertising or publicity.

6. J. C. Levenson, *The Mind and Art of Henry Adams* (Stanford, CA: Stanford University Press, 1968), pp. 96–97, discusses Adams's fiction-writing as both an effort "to recapture the general readers for whom his journalistic pieces had been written" and an effort to earn the approval of a radically limited audience like his friends John Hay and Clarence King, "officeholders both, [who] no doubt enjoyed the impudent suggestion that office and integrity were incompatible—for most people."

7. See, for two among a myriad of possible examples, *MSMC* 49: "The cathedral of Coutances alone has preserved its central *clocher* of the thirteenth century, and even there it is not complete; its stone *flèche* is wanting"; or *MSMC* 24: "William of Malmesbury is supposed to have written his prose chronicle about 1120 when many of the men who fought at Hastings must have been alive, and William expressly said:— 'Tunc cantilena Rollandi inchoata ut martium viri exemplum pugnaturos accenderet, inclamatoque dei auxilio, praelium consertum.'"

8. Dusinberre, *Henry Adams: The Myth of Failure*, p. 202, complains that in the process of parading his own connoisseurship Adams loses his audience: "This is poor training for the superior but untutored American tourist to whom Adams directs his lecture."

9. Henry Adams, *The Education of Henry Adams*, ed. Ernest Samuels (Boston: Houghton Mifflin, 1973), pp. 28–29. Hereafter all citations to this edition of *The Education* will be made in the text as *Ed*.

10. Robert F. Sayre, for example, in *The Examined Self: Benjamin Franklin, Henry Adams, Henry James* (Princeton: Princeton University Press, 1964), pp. 118–21, sees

the "carefully designed puzzle" of this gap in *The Education* as an effort on Adams's part to establish the priority of "universals at the expense of particulars"; while Dusinberre, *Henry Adams: The Myth of Failure*, p. 215, finds it destructive, an "unnatural exercise in self-mutilation."

11.   Levenson, *Mind and Art*, p. 97, describes Adams's 1879 readings of *Democracy* to the Five of Hearts, who "listened to him read chapters of his novel at their teatime meetings and were pleased to find how amusing the ten-o-clock scholar could be at five"; and Arline Boucher Tehan, *Henry Adams in Love: The Pursuit of Elizabeth Sherman Cameron* (New York: Universe Books, 1983), pp. 204–6, describes Adams reading aloud *Mont Saint Michel and Chartres* in 1902 to Lizzie and Martha Cameron, in Cameron's Paris apartment.

12.   See Linda A. Westervelt, "Henry Adams and the Education of His Readers," *Southern Humanities Review* (Winter 1984), pp. 26–29, on the ways in which Adams's insistence on the provisional status, "open to revision by others as well as by himself," of *The Education* functioned in tandem with Adams's resistance to closure in sentence structure and his refusal to synthesize forms of "doubleness," to impose tension and responsibility on Adams's readers. See also John Carlos Rowe, *Henry Adams and Henry James: The Emergence of a Modern Consciousness* (Ithaca: Cornell University Press, 1976), pp. 93–96, on the "unpublishable and incomplete" status of *The Education*.

13.   Raymond Carney's Introduction to *Mont Saint Michel and Chartres*, p. x, also makes this point about the special demands which Adams places on his readers: "We must enter into a specially responsive relationship both to Adams and to the persons and events we will subsequently encounter. . . ."

14.   See Ernest Samuels, *Henry Adams: The Major Phase* (Cambridge: Harvard University Press, 1964), pp. 332–39, for a discussion of Adams's first, privately printed edition, "a gratifyingly comfortable quarto volume printed on heavy paper with wide margins," and the responses (marginal and otherwise) which it elicited from readers.

15.   Alfred Kazin, in *The American Procession* (New York: Knopf, 1984), p. 308, points out: "In *The Education* all friends are flattered by being put into the book." See also James G. Watson, *William Faulkner: Letters and Fictions* (Austin: University of Texas Press, 1987), pp. 13–14, for a discussion of the ways in which the writer of letters writes the correspondent into the text: "the Receiver is with the Sender in the text they share. . . . Failure to recognize and honor the Receiver in a letter threatens the exchange on which each expression in a letterly discourse depends."

16.   See Raymond Carney's Introduction to *Mont Saint Michel and Chartres*, p. xxiv, which includes an especially effective discussion of how "the erasing of the individual as the personal author of value and the controller of meaning" in *The Education* "leads Adams to a nightmare vision of human powerlessness and irrelevance in . . . an apparently 'de-authored' universe." And see Robert F. Sayre, "*The Education*: Henry Adams's Epistolary Last Hurrah," manuscript, pp. 13–15, for a discussion of *The Education* as a "society letter," interested in types rather than in unique personalities.

17.   See Samuels, *Henry Adams: The Major Phase*, p. 334, on Adams's anxiety over Eliot's response to *The Education*, in which he had written in his chapter "Failure (1871)," "In spite of President Eliot's reforms and his steady, generous, liberal support, the system remained costly, clumsy and futile" (*Ed* 304).

18. See Rowe, *Henry Adams and Henry James*, p. 38, on the ways in which Henry Adams and Henry James responded to their sense of "radical cultural discontinuity at the end of the century" by "experiment[ing] with different literary forms . . . [by] trying to find a relation between public and private, to formulate a nexus between the language of consciousness and the names of society," and John J. Conder, *A Formula of His Own: Henry Adams's Literary Experiment* (Chicago: University of Chicago Press, 1970), p. 3, on Adams's "invention of unique literary structures . . . turning from genre to genre in a search for form. . . ."

19. Rowe, *Henry Adams and Henry James*, pp. 56–59, discusses *Democracy* in terms of Madeleine Lee's "quest for the power behind American politics."

20. Henry Adams, *Democracy: An American Novel* (New York: Library of America, 1983), p. 19. Hereafter citations to this edition of *Democracy* will be made in the text.

21. Henry Adams, *Esther: A Novel* (New York: Library of America, 1983), p. 213. Hereafter citations to this edition of *Esther* will be made in the text.

22. See Melvin Lyon, *Symbol and Idea in Henry Adams* (Lincoln: University of Nebraska Press, 1970), pp. 45–56, for a discussion of the symbol of Niagara in *Esther*, especially in terms of a transcendent, natural spirituality.

23. See Conder, *Formula of His Own*, pp. 53–84, for a very helpful discussion of the centrality of Adams's thematic commitment to "relations" between reader and narrator, between past and present, and between disunity and unity.

24. Ibid., pp. 35–46, provides a sustained discussion of the "striking emphasis upon personal feeling" in *Mont Saint Michel and Chartres* which makes it possible for Adams to experiment with the relationship between narrator and reader.

25. Emerson's famous passage appears in his 1836 essay *Nature*: "Crossing a bare common, in snow puddles, at twilight, under a clouded sky, without having in my thoughts any occurrence of special good fortune, I have enjoyed perfect exhilaration. I am glad to the brink of fear. . . . all mean egotism vanishes. I become a transparent eyeball; I am nothing; I see all; the currents of the Universal Being circulate through me; I am part or parcel of God." *Selections from Ralph Waldo Emerson*, ed. Stephen E. Whicher (Boston: Houghton Mifflin, 1957), p. 23.

26. *Benjamin Franklin's Autobiography*, ed. J. A. Leo Lemay and P. M. Zall (New York: Norton, 1986), p. 20.

27. Both Rowe, *Henry Adams and Henry James*, pp. 116–26, and Porter, *Seeing and Being*, pp. 184–202, among many others, stress the centrality for Adams of feeling alienated from sources of knowledge and control and of finding a language and form for achieving some kind of order.

28. Michael Fried's *Realism, Writing, Disfiguration: On Thomas Eakins and Stephen Crane* (Chicago: University of Chicago Press, 1987) is probably the best known, and most radically argued, of the recent discussions which have made this point: Fried claims that writing itself becomes Crane's subject when the frequently repeated figures of up-turned faces become "at once synecdoches for the bodies of those characters and singularly concentrated metaphors for the sheets of writing paper that the author had before him" (p. 100), and that Crane "unwittingly, obsessionally, and to all intents and purposes automatically metaphorizes writing and the production of writing . . ." (p. 120). See also Donald Pease, "Fear, Rage, and the Mistrials of Representation in *The Red*

Badge of Courage," in *American Realism: New Essays*, ed. Eric J. Sundquist (Baltimore: Johns Hopkins University Press, 1982), pp. 155–75, on Crane's insistence on the priority of narrative *versus* war, as opposed to narrative *of* war: "Henry's narrative does not exist as his means of recording events of war but as his principal strategy for taking possession of 'his' life."

29. See James J. Cox, "Autobiography and America," *Virginia Quarterly Review*, 47 (1971), 256–62, on Franklin's conflation in the *Autobiography* of his own "invention of himself, not as fiction, but as a fact both of and in history" with the American Revolution.

30. Among others, Rowe argues, similarly: "In the context of Adams's thought, the conventional notions of 'author' and 'subject' cannot be sustained. If Adams's man is pushed, pulled, and trapped by forces beyond his control, he may hardly be termed the author or originator of his own life." *Henry Adams and Henry James*, p. 122.

31. See Porter, *Seeing and Being*, p. 169, on how Adams's stance as observer positions him with respect to his audience: "It is because of this repressed recognition of his role as participant that Adams feels a responsibility toward his reader."

32. Westervelt ("Henry Adams and the Education of his Readers") discusses both *The Education* and *Mont Saint Michel and Chartres* in terms of Adams's faith in his readers, especially the twentieth-century public to whom his authorization of publication brought the text.

33. See Christopher P. Wilson, *The Labor of Words: Literary Professionalism in the Progressive Era* (Athens: University of Georgia Press, 1985), pp. 1–16, for a discussion of the emergence of a mass literary marketplace in the late-nineteenth-century United States and its effect on the elite republican ideal of the "gentleman amateur" writer. And see Eric J. Sundquist, "Introduction: The Country of the Blue," in *American Realism: New Essays* (Baltimore: Johns Hopkins University Press, 1982), pp. 15–19, for an additional discussion of the effects on realistic literature in the United States of the professionalization of writing and of the "many pressures of the economic and social market."

34. See Shelley Fisher Fishkin, *From Fact to Fiction: Journalism and Imaginative Writing in America* (Baltimore: Johns Hopkins University Press, 1985), especially pp. 3–14, on these developments in American journalism and their effects on imaginative writing.

35. Michael Anesko, *"Friction with the Market": Henry James and the Profession of Authorship* (New York: Oxford University Press, 1986), p. 34.

36. Ibid.

37. See Wilson, *Labor of Words*, pp. 9–11, for a discussion of the transition from the republican ideal of the "gentleman amateur" as a resisting alternative to the bourgeois ideal of productivity, and of the distinction between the elite amateur context of authorship and the ethos of work which came to dominate in the increasingly commercial context of the late nineteenth century.

38. In his Epilogue, pp. 192–202, Wilson (*Labor of Words*) summarizes this argument.

39. See Anesko, *"Friction with the Market,"* p. 11, for an extended discussion of the anxiety over maintaining his professionalism "in the face of a debased reading public" while simultaneously engaging in "calculated maneuvering in the more private

confines of publishers' offices" (pp. viii–ix) which characterized "James's calculated attempt to avoid both the din of commercialism and the silence of oblivion. . . ."

40. Fishkin's discussion of Mark Twain's career as a travel correspondent in terms of the popularity of this form of letters during the last half of the nineteenth century, *From Fact to Fiction*, pp. 55–56, is helpful in appreciating the public course which Adams's writing career could have taken.

Conclusion: The Resisting Letter

1. J. Gerald Kennedy, *Poe, Death, and the Life of Writing* (New Haven: Yale University Press, 1987), pp. 91–96, discusses the ways in which Poe used writing, particularly the writing of letters, to hold off the threat of death: "writing . . . became a defiance of mortality, a resistance to oblivion," as Poe mastered a "rhetoric of dread" in order to issue "calls for help" and "to produce a text that would save him from dissolution."

2. Paul de Man, "Autobiography and De-Facement," *The Rhetoric of Romanticism* (New York: Columbia University Press, 1984), p. 68. A substantial amount of critical work has also amply demonstrated autobiography's creative imperatives. See, as one among many possible influential examples, James Olney's "A Theory of Autobiography," in *Metaphors of Self: The Meaning of Autobiography* (Princeton: Princeton University Press, 1972), pp. 3–50.

3. See Alfred Kazin, "Autobiography and Narrative," *Michigan Quarterly Review*, 3 (1964), 210–16, on the imaginative imperatives of narrative coherence in autobiography.

4. See Robert F. Sayre, *The Examined Self: Benjamin Franklin, Henry Adams, Henry James* (Princeton: Princeton University Press, 1964), especially pp. 121–36, on Adams's "climactic" decision to write his autobiography.

5. See Karl J. Weintraub, "Autobiography and Historical Consciousness," *Critical Inquiry*, 1 (1975), 821–48, on the cultural conditions—particularly the development in the eighteenth century of a conception of individuality and a supporting "historical sense" of change—which made "autobiography possible" in the West. See James M. Cox, "Autobiography and America," *Virginia Quarterly Review*, 47 (1971), 252–62, on the revolutionary American consciousness of Benjamin Franklin's autobiography, which responded to "political necessities" by offering a radical model of self-invention. And see Robert F. Sayre, "Autobiography and the Making of America," in *Autobiography: Essays Theoretical and Critical*, ed. James Olney (Princeton: Princeton University Press, 1980), pp. 146–68, on "the very identification of autobiography in America *with* America."

6. A number of recent analyses have focused on the androcentric biases of "autobiography" and autobiography criticism, which privilege the "representative" voice and the distinct, self-creating "individual" as models. See, for example, Sidonie Smith's opening chapters, "Autobiography Criticism and the Problematics of Gender" and "Renaissance Humanism and the Misbegotten Man," in *A Poetics of Women's Autobiography: Marginality and the Fictions of Self-Representation* (Bloomington: Indiana University Press, 1987), pp. 3–43, on the "complexities of women's public self-disclosure"

and on the gendered status of assumptions about the "representative" voice and "individuality." And see Susan Stanford Friedman, "Woman's Autobiographical Selves: Theory and Practice," in *The Private Self: Theory and Practice of Women's Autobiographical Writings*, ed. Shari Benstock (Chapel Hill: University of North Carolina Press, 1988), pp. 34–62, for a discussion exposing the problematic status of theoretical models which assume that "the healthy ego is defined in terms of its ability to separate itself from others." Both Smith and Friedman rely heavily on Nancy Chodorow's and Carol Gilligan's work on the distinctions between men's and women's experiences of differentiation.

7. See Wendy Deutelbaum, "Epistolary Politics: The Correspondence of Emma Goldman and Alexander Berkman," *Prose Studies*, 9 (May 1986), 30–46, on "epistolary" exchange as a radical political alternative.

8. See Marcel Mauss, *The Gift: Forms and Functions of Exchange in Archaic Societies* (New York: Norton, 1967), "Conclusions," pp. 63–81, for a helpful discussion of gift economies as humane alternatives to the competitive commercial values of modern industrial society.

9. Again, recent feminist discussions of autobiography are helpful in appreciating the stance of resistance which Adams adopted. See Katherine R. Goodman, "Elisabeth to Meta: Epistolary Autobiography and the Postulation of the Self," in *Life/Lines: Theorizing Women's Autobiography*, ed. Bella Brodzki and Celeste Schenck (Ithaca: Cornell University Press, 1988), pp. 306–19, on the challenge to "proper" bourgeois autobiographical form which letters' "fragmentary" form poses; and see Nancy Walker, "'Wider Than the Sky': Public Presence and Private Self in Dickinson, James and Woolf," in *The Private Self: Theory and Practice of Women's Autobiographical Writings*, ed. Shari Benstock (Chapel Hill: University of North Carolina Press, 1988), pp. 272–303, on the strategies which Dickinson, James, and Woolf used in their letters to "resist classification of the self by others. . . ."

10. See Mireille Bossis, "Methodological Journeys through Correspondences," in *Men/Women of Letters*, ed. Charles A. Porter, *Yale French Studies*, 71 (1986), 68, on the tension between "real" collaboration in epistolary exchange and the "fiction-making [that is] possible because the recipient is absent."

11. Ruth Bernard Yeazell, ed., *The Death and Letters of Alice James* (Berkeley: University of California Press, 1981), p. 132. Hereafter citations to this edition of James's letters will be made in the text as AJ. See Felicity A. Nussbaum, "Eighteenth-Century Women's Autobiographical Commonplaces," in *The Private Self: Theory and Practice of Women's Autobiographical Writings*, ed. Shari Benstock (Chapel Hill: University of North Carolina Press, 1988), pp. 147–71, for a very helpful discussion of the ways in which diary writing both reconfirms women's disempowering consignment to a separate private sphere and contests the disempowerment of closure and silence.

12. Jean Strouse's *Alice James: A Biography* (Boston: Houghton Mifflin, 1980) provides an extended discussion of Alice James's ambiguous position in the James family.

13. See Carroll Smith-Rosenberg, "The Hysterical Woman: Sex Roles and Role Conflict in Nineteenth-Century America," in *Disorderly Conduct: Visions of Gender in Victorian America* (New York: Oxford University Press, 1985), pp. 198–99, on "the

role changes and conflicts bourgeois matrons experienced between the 1840s and the 1890s."

14. Strouse gives detailed accounts of James's illnesses, as well as their treatments and probable origins, in her excellent biography. On late-nineteenth-century "female illness" more generally, see Smith-Rosenberg, "Hysterical Woman," pp. 209–16; Anne Douglas Wood, "The Fashionable Diseases," *Journal of Interdisciplinary History*, 4 (1973), 25–52; Barbara Sicherman, "The Uses of a Diagnosis: Doctors, Patients and Neurasthenia," *Journal of the History of Medical and Allied Sciences*, 32 (January 1977), 33–54; and Strouse, *Alice James*, p. 105. Strouse, Smith-Rosenberg, Wood, and Sicherman all posit a power struggle between female patients and their male doctors and family members. While female illness confirmed the imperative of male expertise, it also stymied male medical experts' efforts to find a cure. While female illness passively signaled female weakness and unfitness for society's demands, it also sabotaged the rules of decorum which society prescribed for women. And while female illness may have expressed a deep-seated sense of sexual repression, it also earned women the undivided attention of the male authority figures around them.

15. See Rachel Blau DuPlessis, *Writing beyond the Ending: Narrative Strategies of Twentieth-Century Women Writers* (Bloomington: Indiana University Press, 1985), on twentieth-century women writers' subversive refusal of obligation to the conventions of closure in the romantic novel: "Writing beyond the ending begins when authors, or their close surrogates, discover that they are in fact outside the terms of [the romance plot's] scripts, marginal to it" (p. 6).

16. See Walker, "'Wider Than the Sky,'" pp. 272–303, on the centrality of "balance, or more often a tension, between the personal and public lives" for women writing autobiography.

17. See Patricia Meyer Spacks, "Selves in Hiding," in *Women's Autobiography: Essays in Criticism*, ed. Estelle C. Jelinek (Bloomington: Indiana University Press, 1980), pp. 112–32, on women's consignment to private forms like letters and diaries and women's reticence about calling public attention to themselves in published autobiographies. And see Patricia Meyer Spacks, "Female Rhetorics," in *The Private Self: Theory and Practice of Women's Autobiographical Writings*, ed. Shari Benstock (Chapel Hill: University of North Carolina Press, 1988), pp. 177–91.

18. See Nussbaum, "Eighteenth-Century Women's Autobiographical Commonplaces," pp. 156–64, for a corroborating discussion of the eighteenth-century woman's diary as both "a place to contest the closure of 'self' and text," "a site for the contest over the privatizing of woman"—and a means of negotiating "splittings" between public duty and private need, which "suppresses the threat of conflict by relegating it to the private sphere."

19. Whitman's "Democratic Vistas," in *Leaves of Grass and Selected Prose*, ed. Lawrence Buell (New York: Random House, 1981), p. 470, amply articulates his formulation of literature's role in achieving the democratic future which he envisioned for America: "what finally and only is to make of our western world a nationality superior to any hither known, and outtopping the past, must be vigorous, yet unsuspected Literatures, perfect personalities and sociologies, original, transcendental, and expressing (what, in highest sense, are not yet express'd at all,) democracy and the modern."

20. See Justin Kaplan, *Walt Whitman: A Life* (New York: Bantam, 1982), p. 200: "In an era of triple-barreled literary eminences who uttered their names in Jovian trochees and dactyls—William Cullen Bryant, John Greenleaf Whittier, Ralph Waldo Emerson, Henry Wadsworth Longfellow, James Russell Lowell—Walter Whitman had chosen to follow the populist examples of Andy Jackson, Kit Carson, and Davy Crockett. The change was more than nominal—it was organic, revolutionary."

21. Edwin Haviland Miller, ed., *Walt Whitman: The Correspondence*, Vol. III: 1876–1885 (New York: New York University Press, 1965), p. 201. Hereafter each volume of Whitman's correspondence—including Volume I (1842–1867, published 1961); Volume II (1868–1875, published 1961); Volume IV (1886–1889, published 1969); Volume V (1890–1892, published 1969)—will be cited in the text as WW1, WW2, WW3, WW4, or WW5.

22. In this resistance to hierarchy, Whitman's letters shared his poetry's equally political commitment to catalogue rhetoric. See Lawrence Buell, *Literary Transcendentalism: Style and Vision in the American Renaissance* (Ithaca: Cornell University Press, 1973), p. 167: "One reason for its American popularity is that catalogue rhetoric seems an inherently 'democratic' technique. . . . It . . . adheres to a sort of prosodic equalitarianism: each line or image is of equal weight in the ensemble; each is a unit unto itself."

23. See Kaplan, *Walt Whitman*, pp. 38–39, on Whitman's shrewd involvement in his own portraits: "In the self-absorption of old age Whitman became his own iconographer. . . ."

24. See Miller, WW1, p. 6: "in [his letters to soldiers], his prose was plain and colloquial, as befits communications addressed to young men who had little schooling and less command of language. But the drafts of these letters, interlined and filled with stricken passages, frequently reveal uncertainty and caution."

25. See Robert K. Martin, *The Homosexual Tradition in American Poetry* (Austin: University of Texas Press, 1979), p. 7: "Whitman's own life was marked by the same pressures toward sexual conformity that now lead to critical distortions. He seems to have felt the need to act out a role, to hide behind the mask of the 'tough.' And he had to learn the strategies of concealment, which, at least until recently, all of us had to learn as homosexuals in a heterosexual world."

26. See Kaplan, *Walt Whitman*, p. 311, and Paul Zweig, *Walt Whitman: The Making of the Poet* (New York: Basic Books, 1984), p. 193, on Whitman's initial contact with Doyle. And see Zweig, pp. 193–94, for a quoted entry from Whitman's journal in which Whitman refers to Doyle as "164" (P is the sixteenth letter of the alphabet, D is the fourth), in an effort to mask what he himself referred to as "*cessant enormous &* [enormous] PERTURBATION."

27. See Lewis Hyde, *The Gift: Imagination and the Erotic Life of Property* (New York: Vintage, 1983), pp. 188–189, on Whitman as Doyle's literary mentor.

28. See Kaplan, *Walt Whitman*, pp. 359–64, for a narrative of Whitman and Stafford's relationship.

29. Whitman's comment appeared in a letter to the critic William Gilchrist, through whom Anne Gilchrist had arranged in 1869 for Whitman to send her a copy of *Leaves of Grass*, and who later gave Anne Gilchrist permission to write directly to Whitman. See Kaplan, *Walt Whitman*, pp. 327–28, on Gilchrist's review.

30. See Sandra M. Gilbert and Susan Gubar, *The Madwoman in the Attic: The Woman Writer and the Nineteenth-Century Literary Imagination* (New Haven: Yale University Press, 1979), p. 51, on the distinction between the "anxiety of authorship," felt by women, and male writers' "anxiety of influence" and anxiety about creativity. Gilbert and Gubar work here from their opening question about the gendered power dynamic which shapes the act of writing: "Is the pen a metaphorical penis?" (p. 3).

31. See Deborah Kaplan, "Representing Two Cultures: Jane Austen's Letters," in *The Private Self: Theory and Practice of Women's Autobiographical Writings*, ed. Shari Benstock (Chapel Hill: University of North Carolina Press, 1988), pp. 222–29, on the ways in which Austen exploited the opposition between the male-dominated gentry culture and the culture of female social and kinship networks which her letters had to negotiate, in order to undermine publicly authorized assumptions about the status of "triviality."

32. See Amy Kaplan's Introduction to *The Social Construction of American Realism* (Chicago: University of Chicago Press, 1988), especially pp. 8–10, for a discussion of realism's struggle for control over an increasingly elusive reality, and its effort "to assuage fears of powerlessness."

33. See Smith's "Coda," *Poetics of Women's Autobiography*, pp. 174–76, for a helpful discussion of the subversive power of the marginally literary voice. Speaking about women's autobiography, Smith writes: "voices from the margins are louder at the moment of cultural instability. Moreover, the breakdown of a hegemonic conception of selfhood has fostered the collateral breakdown of canonical literature's hegemony."

34. Mark DeWolfe Howe, ed., *Holmes-Pollock Letters: The Correspondence of Mr. Justice Holmes and Sir Frederick Pollock, 1864–1932* (Cambridge: Harvard University Press, 1941), 2:18.

35. Raymond Carney also discusses the creative potential of alienation for Adams, in his Introduction to Henry Adams, *Mont Saint Michel and Chartres* (New York: Viking Penguin, 1986), p. xxxii: "[Adams] defines the possibility of a state of imaginative alienation from one's own experience that is not destructive or desperate but potentially creative and invigorating and liberating."

Index

Wisconsin Studies in American Autobiography

WILLIAM L. ANDREWS
General Editor

Robert F. Sayre
The Examined Self: Benjamin Franklin, Henry Adams, Henry James

Daniel B. Shea
Spiritual Autobiography in Early America

Lois Mark Stalvey
The Education of a WASP

Margaret Sams
Forbidden Family: A Wartime Memoir of the Philippines, 1941–1945
Edited, with an introduction, by Lynn Z. Bloom

Journeys in New Worlds: Early American Women's Narratives
Edited by William L. Andrews

Mark Twain
Mark Twain's Own Autobiography:
The Chapters from the North American Review
Edited, with an introduction, by Michael J. Kiskis

American Autobiography: Retrospect and Prospect
Edited by Paul John Eakin

Charlotte Perkins Gilman
The Living of Charlotte Perkins Gilman: An Autobiography
Introduction by Ann J. Lane

Caroline Seabury
The Diary of Caroline Seabury: 1854–1863
Edited, with an introduction, by Suzanne L. Bunkers

Cornelia Peake McDonald
A Woman's Civil War: A Diary with Reminiscences of the War,
from March 1862
Edited, with an introduction, by Minrose G. Gwin

Marian Anderson
My Lord, What a Morning
Introduction by Nellie Y. McKay

American Women's Autobiography: Fea(s)ts of Memory
Edited by Margo Culley

Frank Marshall Davis
Livin' the Blues: Memoirs of a Black Journalist and Poet
Edited, with an introduction, by John Edgar Tidwell

Joanne Jacobson
Authority and Alliance in the Letters of Henry Adams

DATE DUE

DEMCO 38-296